Voices of Recovery

Sex Addicts Anonymous

Literature Committee Approved 2018

First Printing, October 2018

SEX ADDICTS ANONYMOUS is a registered trademark® of the International Service Organization of SAA, Inc.

ISO
P.O. Box 70949
Houston, TX 77270
800-477-8191

Website: saa-recovery.org
Email: info@saa-recovery.org

ISBN: 978-0-9892286-7-1

Printed in the United States of America

Cover Image Copyright: rozum / 123RF Stock Photo.

Table of Contents

of the International Service Organization of SAA, Inc.

Foreword

This book is the response of the International Service Organization (ISO) of Sex Addicts Anonymous (SAA) to the request by members of the fellowship and the Conference delegates for a meditation book written and produced by the fellowship of SAA. Guided by the following Vision Statement, the ISO Literature Committee welcomed meditation submissions from members around the world:

The SAA Meditation Book carries the message of recovery by collecting into one volume diverse voices of the SAA fellowship to serve as a resource for meditation and prayer for the addict in recovery and the sex addict who still suffers.

This book is not the work of a single person. Numerous individuals have donated their time and talents to writing, reading, selecting, and editing meditations. This book is a labor of love for the fellowship and each member's recovery.

Each meditation is a reflection of the individual member's own experience, strength, and hope in their own recovery process, and is not meant to represent SAA as a whole. The meditations may be read daily based on the date, by topic using the index, or by any other way the reader or group desires.

We pray that this book will aid individuals in their recovery and assist groups in carrying the SAA message!

In Deep Gratitude,
The ISO Literature Committee

ॐ

> "Continuing to apply them on a daily basis
> keeps us spiritually fit <u>and</u> growing in recovery."
>
> *Sex Addicts Anonymous*, page 61

The following has been attributed to many different musicians: "I must practice daily. If I miss one day, I can hear it in my playing. If I miss two days, the band can hear it. And if I miss three days, the public can hear it."

My recovery practice includes: attending meetings, praying, reading the literature, making calls to others in recovery, working the Steps (including my daily Tenth Step inventory), and engaging in my outer circle. If I skip my recovery practice for one day, I can feel it. I am more vulnerable to small irritations and temptations—I am just not quite right. If I skip two days, I am prone to impatience and fantasy. If I skip three days, I start developing resentments and I am off in my head with addictive plans and schemes. I'm never sure how much others notice, but in all cases, I am further away from the people in my life, I no longer live in serenity, and I return to the chaos of my addictive life.

To me, recovery is an artistic gift to the world. It allows me to make beautiful life music. I make the world better by practicing my daily recovery plan.

I can give myself and the world a gift by practicing my recovery today.

"Honesty, willingness, courage, humility, forgiveness, responsibility, gratitude, and faith are just some of the names we give to the spiritual principles that gradually come to guide us in our lives. As we progress through the program, establishing conscious contact with the God of our understanding, we become aware of these principles within us—like gifts that were always there, unopened until we were ready to receive them."

Sex Addicts Anonymous, page 61

After a relapse, I contacted several SAA members to be honest about my situation and to reconnect with the fellowship and the program. One member sent me an email with a short but profound message: I love you.

How do we know what is good for us? I had never wished to be a sex addict. In recovery, I never wished for relapse. Yet in the very worst of my fears, I found my greatest strength and courage. And when I admitted the scary truth, I found a loving Higher Power. In this case, it was expressed through the love and understanding of other recovering sex addicts. Even my doubts became signposts that the God of my understanding is close by. When I admitted my doubts, that still, small voice would say, "It's ok, I'm right here."

We have all sat in fear and disclosed the truth about what we have done. In our cross-wired beliefs, we were expecting hatred and rejection when we revealed ourselves. Instead, among the fellowship of Sex Addicts Anonymous, we experience love and acceptance.

My Higher Power has provided a safe place to practice honesty—the rooms of SAA.

ଔ

> "We would spend increasing amounts of time
> in fantasy, which tended to alienate us from
> others and from a real sense of ourselves."
>
> *Sex Addicts Anonymous*, page 70

It seems that much of my fantasy and intrigue, as well as my acting out, served to numb a pain that I don't understand. I have a fear of seeing who I really am. My behaviors and daydreaming have masked something from others as well. Can it be so hideous that I must hide it at all cost? I experience fear in the prospect of looking under the mask. Sharing with another person I trust helps me with my fear. Reaching out to a power greater than myself assists me in imagining an alternative to gloom.

The familiar track promises more loneliness, frustration, and alienation from others. Each day I get a little older and more isolated. Now what if I set the distractions aside—what if I leave the bubble? Through working the program I have much to gain: inclusion in a nurturing fellowship and, eventually, society as a whole. I may well be shocked (in a nice way) to experience what is at the core of my being.

~

I endeavor to discover my true self by peeling away the layers one step at a time.

> "Looking at areas of unmanageability in
> our lives can help us recognize our defects,
> when we identify our responsibility for
> events that felt painful or out of control."

Sex Addicts Anonymous, page 41

When I came into recovery, I truly felt superior. I believed I was above the average human being and didn't want to believe that I, too, might have character defects. Arrogance and grandiosity formed a protective shield against my inner sense of shame.

Yet my life was in shambles in so many ways. Unmanageability was all around, and my strongest denial did not work anymore. Identifying the painful events in my life, owning up to my part in them, and bringing my character defects out into the light were anything but fun. But, it was the first time I actually felt what positive humility means, how honesty feels.

I comprehended the joy of understanding what "whole" means, and what "true-to-myself-and-others" is like for me. Accepting my mistakes and shortcomings, I could embrace the happiness of being part of humanity.

~

Today I will remember that being entirely ready to accept God's help allows me to be completely human and imperfect.

CR

> ". . . Recovery does not mean that you stop
> having problems. Rather, you get to have
> problems that are not sexual ones."
>
> *Sex Addicts Anonymous*, page 113

When I was acting out and life got difficult, I turned to my addiction as a cure for ills I literally didn't know I had. It never worked. When I was done acting out, my problems were still there, sometimes compounded by my acting out.

When I entered the program, the biggest problem I had was my addiction. Becoming sober was a big deal. After a while, I learned to rely on spiritual practices instead of a sexual high. I also came to believe that no matter how difficult a situation, my Higher Power was there for me.

Once the practices to maintain my sobriety were well established, other problems that I hadn't dealt with came to the forefront. I began to deal with the truth about my finances and got a job after eighteen years of self-employment. And when I had trouble finding a suit in my size, I realized it was time to lose some weight. It's not that I didn't have these problems before, it's just that acting out and then getting sober took my focus away from them. Now that I have sobriety, I can finally take care of myself in other ways.

Today I am grateful for the problems in my life. They seem to be a form of fierce grace, designed to grow my acceptance, accountability, and serenity. Every time I choose spiritual principles, my sobriety grows.

~

No matter how difficult a situation, my Higher Power is there for me.

જ

> "With spiritual awareness comes the
> responsibility, the desire, and the need
> to help other suffering sex addicts, just
> as help was <u>freely</u> given to us."
>
> *Sex Addicts Anonymous*, page 59

Before starting my recovery journey, I made little time for anyone or anything but my addiction. By staying sober and working the Twelve Steps, I have gained a new spirituality and a new freedom. Suddenly, all of the time spent on my addiction became available for spiritual growth and working with others.

My sponsor pointed out from the beginning that any addiction indicates a spiritual impairment, and that only a spiritual solution can remedy a spiritual flaw. He taught me how to internalize an attitude of gratitude as I offered my experience and hope to others in the program.

As others have selflessly guided me in my spiritual growth, I similarly strive to make myself available to those seeking this spiritual solution. By getting outside myself and making myself available to others, I have been able to be a bit less selfish and self-centered, which in turn allows progress in my own recovery journey. My best vehicle for demonstrating gratitude is simply making myself available to others and honestly sharing the struggles and joys that recovery from sex addiction has created in my life.

Sobriety and recovery equals freedom. When I am truly grateful for this gift, I can be a conduit where my Higher Power can work through me for the benefit of other sex addicts.

God, let me demonstrate my gratitude for recovery by sharing what I was freely given.

℘

> "An important part of my recovery is to share
> my experience with other sex addicts who are
> trying to find a way out of the insanity."
>
> *Sex Addicts Anonymous*, page 302

Early in recovery, I couldn't imagine the day I would carry this message to others as suggested in Step Twelve. Today, however, if I am open, Twelfth-Step opportunities present themselves fairly often. I have to be willing to swallow my pride and timidity, and to act. After seeing people die from addiction, including sex addiction, I swore I would not pass up another opportunity to carry the message of recovery. This steels my resolve.

Hurting people are everywhere. I have shared about Twelve-Step recovery at work, at church, and at other recovery meetings if I think our fellowship could help someone struggling with a sex or intimacy issue.

I rarely declare that I am a sex addict or member of SAA, but I talk about my fear of intimacy and its destructive effect in my life. I say I have found it helpful to talk about my struggles with people who have similar issues and are finding solutions. I share some of my less-sensitive insane thinking. I believe I am planting seeds whenever I am willing to open up.

Sharing the message of recovery isn't always comfortable, but it always connects me to my Higher Power and others. Giving away healing is the most healing thing I do. It takes courage and humility, but I believe God supplies these if I am open and willing.

~

Hurting people are everywhere. Help me see and take opportunities to plant seeds of healing.

⁊

> "When we practice new ways of acting
> and thinking, we show that the program
> works, and we offer hope to others
> who are seeking a new life."

Sex Addicts Anonymous, page 60

When I came into SAA, it was not to raise my self-esteem. I was thinking about run-ins with the law and the time I ran out the door because my acting-out partner, suffering buyer's remorse, tried to kill me. I had grown to think of myself in terms of my addiction. I believed that all I had to offer was my sexual repertoire, though it continuously proved insufficient in keeping relationships.

When I created my circles, the inner and middle were easy, but the outer circle stymied me. I could only come up with activities that were expressly recovery: meetings, prayer, meditation, service, etc.

My sponsor suggested I think back to before my addiction kicked in. This unlocked a door. I revisited creative pursuits from my youth, and later added new practices like exercise. Soon, more new activities appeared, like adopting a pet and keeping the house clean. My outer circle keeps expanding.

After achieving some recovery and building my outer circle, I discovered I had much more than sex to offer. I began to find my true gifts and put them into action. Before I thought I could only offer behaviors that put me at genuine risk, I now have the fulfilling sense of being able to offer my true self.

~

Much of the serenity and happiness I now have stems from being able to offer my real self to others.

ℭℛ

> "The lightning jolts of terror I registered then,
> I would come to understand as Higher Power
> surges shocking <u>my</u> heart back to life."
>
> *Sex Addicts Anonymous*, page 114

As a physician, I have witnessed the miraculous capacity of electrical shock to restore life to patients who might otherwise be considered dead. As an addict, compulsively striving to avoid pain at all cost, I progressively deadened myself to this life force. At the end, God could only reach me through the violent shocks that comprised my bottom and my turning point.

My experience since entering recovery is that my Higher Power's love is a current that permeates everything. With every meeting, admission, amends, prayer, and act of service, I scrape off the corrosion that blocked this current from my heart. By establishing a daily practice of meditation, I consciously invite the current of my Higher Power as a more continuous flow of life and love through my heart. It's always here, free, for everyone and everything. It doesn't judge. All I have to do is be still, be how and who I am right now, and be open. God can handle the rest.

~

In connecting with the healing energy of my Higher Power, I welcome the surges of energy—joy, pain, compassion, peace—that may come with this life-giving connection.

✖

> "Often we may need the help of other members...
> another sex addict can bring us back to earth."
> *Sex Addicts Anonymous*, page 63

Lately I've felt that the more willing I am to let my Higher Power take over, the more doors open for me. I am grateful for the opportunities I have had in recovery. The most important door, however, was the one I walked through to get to my first meeting and I don't know if I could have done it alone. I stood outside the door for what seemed like an eternity. I was gripped by a fear I couldn't yet fully understand.

Just then a man walked up, carrying boxes of goodies and asked if I was looking for AA. I shook my head no; I was crying. He leaned in and said in a whisper, "SAA?"

I could barely move, but my head shook yes and he told me that it was just inside that door, gesturing with his shoulder. Then he asked me if I could open the door for him. It was a simple request, so I did. And once that door was open, I had to walk inside. At first, the fear blocked me from hearing anything. The fear got louder when I realized I was the only woman in the room. A man sat down next to me and welcomed me to the meeting by handing me some of the pamphlets. That simple gesture helped to calm my fear and open my ears.

After hearing just one share, I knew I was home. I know my Higher Power chose that meeting for me. I was welcomed with open arms and I have never stopped feeling the love and genuine care that the men in my group share with me.

~

Thank you God for all the doors you open for me.
Continue to guide me through them.

CR

"A slogan that expresses one of the fundamental
truths of the program is 'one day at a time.'"
Sex Addicts Anonymous, page 65

There is a species of bamboo that doesn't break
through the ground for the first four years after being
planted. Nonetheless, it must be watered and tended
regularly. Just think of getting up every morning to
water a spot on the ground that is marked for this
bamboo—not even a sprout or mound in the dirt, never changing, not a sign of movement or growth year
after year. After five years, a small sprout shoots up
through the dirt. Then, over the next six weeks, it can
grow ninety feet high to maturity.

My journey through the Twelve Steps has been similar. If am willing to do whatever it takes to stay sober,
if I have the patience to maintain my daily practice, if
I work the Steps with my sponsor, if I attend meetings
and share in the fellowship; I will come to realize that
the roots have built up to support a new me. I may not
notice anything for a long time, and in my case, I don't
always see the sprouts right away after they appear.
But gradually, I find myself growing in newness of life.

Just ask the old timers how they got their five, ten or
twenty year chip. They will say, "One day at a time."

May I walk this day in sobriety, one day at a time.

ભ

> "Personal disclosure is easier for us when
> we can trust that our presence and what
> we share will be kept confidential."

Tools of Recovery, page 4

At my first SAA meeting, I was terrified and suspicious. Anonymity assured me there would be none of the punishment and rejection that I associated with any discussion of sexuality. I listened to the stories of other sex addicts, and realized that the harshest judgment was my own. The group members would not rat me out or attempt to publicly embarrass me. I came to see my fears both as expressions of my own shame about my acting out behaviors, as well as of my grandiosity in thinking I was important enough for others to want to harm me.

Some of my fear of punishment was justified, both for my offender behavior, and as an artifact of the moralistic background of my formative years. I did not know what healthy sexuality was, and I am still learning. Anonymity provided me an emotionally safe environment to hear others and eventually ask my own questions. I was able to identify those with whom I could practice that rarest of gifts—trust. I was able to reach out for help.

The safety created by the spiritual foundation of anonymity was fundamental to my early recovery, enabling me to ask for help without the fear of punishment or rejection. It enabled me to begin discovering the ability to trust others—appropriate others—and to be open and honest in my recovery.

~

Anonymity provides the safety I need to practice trust and honesty.

ལ

> "I can take it a step at a time and gradually
> work my way toward spiritual health."
> *Sex Addicts Anonymous*, page 324

The religion of my youth had very exact descriptions of God and how to be a supplicant. God was personified in the leaders of the religion and I experienced God as abusive. As a result, Step Three was very difficult for me to accept and work. Even though it says "as we understood," my understanding was not acceptable to me.

Working with my sponsor, I was able to accept the notion of a Higher Power by first acknowledging that many powers are greater than I, and by recalling moments of powerlessness even before joining SAA. But I needed to find a power that was loving, that allowed conscious contact, and that was helpful to my recovery.

I learned that spirituality is usually an action that connects me with something greater. I have found that I can establish conscious contact with my higher values of honesty, kindness, service, and compassion. I have learned that being still and observing nature connects me with something greater. I have learned the power of gratitude and have developed a practice to improve my ability for gratitude. One of the greatest sources of understanding and experiencing my Higher Power is in witnessing the experience, strength, and hope of my sisters and brothers in recovery. I attempt to connect with program friends on a daily basis.

~

I am grateful for this ongoing spiritual awakening.

ભ

> "We find that spiritual principles can guide
> us in the everyday challenges of life, and
> they can help us face even loss, grief,
> and death with fortitude and grace."
> *Sex Addicts Anonymous*, page 61

My father died three years ago. Choosing photos for his memorial service was excruciating, knowing the truth underlying the camera-ready moments. Now my mother is dying and her disease manifests symptoms reminiscent of my painful childhood. My insides feel untethered, as though gravity doesn't exist.

My grief often comes out as anger. It rises from the deepest part of my stomach, aching to be seen. By the time it reaches my heart, I feel I must release it or I will disappear. The release often leaves catastrophic debris in my relationships. How do I take care of myself while caring for my ailing parent? How can I be the daughter I want to model for my son? I pray, "Please keep my heart open and help me see my true nature: gentle, loving, vulnerable, kind."

I share my pain in SAA meetings, believing your lives are happier than mine. I tell you that I want either someone to take care of me, or power of control. You nod and smile, invite me to coffee, and make sure I have phone numbers. I work steps with my sponsor and keep close contact with God and the fellowship of SAA. In the midst of pain and confusion, my feet can still find solid ground.

~

God, help me feel the mixed emotions of life's changes without losing my true self. Help me remain vulnerable so that, on the other side of grief, I may feel authentic joy.

ભ

> "We can also list the things we feel guilty about.
> We look at things we did that we knew were
> wrong and about which we feel remorse."
>
> *Sex Addicts Anonymous*, page 36

I used to confuse guilt and shame, but now I know that guilt, or recognizing a wrongdoing, can be a good thing. Shame, a feeling and belief of being defective or not good enough, is not healthy. Guilt is a sign that something needs to be addressed, like an indicator light in a car. Just as letting a problem persist for too long in a vehicle can cause expensive or even irreparable damage, putting off working a step can have undesirable consequences, too.

Working the Steps around guilty feelings keeps me from the hopelessness of shame, and moves me into the transformative light of grace and self-acceptance. Taking responsibility for my actions empowers me and everyone else. I cease being a victim as I promptly own my part and make amends. With help, I accept what I can't change, and I'm given courage to let it go. I also ask God to heal the wounds in me that add to the problem, and to help me find strength and courage to do the right thing. Through this process, my guilt is removed and replaced with forgiveness.

～

God, help me not to fear guilt, but to recognize it as a signal to work the Steps.

ॐ

> "In gratitude, we seek opportunities for
> service to God and our fellow sex addicts.
> Our path leads to Step Twelve."
>
> *Sex Addicts Anonymous*, page 58

After a year sober, I hit a period of intense anxiety. I was not prepared. My disease knocked me over and ran rampant for six months. I continued to attend meetings, talking openly with my sponsor and others. I picked up so many white chips that I finally gave up.

Openly acknowledging my anxiety, I recognized that it wasn't based in present reality. This helped me experience it raw, without trying to run or hide. I read literature, prayed, and meditated. Sometimes praying would pull me, emotionally drained, out of my wrenching feelings of inadequacy. As I continued to open up, a small chink in my self-hatred armor cracked open. I began practicing gratitude, especially gratitude that I could open my soul to others without being rejected.

I tried to be of service, sharing openly with others who were suffering. During this time, I realized a foundational truth of all Twelve-Step programs: the most healing thing I can do for myself is to offer healing to others. I began to offer service as often as I could, and every time I did, I experienced love. I always got more than I gave. I've been sober a while now, and I owe it to lessons learned from my greatest anguish.

~

When I give, I live.

ଓଃ

"In taking the Tenth Step, we commit to keeping
our house in order, whether old failings reappear
or new ones arise, as they inevitably will."
Sex Addicts Anonymous, page 52

At a meeting the other day, the secretary may have
gotten a little pushy when distributing the readings.
Another member responded a little sharply. The member was angry and the secretary was hurt, so one of
them brought it up as a meeting topic. It made for a
great meeting.

Most of those who spoke admitted that they were often on both sides of this experience—mad and hurt
about many little things in daily life. Some noted how,
if they are not careful, these hurts and angers can blow
up and ruin their entire day. One said that it was like
part of him was just waiting for something he could get
worked up about. He called it head trash.

I was stunned. These people, many with a decade or
more of solid recovery, were telling the story of my daily life. I was surprised to learn that I was not the only
one who can overreact to the smallest provocations.

Then the wisdom of the program shone through. I
take daily inventory to deal with this very tendency.
My addicted mind can find things to get emotionally
overwrought about on any given day. Step Ten is a
daily way to clear out any accumulation of head trash.

~

*I sort through my thinking every day, so I can haul out
what doesn't work and keep my serenity.*

ை

"The message is not that we sit passively
and wait for things to happen. Rather, it is
a shift in our attitude in which we admit
that we don't always know where we should
be going or how <u>we</u> should get there."

Tools of Recovery, page 19

As a practicing addict, I felt a compulsive need to be decisive and to control outcomes. The inevitable fruits were frustration and alienation. This yearning for control ultimately stems from fear that my needs may not be met. Admitting that I don't always know what to do or how to respond is a large step toward living a serene and real life.

In my experience, the forces at work in any situation are as varied and powerful as a winter storm, and I can manage these forces about as well as I can a typical blizzard.

In recovery I am free to let go of my fear and my need (to try) to control situations that are beyond my power. I can then allow life to unfold in its own way and know that my needs will be met. Perhaps more importantly, I can then put my energies into those things over which I do have control, like my well-being, my responsibilities, my life.

Allowing things to be as they are is not necessarily a sign of weakness or passivity. It can also be a sign of strength and of confidence in my Higher Power.

~

Higher Power, help me see what is mine to care for, and grant me the courage to act with grace.

ભ

> "Willingness to change routines
> that threaten our sobriety helps us
> stay out of our inner circle."
> *Tools of Recovery*, page 14

Even before I got into recovery, I was aware of many routines that fed my addiction. To gain abstinence, I had to be willing to change my actions. With the help of my sponsor, I cataloged those routines, and then took steps to introduce new routines and eliminate old ones. The first new routine was to start my day by getting on my knees and asking my Higher Power for the willingness and ability to get through this day sober.

Most, if not all, of the routines I addressed in the beginning were physical: people, places and behaviors. By changing these routines, I was able to achieve abstinence.

But true recovery is abstinence coupled with spiritual growth. As the sexual obsessions began to dissipate with abstinence, I discovered mental and emotional routines that threatened this sobriety. My mental criticisms of others reflected harsh judgments about myself, leaving me isolated, lonely, and vulnerable to slips. To maintain sobriety, I had to change these routines too, first by identifying them through my resentments (Steps Four and Five), and then working the Sixth and Seventh Step on these defects of character.

Today, I am more conscious of my attitudes toward myself and others, and I am willing to change those routines of the heart and mind that threaten my sobriety and serenity.

~

This is a program of action. Grant me willingness to take new actions—actions that reflect health, courage, and love.

ଔ

"The Sixth Tradition wisely identifies *money, property, and prestige* as potential obstacles to effectively carrying our message of recovery."

Sex Addicts Anonymous, page 86

Before coming to SAA, many of us defined ourselves and our self-worth in terms of money, property, and prestige. Many of us, if we are honest with ourselves, still do. Our tendency to judge ourselves and others by what they have rather than who they are keeps us in anxiety and isolation, worrying about whether we are "getting ahead," or wondering whether our next human interaction will leave us feeling one-up or one-down.

How healing it is, then, to come to an SAA meeting—a group that holds no property and usually very little money. Prestige, at least as the outside world defines it, means nothing here. And yet it is in our meetings that we begin to understand who we really are, and come to appreciate our true value. We value, too, the other members of our group, even though we often have no idea what they own or what they do when they leave the room.

The new life we discover in SAA brings with it new values. Most importantly we learn to value ourselves, and the people in our lives, without regard to status or wealth. We learn to see, and to love, the person within.

~

May I learn to see others and myself in terms of spiritual values.

ॐ

"Because of the nature of our addiction, we are careful about touching or giving hugs to others in the fellowship without permission."

Sex Addicts Anonymous, page 12

As a child, I lived in a world without boundaries. The house I grew up in had rules such as, "no locks on the bathroom," and "no private telephone conversations." As a practising sex addict, my boundary-less sexual world seemed exciting and fun. In reality it was frightening and definitely not safe.

I was terrified. On one day, I would be afraid of other people; the next day, I would be desperate for human contact; the next, I couldn't be touched. My life was a constant bouncing between extremes of terror and neediness. In fact, when I came to SAA, I was so afraid, I could only come with a friend, and I tried to hide in his shadow.

I was so relieved to find myself in a place where other recovering sex addicts were respectful of me physically. Many spoke to me kindly and gently, without moving towards me. Many offered to hug me, and made it clear that my options were open. And others gave me the best hugs I had ever had because I was now free from acting out. Those hugs may have felt strange at first, but, best of all, they felt safe.

I am grateful for the many types of relationships I can have in my life today, and the many kinds of physical connections they give me.

⁂

"But with others of like mind, we discover
a new courage and a new faith."

Sex Addicts Anonymous, page 13

For many years I felt so alone. Isolated in addiction,
I was convinced I was unique, different, and alone.
I thought I was the only person who struggled with
compulsive sexual behavior. Lost in this world, it is so
easy to give up and give oneself over to the compulsion
and obsession. And that's what I did for years—just
gave up.

When I first heard of SAA, I was amazed. Being convinced I was alone, I found it hard to believe that there
was an entire fellowship dedicated to this issue. Being
with others of like mind means two things to me. The
first like mind is that all of us in the fellowship of SAA
know the disease of sex addiction. Each face I turn to
in a meeting knows the pain, the suffering, and tor-
ment of this disease. I am not alone; we are not alone.

The second like mind is that each of us is determined
to seek a spiritual awakening and an end to active sexual addiction. Every time I sit in a meeting, I know
the faces I'm seeing are all there sharing in a common
solution. When I share in this common solution by attending meetings and working the Twelve Steps, I avail
myself of the collective wisdom of the thousands in
the fellowship. I cannot help but discover courage and
faith in this light.

*Have I discovered faith in a common solution and the
courage to walk the Steps?*

CR

"We found ourselves isolated and
alone. We felt spiritually empty."
Sex Addicts Anonymous, page 4

I did not play baseball that year because I could not see the ball until it hit me. Dejected and unwanted in fifth grade, I isolated from classmates, withdrew, and was mocked by the jocks. Finally, I had the chance to see an eye doctor. The exam resulted in the diagnosis of legal blindness. But, it was correctable with special glasses. I was able to see! The first day back to school with my new glasses, I realized the teacher was writing on the blackboard and I could read it from the back of the room! I played baseball and caught a high hit to left field. I was able to throw the ball to third base to make two outs. No longer unwanted, no longer isolated, and no longer mocked, my life had changed.

In my addiction I was legally blind to the realities of my life—the pain I was feeling and the hurt I was causing. Damaged lives were all I knew. I felt unwanted and withdrawn from the people I love the most. I felt no hope in my scant awareness that something is horribly wrong with me.

Working the program of SAA, another form of blindness is healed. I am now able to participate with others, recognize my and others' emotions, and I know how to make amends and maintain relationships. I am able to live life with a new freedom.

Through the lens of the Twelve Steps, a new universe is opened for me.

☃

> "We look at how we have neglected our physical, emotional, mental, and spiritual needs.
> We examine the ways in which we allowed others to abuse us and treat us poorly."
>
> *Sex Addicts Anonymous*, page 36

Forgiveness means letting go of the hope or expectation that I can change the past. Today, I can accept that, and that's all that I'm invited to agree to by saying the word forgive. This brings a huge sense of peace.

In the past, I felt forced to forgive as part of being a good person, but it often meant allowing other people to own my power. It allowed me to be bullied and victimized, and it created the false belief that that's what I deserved and what life had to offer me.

Forgiveness does not mean I'm going to fix or change the person, their behavior, or the relationship. Also, forgiveness does not mean giving up my boundaries, or being exposed and vulnerable to people who don't deserve my trust.

Now, forgiveness means loving myself enough to let go of the past and its grip on me, choosing to focus on today and all the wonderful things it has to offer me, including the Steps and all the tools and gifts of recovery. Forgiveness means honoring and caring for my greatest gift and responsibility—my life. Today, I have a choice.

God, I thank you for recovery, for forgiveness, and for my ability to be open to a wonderful present.

ભ

"At the same time, we don't claim that our program is the only way to recover, or oppose those who believe differently. Our only interest is to inform people about the SAA program, to the best of our ability, and not to try to argue or convince."

Sex Addicts Anonymous, page 93

This passage from SAA's Tradition Ten is appealing and refreshing. In the early days of Twelve Step programs, when they were seeing prodigious successes where others had failed, those founders were the first to say that the fault was not in the other approaches, but in the nature of the disease.

Even if I am not religious, I may get help and learn from religious people. If I have problems that are best treated medically, it is likely wise to pursue medical solutions, as long as I consult with my sponsor, my conscience, and my Higher Power before taking any drastic actions. Numerous times in my recovery, I have found the guidance and support of a professional therapist to be very helpful.

The idea that any approach holds all of the answers lacks the very humility I seek as a healing source in my recovery. When I carry the program of SAA to other sex addicts, I need not reject or belittle the idea that they may also find help with a therapist, medicine, or the religion of their choice. To do this might discourage others from finding a solution to the incredibly complex problem of sexual addiction, and also carry a message of intolerance and conceit.

I will respect the choices of others in SAA as they pursue their recovery.

> "For most of us the First Step was diametrically opposed to one of our core beliefs: that we were in control and if we just tried a little harder or tried one <u>more</u> time we'd have it."
>
> "First Step to Recovery"

I finally realized my life was unmanageable as I stared down at a pair of yellow socks that looked like someone had skinned a certain cartoon sponge. I was on suicide watch at the local hospital. No one knew where I was. I had been picked up by a police officer and involuntarily committed. They had taken everything: my phone, my computer, even my socks. I had become a non-person.

Up to this point, I had explained away every consequence of my addiction. There was no explaining this away. Without a doubt my acting out had landed me here, wearing yellow socks in a locked mental ward.

I needed this experience to finally face the utter bankruptcy of my own abilities and ideas. Maybe I had never truly been present enough or honest enough to recognize it. This painful moment became the touchstone for my recovery.

I keep the yellow socks to remind me. My admission of powerlessness and unmanageability opened the door for change, and it keeps me coming back and working the program. I am not in control of my disease. Fortunately, I can bring it to my Higher Power and to the tools and fellowship of SAA for expert care.

For today, I offer my addiction and my life to the loving care of one more qualified.

∞

"I only have to be awake enough to notice, or
smart enough to remember to turn to God when
I need help, or even to express gratitude."

Sex Addicts Anonymous, page 289

The electricity in my house was out for a short time
while the line was repaired. I was in the basement
with no windows when the electricity shut off, and I
was plunged into darkness. However, I went upstairs
where light was streaming in, and things seemed so
normal that I promptly forgot I had no electricity. Only
when I opened the dark fridge or futilely tried the mi-
crowave did I remember. I felt foolish and frustrated as
I continued to fail at things I thought I should be able
to do. I couldn't make things happen.

Though I've been granted, by the grace of God, a re-
mission from my acting-out behaviors one day at a
time for some time, I need to be reminded that I'm also
powerless over my intimacy-avoidant behaviors. I can
still assume that, on willpower alone, I should be able
to let go of my need to control everything and everyone, to open up and share my feelings, and to allow
my partner to nurture me emotionally and physically.

But God lets me squeeze the steering wheel until my
failures show me, again, where I am powerless. Then I
pray for understanding, strength, and help; and seek
encouragement and support from program friends.
The big difference now is that I am open to the signs
and willing to change.

God, give me the courage to love more fully today.

❧

"We may never be able to fully understand
what those we have harmed have gone through,
but we can ask for the willingness to have this
understanding given to us, in God's time."

Sex Addicts Anonymous, page 48

I struggle to understand what harm I may have
caused some people from my past. Over the years,
some people have cut off contact with me, but I cannot
recall what I may have done to cause this. Something
lingers in my memory: a sense of guilt and remorse,
maybe accurate, maybe not.

I may not be able to get into their heads to understand if I have done something to impact them, but I
am reminded that my Higher Power can help me if I
am willing to ask. It may take time and require a great
deal of patience, but I believe it is worth the effort. If it
is meant to be, the opportunity will present itself. I just
have to be ready and willing.

In the meantime, I can continue to acknowledge the
harms I remember causing others. In going through
the process of identifying those I have harmed and
being specific about those harms, I am able to move
forward in Step Eight. With each person I identify and
with each action I take ownership of, I come that much
closer to healing my past. Calling upon my Higher
Power, and with the support of my sponsor and fellows
in SAA, I discover the willingness to make amends to
those I have harmed.

～

I can do what I can do. Today, that is enough.

❧

> "We were often depressed and dissatisfied
> with our lives; we were resentful and
> blamed others for our unhappiness."

Sex Addicts Anonymous, page 7

Funny thing about my resentments: I treasured them because they made me feel powerful, and I denied them because I was ashamed to have anyone know I harbored them. I loved them and felt guilty about them at the same time. So I disguised them behind a fake smile, fake warmth, and by manipulating and ignoring people.

I veiled my resentments with sarcasm, teasing, gossip, mocking, and "constructive criticism." I hid them behind non-verbal actions like crossing my arms, rolling my eyes, and sighing. I even tried to soften resentments by relabeling them as grudges, hurts, or disappointments. These are only a few of the ways I kept from facing how deeply resentful I was.

When it came time to inventory my resentments in Step Four, I had to face the disguises, veils, hiding places, and misleading labels. I had to give up feeling powerful for being truthful. Gently and honestly, I started to face all the anger, pain, and jealously that I had been trying to avoid. My resentments had been a cover for these more personal and vulnerable emotions.

For perhaps the first time in my adult life, I was consciously trying to be emotionally honest with myself and others. As I worked through my resentments and related feelings, another funny thing happened. A more genuine person came out. The true me started to emerge.

~

My resentments hide the real me. As I work through them, my best self can appear.

> "Changing old routines that are
> associated with our addiction is an
> important tool for staying sober."

Tools of Recovery, page 13

I immediately felt at home in SAA, but worried that
you would not accept me. I was married to a woman
but acted out with men. I helped others but couldn't
help myself. You welcomed me; no one shamed me; I
belonged. I took your suggestions: went to meetings,
found a sponsor, made phone calls, and started the
Steps.

In addiction I would sexualize uncomfortable feelings
into acting-out fuel. A month ago I was at work on a
Friday, my traditional acting-out day. It was a slow
day. I felt uncomfortable, and all the old pain and fear
came back. I dipped into what my sponsor and I call
dysphoric recall—regret, shame, and hopelessness.

But this time, I had choices for addressing those uncomfortable feelings and memories. I made phone calls
and texts to my sponsor and program friends. I even
had the courage to let my wife know what was going
on. She appreciated my trust in her. The day came and
went, and I stayed sober.

I'm still me and can still struggle with negative self-
talk like, "I don't deserve grace, forgiveness, or belonging." When the old tapes re-emerge, it's a clue that
something may be going on in me, and I need to reach
out. With the tools of recovery, I can recognize those
uncomfortable feelings for what they are and let them
pass as they always do.

*This feeling will pass whether I act out or not. Today, I
have choices.*

ભ

"We ask for and accept help, reaching out
to other recovering sex addicts on a regular
basis, instead of <u>living</u> in secrecy. "

Sex Addicts Anonymous, page 31

Secrets can be devastating to my sexual and relational sobriety. They can be a back door through which the ills of my addiction can pass. When I start to be selective about the information I share with my sponsor, I set myself up for relapse.

One addict really does know when another is setting himself or herself up. When I start to go underground and isolate, there is no opportunity to do a reality check or halt the progression or cycle. Owning my thoughts and behaviors to another recovering addict can stop the downward spiral.

I have learned that the thoughts and behaviors I try to keep secret are shame-based. The fact that I try to hide them is a clear message that they are unsafe and can wreak havoc in my life. Bringing them out into the light exposes them for what they are—phantoms without substance. It also helps me stay accountable to myself and to life.

~

Today I contract to share secret thoughts and behaviors with another recovering addict.

> "I know that I am on track spiritually when
> I am able to be honest with myself and be
> present both with my feelings and with the
> moment at hand, no matter what it is."
>
> *Sex Addicts Anonymous*, page 130

Feelings are real, but they are not necessarily based in truth. This reminder has been helpful when powerful emotions such as resentment, fear, loneliness, shame, or self-loathing have pulled me in the direction of acting out. Yet acting out is never a viable option.

In the moment, any feeling can be so intense and pervasive that it seems to be my whole world, my entire perception of reality. A familiar slogan of Twelve-Step programs reminds me that "This too shall pass." If I can stop for a moment and ask for God's grace, then I can choose sobriety and recovery.

Steps Ten, Eleven, and Twelve bolster me in the onslaught of powerful emotions. Taking personal inventory helps me to keep things in balance. Immersing myself in my Higher Power's presence through prayer and meditation re-centers me. Engaging in service moves my focus outward. Most importantly, each step keeps me sane and sober.

I can give myself and the world a gift by practicing my recovery today.

ଔ

"Boundaries may also be limits we set and
maintain with others in our lives. We learn
how to let other people know how we wish to
be treated and what kinds of behavior we will
and will not accept. Unless we accept personal
responsibility for establishing and sticking
to healthy boundaries in our relationships,
we run the risk of harboring resentments or
casting ourselves in the role of the victim."

Sex Addicts Anonymous, page 64

Bumping up against limits is not easy for me. From
that first painful moment I was told no, my world
seemed smaller, restricted. I no longer felt that I was
fully free or fully in charge.

In time, I have learned that I, too, can set limits. By
saying no, I define my likes and dislikes, my principles, my values, myself. Paradoxically, it is only when
I can say no that I can freely say yes. Healthy limits
and boundaries free me by making the world safe for
my exploration.

~

*May I respect my own limits and those of others. May I
find new freedom and safety.*

ભ

> "A profound turning point in my recovery
> happened when I faced and embraced the
> pain of the emptiness I felt inside, which
> I had tried to fill with so many fixes."
>
> *Sex Addicts Anonymous*, page 130

After working a very difficult Fourth Step, I was sure that Step Five was going to be less painful. As it turned out, Step Four uncovered and brought to the surface many unsettling emotions—emotions that I had successfully locked away in unfettered avoidance. Thank God for my sponsor, who guided me through this personal upheaval with a sense of grace, clarity, and perspective. I had no idea that working these Steps could help me rediscover myself on a level that continues to enhance integrity and diminish shame.

Many years of addiction and self-hatred programmed me to wallow in self-pity, entitlement, and a never-ending cycle of self-criticism. Ironically, it was the deep reflection and recalling my most despicable, shameful behaviors that allowed me to be more gentle with myself. Trusting others with this awful information of my past opened the door for an honest journey into the moment. No longer do I dwell in shame. I am accepted lovingly by my sponsor and by my brothers and sisters in recovery. I can embrace God's will with the renewed faith that every day is an opportunity to make a new past.

As I look back on my life since coming to SAA, I am proud of who I have become and excited about the new relationships I have made. None were more important than a relationship with God.

May you find God now!

"While in the throes of tension, anxiety, or insistent sexual urges, some find it helpful to recite [the Serenity Prayer] over and over."

Tools of Recovery, page 17

I became a meditator years before I got sober. I studied with disciples and practitioners, went on silent retreats and vision quests, and sat in zendos, ashrams, and sweat lodges. All the while, I acted out.

I used meditation to escape anxiety and blot out the fact that I wasn't happy with my life or comfortable in my skin. Once, sitting before an acknowledged master, I was told, "You are trying too hard, sitting too tight in the saddle." I didn't know what to do with this, but I felt it was true. It wasn't until I hit bottom that the path was cleared for my discovery of SAA.

When I came to the rooms and was surrounded by fellow sufferers, I was ready to learn and use the Serenity Prayer. There were times in early sobriety when I was in such pain that I struggled to remember the words. There were times when I said the prayer dozens of times in a row just to exorcise the fear and unfamiliarity of living as a known entity, a recovering addict, for the first time in my life. But the prayer has a context. The fellowship of other addicts, and saying it together, give it a power and meaning beyond my wildest dreams. Now, almost twelve years later, the power of serenity is a constant in my life.

God, grant me serenity.

ca

> "When I'm in judgment of someone else, I
> have no peace, so I try to stick to taking my
> own inventory instead of everyone else's."
>
> *Sex Addicts Anonymous*, page 326

When my sponsor encouraged me to journal about the defects I was least willing to be rid of, I quickly identified judgmental thoughts. I proudly had no patience with people who think the rules don't apply to them. The beauty of this faulty belief system is that I got to be the sole arbiter of other people's motives.

In traffic one day, a driver in front of me turned left where a sign indicated no left turns. I went straight into judgment. I was righteously indignant for days. Any time I passed the intersection, the anger and feeling of superiority returned.

Through discussions with my sponsor and others, I acknowledged that the driver of the car was just as likely a good person who simply made a mistake. Heaven knows, I don't want to be judged solely by my mistakes!

If I sit in judgment and scorn of others, I lose my humility, I isolate myself, and I leave no space for empathy, understanding, forgiveness, or love. Now, I have tools. The Serenity Prayer and the Third Step remind me of what I actually have control over. My Fifth and Eighth Steps keep me from getting too self-righteous. The kindness and acceptance I have experienced in SAA reminds me of the power of love.

Thank you for showing me another way.

ॐ

> "Learning to seek the will of our Higher Power
> through group conscience takes time, patience,
> and good will. Love is the force that guides
> our service activities, rather than the familiar
> methods of human power and control."

Sex Addicts Anonymous, page 80

To me, group conscience meetings are an important part of a group. During one of my first group conscience meetings, our group discussed an idea that I thought would allow newcomers to be better able to find our meeting. We had a vote, but the motion wasn't approved. I felt disappointed and thought we were denying addicts an opportunity for help, but I knew that we would be all right.

In addition, my sponsor told me that he would continue to attend the meeting because he needed the meeting more than the meeting needed him. To me, this was an example of the principle of surrender by putting the group first and then letting God work in our groups. It is important for me to speak my conscience and to allow others to do the same. If it's the right thing to do, it will eventually make itself apparent.

I find group consciences rewarding because I also feel a deeper connection to other recovering sex addicts and to the fellowship as a whole. In addition, I realize that a loving God is acting as the ultimate authority.

~

Grant me courage to speak the truth as I see it, and serenity to let others do the same.

ॐ

> "In writing about envy, we may look at
> all of the ways we compare our insides
> with the outsides of others."
>
> *Sex Addicts Anonymous*, page 35

Looking back, I see how my life crawled forward from a lonely, isolated childhood, through a self-conscious adolescence, and finally into an adulthood where envy was always a passenger on life's bus. I did not compare myself from a standpoint that others were smarter, stronger, better looking, or more popular, but more so from what I saw when viewing my image in life's mirror. I saw a lanky scarecrow, a runny-nosed kid who wore tweed jackets and a bowtie. I had taught myself to dislike this image.

Over the years, I kept the impression that I was still the little boy I had perceived as ugly. In this prison, I avoided close friendships, belittled my abilities, and found reasons to fail. In this whirlwind of self-deprecation, my sex addict found his home.

My work in recovery has brought many gifts, some immediately obvious and others growing subtly in the background. Of the subtle gifts, a growing acceptance of self has blossomed from the love and acceptance of my friends in the fellowship, and from the love and grace of my Higher Power. This acceptance has allowed love to flow to the surface. Finally, the carnival of madness I call my negative self-perception has vanished. Now, the mirror's most unpleasant tasks are to check for that annoying spot on my shirt or to see if my tie is straight.

~

I am a precious child of a loving God. I need not compare myself to others.

⋘

"What has recovery given me? Everything.
Recovery has graced every aspect of my life."
Sex Addicts Anonymous, page 316

I am so grateful I am a sex addict! If you think I'm crazy, I would certainly understand. My acting out was causing cognitive dissonance. I didn't want to be the person I quite apparently was when I was practicing this disease. I wanted to be a loving person, but I couldn't stop acting out, and it was killing me inside. However, because of the ravages of my sex addiction, I started going to SAA meetings, arguably the best decision I have ever made.

I am not only free from inner circle behaviors for over a year, I have blessings I never could have imagined for myself. I have become more honest with myself and others than I thought possible. I have started to be truly present with others and experience honest intimacy. I have made friends with some amazing people. I am starting to love and accept myself. I am becoming courageous. I am learning how to handle my emotions in a healthy way. I am becoming a whole, integrated person.

I am grateful to this program and the amazing people in it, and to my Higher Power, who directs my recovery. None of this would have happened if I hadn't been sick and miserable enough to stumble, ashamed and dazed, through the doors of SAA.

~

Little did I realize that recovery is so much more than mere sobriety. I am healing, and I am living.

> "Being a sex addict felt like being trapped
> in endless contradictions. We sought
> love and romance, but when we found
> it, we feared and fled from intimacy."
>
> *Sex Addicts Anonymous*, page 6

I never understood why I would avoid sex with my loving, beautiful partner but crave sex with strangers. I would make excuses not to be sexual, then sneak off to masturbate to pornography or act out with prostitutes. I told myself I had sexual needs that others weren't evolved enough to understand.

I now see the complete insanity of my behavior and the belief system behind it. I wasn't some special being; I was a sex addict desperately fleeing intimacy, terrified of vulnerability and my own feelings. By acting out, I built walls to keep my partners and friends at a safe distance, and I used porn and sexual obsession to numb myself.

I first discovered true intimacy in the rooms of SAA. I found a safe place to express my feelings and forge true connections with others. I could share from my heart without fear of judgment or ridicule because these people are just like me—imperfect and beautiful, and in the early connections I forged with my sisters and brothers in program, I found my Higher Power.

My sex addiction is an intimacy disorder, but in SAA I learn to be vulnerable and share from my heart. I am safe and no longer alone.

Just for today, I pray for courage to share from my heart.

> "To make the Third Step decision is to
> surrender. We give up the belief that our
> intellect, our knowledge, our judgment, and
> our will could successfully guide our lives."
>
> *Sex Addicts Anonymous*, page 30

"You're right where you're supposed to be" was a saying I often heard in the fellowship. These people obviously did not understand me if they thought that was helpful. I hurt. A lot. I needed to be someplace else. My vehicle to that place, acting out, was no longer a viable option, so I was miserable, and they obviously did not understand.

But, since they said they had a solution that would work, and more, I kept coming back, wanting to be anything other than me here now. I still did things my way, and I continued to hurt. A lot. Not overly enthusiastic about Step Three, I was nonetheless miserable. Knowing I could not manage sobriety or my own life, I gave surrender a shot.

Without the desperation and misery, I would never have stayed for the miracles that come with abstinence and walking a spiritual path. I have learned that when (maybe especially when) the pain becomes unbearable, I am reaching another level of surrender, a new area of growth, again, exactly where I'm supposed to be. On my own unaided power, I make messes, but if I just do my small part in accordance with this program and leave the rest to my Higher Power, my Higher Power takes those messes and makes miracles.

For this moment, I'm right where I'm supposed to be.

&

> "By admitting that powerlessness extended
> to compulsive sexual avoidance, we made it
> possible to move from a kind of superficial
> abstinence into deeper sobriety."
> "Recovery from Compulsive Sexual Avoidance"

Superficial abstinence really describes me when I joined SAA. I'd withdrawn from acting-out behaviors right into avoidance of any sexual behavior. I started identifying myself as a sexual anorexic, somehow knowing the description fit. I didn't grasp how deep it went until I met program members who understand both aspects of the addiction: acting in and acting out.

Losing interest in sex with a committed partner was nothing new to me. Understanding why I cheated, lied, and acted out with everyone but my partner was a revelation. Introverted in the extreme, I recharge my batteries with alone time. But when acting out, I badger myself into acting like an extrovert and tend to connect sexually with extroverts. Talk about setting myself up, not to mention false advertising!

When I read the pamphlet on avoidance, I could honestly say no to only two of the eighteen questions. Hearing other SAA members describe similar behaviors finally got my attention. I began to acknowledge my avoidant behaviors: lack of self-care, self-sabotage, self-mutilation; and sexual, social, and emotional isolation. With better understanding of my addiction— both extremes—I'm more able to recover and find some balance in my life.

~

You mean my Higher Power might actually want me to enjoy healthy sexuality?

"Practicing new ways of behavior can
help open our hearts to the spiritual
changes God wants for us."
Sex Addicts Anonymous, page 42

When I listed my defects in my inventory, I became discouraged. I felt overwhelmed. It was tough enough to deal with addiction and abstinence. It was painful seeing my defects listed so plainly. When I came to Step Six, I thought, "Well that's not very practical. All I need is to be 'entirely ready'?"

A partial answer came when I studied the section on Step Six in Sex Addicts Anonymous. The words willing and willingness appear eight times. When we begin the program of SAA, we acknowledge that we are willing to do whatever it takes, willing to change our way of life. Ah! Now we're talking action! I can allow myself to be ready for change as I let go of old ways of approaching life.

Many of my old ways of approaching life are now character defects, but on the other side of every defect is an asset. It will take time to replace my defects and discover my assets, but there are things I can do right now. I can ask myself, "What am I doing now—a good action, or a bad action? Is my mind clear, or is it filled with desire, or anger, or …?" As I develop awareness of my thinking and behavior, I begin to learn how and when my defects activate. I can ask my Higher Power for alternative actions, and I can grow in willingness for Step Seven.

I can be the change I want to see, one step at a time.

ℂℋ

> "We cannot afford to be complacent
> or to live unconsciously."
> *Sex Addicts Anonymous*, page 62

I am a sex addict, and if I want to stay sober, I must be vigilant. I have a number of months of continuous sobriety from my inner circle behaviors, and a better life than I ever experienced before. If I want to keep my new life, I cannot rest on my laurels. I must keep up with my spiritual practices, which include working the Steps and using the tools of Sex Addicts Anonymous.

I recently went on a spiritual retreat for a week. Admittedly, I was secretly hoping to have a vacation from my rigorous program practices—the phone calls, the meetings. I reasoned that I was going to a meditation retreat, so I could relax my program work while there.

Fortunately, my Higher Power intervened, and two people I know from SAA arranged to take me to a meeting. I was picked up at my hotel and whisked away to an SAA meeting. I knew God was in charge, and I smiled. It was a great meeting, and I was able to get to another meeting on the phone during that week.

Because of this intervention by my Higher Power, I was made aware how, during this retreat, I could have been in active addiction. My mind would have been in a totally different realm. It would not have been a meditation retreat focused on God, it would have been instead focused on my disease. I can never be complacent or live unconsciously, even in the midst of the most spiritual circumstances.

~

Everyday is a new day to be vigilant about sobriety from sex addiction.

F

"We have found that one of the reasons
this process works so well is precisely
because we <u>do</u> it ourselves."

Sex Addicts Anonymous, page 83

When I first started attending SAA meetings, I felt
pretty passive. I wasn't sure what was going on, what
was going to happen, and what was expected of me. As
I kept coming back, however, I started to gain a sense
of what meetings are about, what the service roles are
in my groups, and what I can do to help.

I think it's important to remember that Tradition
Four not only liberates our groups from outside control, it also places the responsibility for the conduct of
our groups squarely on each of us. There is no group
without our individual service. Passivity is a natural
place for a newcomer to start, but it's not a place to
stay. There are meetings to lead, business meetings to
attend, phones to answer, members to sponsor, conferences to organize. If I leave these things for others
to do, I am missing out on a vital element of recovery.

As we say, "It works if you work it." Part of working it
means being an active participant in my group and in
SAA as a whole.

~

*May I gratefully accept the autonomy, freedom, and
responsibility that are mine as a member of SAA.*

☙

> "Every SAA group ought to be fully self-supporting, declining outside contributions."
>
> *Sex Addicts Anonymous*, page 87

In my process of growing, recovering, and ultimately, growing up in SAA, I have seen my understanding of the Seventh Tradition grow and change with me. When I first came into the rooms, I was told, "The Steps will keep you from committing suicide, and the Traditions will keep you from committing homicide." In other words, if it was a problem with myself, find the step that applies. If it was a situation with someone else, it might be a tradition that applies.

My sponsor showed me how I could put my name in this Tradition in place of "Every SAA group," and I could quickly see how often my acting out was connected with wanting others to support me when it was actually my job to do so.

As the years pass and I become more and more self-supporting, I have seen how my relations with others have improved. Today, I see that this is more than just "the money tradition." It is a way of living both independently and interdependently with others.

～

God, help me be open and willing today to see where I can improve my practice of being self-supporting. May I also see where I excel at it.

ca

"As we grow in humility, we gradually
come to view our lives, and even
our problems, with gratitude."

Sex Addicts Anonymous, page 44

When I first walked into SAA, gratitude was unfathomable to me. I wondered how in the world SAA members could refer to themselves as grateful recovering sex addicts. How can you be grateful for the wrecked lives we bring to these rooms?

Over time and probably repeated mentioning, it dawned on me that these people have gratitude because they practice gratitude. I learned that gratitude can be developed. If resentment is one of the main feeders of our disease, I've found gratitude to be one of the best medicines.

In my addiction, my mindset was one of self-pity, of how I had been wronged or was owed by the world. When I came to realize that the universe does not play favorites, and that I am not entitled, I could then cultivate gratitude for what I do have. When I acknowledge that all my good and bad experiences will eventually, often quickly, fade, I can develop non-attachment and appreciate life for what it is. I no longer have to cling to the past or grasp for the future. I can just be present.

~

May I bring awareness, not to all my unanswered expectations, but to all the ways my life is made rich, right here, right now. May I recognize life's passing nature and be thankful for all I have, right here, right now.

ભ

> "At meetings we learn that we can
> trust others to know who we really are,
> and still be accepted by them."
>
> *Sex Addicts Anonymous*, page 11

When I first came into the program, I did not trust myself. Mainly, I did not trust my emotions; I thought of them as my enemies because they betrayed me. I thought they made me weak, and I had to be strong in all circumstances. I was always on guard, watching myself. I also did not trust other people. I believed that if I let anyone get close to me, they would leave me or betray my secrets, so I was always on guard watching them, too. I was exhausted and lonely, and felt trapped in the belief that this was just how life went. Needless to say, my addiction thrived in this environment.

A turning point in my recovery began when I tried, slowly, trusting myself enough to acknowledge my emotions, and then trusting others enough to share my emotions with them. As I began to acknowledge and express what was going on inside me, I discovered that it was easing my loneliness and pain. I also learned that my emotions were a great source of information about how I interpret the world around me.

In the process, I realized that, by trusting my emotions and then trusting my group and my friends, I was trusting my Higher Power as well.

By simply acknowledging my feelings, I can open the door to trust and to healing.

❧

> "Although our experiences are different,
> certain aspects are common to many of us."

Sex Addicts Anonymous, page 59

My first impression of Twelve-Step programs was of cookie-cutter, superficial recipes for what I considered a very serious problem. Elsewhere, I had heard gurus and self-appointed experts lay out their simplistic solutions, and I was wary. Instead, I found the Twelve Steps to be a powerful tool for digging deeply into the individual essence of my addiction—the beliefs, actions, and consequences that were making my life unmanageable.

I learned that this is a life-long, life-changing, spiritual program. I emphasize spiritual because part of my life experience included an abusive religious background. Accepting what others called God was a big challenge for me. Being asked and allowed to discover my own Higher Power helped me accept the differences between me and others in the program. Through the steps, my sponsor, my group, and my readings, I found my Higher Power. Sharing my inventory with my sponsor helped me discover and accept myself, warts and all. I began to see new possibilities and make healthier choices.

In looking at the true nature of my addiction and the solution, I found common ground and fellowship with other program members. I learned to set aside superficial differences and focus on the profound, common message of healing through a fellowship of people with similar struggles and a common solution.

～

May I continue to look for similarities, knowing that we are all on the same journey.

ରେ

> "In our addiction we held onto the belief that
> we were in control of our sexual behavior
> and could successfully manage our lives."
>
> *Sex Addicts Anonymous*, page 22

It wasn't until I started to work the SAA program that I could finally admit I had a problem. My sex addiction was destroying me. It was out of control. Like a caged wild animal, my acting out behavior had broken free and I was completely powerless to stop it. I had to admit defeat and let go in order to see how insane I had become. My resistance, though, was strong. My sex addiction has always been grounded on one fundamental human need: safety.

As a survivor of childhood incest, I was never safe. By acting out, my primary instinct was to gain control over people, places, things, and myself. I tried to play God and successfully run my sex life in the only way I knew—to win. Step One teaches me the miracle paradox of recovery: to truly win, I must admit defeat. Only by admitting and ultimately accepting that I am 100% powerless over my sex addiction and that my life is unmanageable, can I begin the life-saving journey of the Twelve Steps. I can now accept that the moment I begin to practice Step One, I won. I let go of my way, which never worked, and allowed my Higher Power to heal me from the inside out.

~

Step One grants me the humility I need to let go of control and trust my Higher Power.

> "The middle circle is where we place
> behavior of which we are <u>uncertain</u>."
>
> "Three Circles"

One focus of my recovery is shifting my attention from strangers to people I know. For much of my life, humanity was the collection of people I saw but did not really know. These included pedestrians on the street, drivers or passengers in cars and buses, and patrons in stores, libraries, or other establishments.

I interacted with these strangers largely through eye contact. Never was I to get beyond a fantasy relationship. I blamed people for not being more open, yet it was I who was closed off. I pushed away any individuals who seemed open to me.

In recovery I am attempting to avoid the frank eye contact with strangers, and have put this in my middle circle. Most importantly, I am taking baby steps toward strengthening my friendships and meeting new people. The loving fellowship of SAA provides me with wonderful opportunities to actually get to know people.

Let my eyes help me see those I would befriend.

ભ

> "Putting slippery behaviors in our middle
> circle is a way of warning ourselves when
> we are in danger of acting out."
> *Sex Addicts Anonymous*, page 18

These are the times, surroundings, behaviors, and thoughts that could easily lead me to my inner circle. Staying at the edge through self-will sets me up for self-sabotage and a return to that darkness we know all too well. But I don't have to, not anymore! When my mind gets cluttered in uncertainty whether a certain item is unhealthy or putting me at risk, I can find relief in a simple tool.

I write down the times, behaviors, surroundings, and mind-sets that jeopardize my sobriety and serenity. I then share what I write with my sponsor. Before doing this, my thoughts are vague, coated by denial. By writing the situation down, it becomes defined, concrete, and clear. I see it for what it is. Also, putting the situation down on paper immediately calms my mind and eases my emotions.

Sharing honestly with my sponsor helps me further identify and define these behaviors. I can then put them in my middle circle if indicated.

~

Today, I have a choice, and I choose to expose my shadows to the light.

☙

"When we accept that our way
doesn't work, Step Two opens the
door to a new way that does."

Sex Addicts Anonymous, page 25

I remember a time in my recovery when I believed
that long-term abstinence was impossible. I had always taken my recovery in SAA seriously, but inevitably, it seemed, I would relapse in despair, frustration,
and shame. One time, after two years of abstinence, I
relapsed directly into some of the worst behaviors of
my life. I felt that the SAA program, the Twelve Steps,
and God had failed me. But then I looked at my sponsor and a few others in my meetings and saw that they
were living examples of the miracle of recovery.

I looked closer at Step Two and found that the quanti-
ty of my efforts wasn't the problem. It was the quality.
I hadn't made room for my Higher Power to guide and
assist me in the process. I realized that I had franti-
cally worked the program, believing that what I saw
was what was there. My own will tends to be short-
sighted, selfish, frightened, and pleasure seeking, and
I was missing a lot. I learned instead to focus on my
relationship with my Higher Power, listening for and
acting on God's will, not mine. When I did this, long-
term abstinence and recovery became a reality for me.

*Rather than relying on my addict mind, I can improve
the quality of my actions by looking to my Higher
Power for guidance and courage.*

"Best of all, the secret is out. There's something liberating about sitting in a room announcing to others ... that I am a sex addict."

Sex Addicts Anonymous, page 192

I recently gave my First Step presentation to my home group for the second time. The contrast between this and the first time couldn't have been more dramatic. The first time, I felt like the narrative was radioactive. It was hard to make myself work on it. It was like my computer had a repelling force as I sat in front of it. I left out major parts of my sex addiction story. And, I felt triggered for several weeks afterwards.

After later hearing a First Step that went into details very much like those I left out, I felt encouraged to look at mine again. I was eager to write down the details I had omitted. I was still fearful beforehand, but there was practically no sense of being triggered before or after. Instead, I felt an enormous sense of relief. I felt raw and vulnerable while giving it the second time, but I was floating on a cloud for days afterwards.

The walls were down, the shameful secrets were out, my burden of shame is lighter, much lighter. What a release! This is the miracle of the Steps.

My secrets are toxic. To let the light in, to be known and still accepted, is healing.

ca

> "Whenever we ask for this help, we invite
> God into our lives in a new way."
> *Sex Addicts Anonymous*, page 43

I'm not very good at receiving from others. At the same time, I tend to hoard things. In my mind's eye, I see my hands piled with useless junk. I can't receive or hold anything new until I put something down. Likewise, I can't fully receive God's love and healing until I give up what's blocking me from accepting it.

The Steps help me identify the self-will that prevents my healing and growth. But I can't change my own programming; all I can do is become willing to allow God to change it. Demanding that God do that for me doesn't work either, but when I invite my Higher Power to remove my resentment, impatience, fear, and the other things that impede my recovery, and when I humbly ask to be filled with love and light instead, I can feel my nature changing.

As I do things that strengthen my relationship with God, that connection increases my sense of self-worth. When I surrender my character defects to my Higher Power, it leaves my heart free to receive what God wants to give me.

~

God, please take from me whatever hinders my progress and give me what I need to grow.

ʘ

"Sometimes we need to call people to help start
our day. At other times, we may need to check
in about current thoughts and behaviors. Some
suggest calling three people every day in order
to build and maintain a support system."

Tools of Recovery, page 10

Over the years I have come to love the slogans. They
encapsulate a lot of wisdom in a few words, and can
readily be called up to guide an action or decision. One
such slogan is "let it begin with me."

I was always hesitant to start anything new in recovery. The actions often seemed trite, scary, or both.
Some years ago, someone at a meeting said, "I need
to rat out my addict." I was immediately struck with
the importance of this. I decided to do it, which meant
action. After years of making very few phone calls, I
started making regular phone calls to program friends.
I let it begin with me.

Making those calls, I couldn't expect the other person
to rat out my addict. Again, I had to let it begin with
me. I needed to practice rigorous honesty. I checked
in regarding my insanity, feelings of being triggered,
whether or not I acted on those feelings, why I might
be feeling triggered, etc. Those calls have changed my
life. My addict has been withering ever since.

~

*When I let it begin with me, I am free to take
responsibility for my own recovery.*

cs

"On the other side of every character
defect is a character asset."

Sex Addicts Anonymous, page 42

My sponsor asked me to find the kernel of good in
each of the character defects uncovered during my
Fourth Step. What could possibly be good about obsession, self-hatred, and seething resentment?

Through work and patience, I learned that most of my
character defects are misdirected virtues, attributes
designed to help me. At the root of obsession I discovered passion; at the root of self-hatred are awareness
and desire to be and do my best; and at the root of
many resentments is the need to set healthy boundaries in relationships.

Each defect started as a good seed, designed to grow
and bear fruit. As an addict, I neglected the plants.
I did not nourish them or prune the branches. Like
many fruit bearing plants, if not cared for, my personality traits cease to bear good fruit.

In Step Seven, I'm not asking God to remove a part
of me. Instead, I'm asking God to remove the snarled,
dead branches. As God prunes, I can watch the virtues emerge and see them bear good fruit in my life.
While this is an exciting premise, I must remember
that pruning is painful. I need courage, compassion,
acceptance, patience, and the loving support of God
and the SAA fellowship to undergo this lifelong challenge, one day at a time.

*For today, I am willing to endure the pruning that can
transform my defects into the fruitful gifts they were
designed to be.*

ଓଃ

> "Humility means being teachable,
> vulnerable, and open."
> *Sex Addicts Anonymous*, page 43

In my youth, I believed I should know everything and be right about everything, even when I didn't know. This included discussions with people who knew more than I. As my addiction took over my life, I did not notice that I was increasingly closed-minded.

Looking back, I now see how my addictive, closed mind presented itself. I had to be right. I claimed knowledge I did not have. I tried to predict the future. I was pessimistic and always looked for the worst possible outcomes. I discounted others whose ideas differed from mine. I was brash and boastful, trying to appear informed and wise. I thought I was controlling my world.

After starting to live by the Twelve Steps, I was confronted with my closed mind and how it contrasted with the recovery I saw in others. I had to face the truth that my closed mind made my life unmanageable. That was almost as painful as seeing how my addiction had made my life unmanageable. To my surprise, surrendering both my addiction and my closed mind relieved a lot of pain.

For the first time in my life, it became all right for me to say, "I don't know." Admitting I don't know opens me to learning from experience and from other people. "I don't know" became a key part of my daily practice. It created an intellectual and emotional freedom I had never known.

~

Admitting I don't know something opens doors.

☙

"Healthy sexuality is a spiritual
experience that is worth working for."

"Abstinence"

In Sex Addicts Anonymous, our inner circle consists
largely of "addictive sexual behavior" or "acting out."
According to my sponsor, for me, that included masturbation and fantasy.

My addiction was hardcore, the acting out hardcore,
the fantasies hardcore. I did and thought about doing
things—some illegal, many extreme—since I was very,
very young.

I signed on to my sponsor's inner circle definitions
because he knows how denial works. For a person
like me, there wasn't room for half-measures. I had
to accept that I had to turn over all of my sexuality
to a Higher Power if I was going to ever have a loving,
healthy relationship.

For me, giving up fantasy, and masturbation—let
alone the porn, prostitutes, and hook-ups—has giv-
en me clean time—years of it. For twenty-five years,
I thought this was impossible. Now it's come true.
Sobriety unfolds for me only in honest abstinence. I
am not numbing out with sex. One day I can know
a loving sexuality with someone else, in commitment
and intimacy, because I am sticking with the program
that has been laid out for me by those who wouldn't
cosign my addict.

~

A hardcore spiritual change awaits me through
hardcore surrender. The anguish does become
replaced with love.

> "Gratitude provides a needed perspective
> on our problems and helps us feel
> connected with our Higher Power."
>
> *Sex Addicts Anonymous*, page 53

I have found that my urge to act out arises most frequently when I am feeling sorry for myself and am experiencing my core dysfunctional beliefs about myself. One of the most powerful tools I have found to turn those self-defeating messages around is to practice gratitude. For me this is a difficult thing to do, and I have found that it takes practice.

Sometimes I have to become what I call primitive in my gratitude list. I have to start by being grateful to be alive. I move on to remind myself that today I have a roof over my head, and I have enough to eat and drink. I then move to higher levels of gratitude by reminding myself that I have family and friends. These people care about me even if they are critical of my behaviors or are telling me how much I have hurt them. If they didn't care, they wouldn't tell me; they would just avoid me.

Eventually, I can get past thinking about myself to the point that I can be grateful to be of service to someone whose needs I consider and treat with respect. Meetings often provide such opportunities.

Sincere gratitude can replace the bondage of self and strengthen recovery.

ରୁ

> "We realize that everything we have been
> through helps us to be of service to others.
> We learn that the world is a much safer place
> than we had ever known before, because we
> are always in the care of a loving God."
>
> *Sex Addicts Anonymous*, page 61

The message I choose to carry is one of gratitude and recovery. For much of my life, I stared at the demon of my addiction, under its control and unable to recognize the damage until I had lost much that was precious to me. I share my story with others in the hopes that it may help someone in time to save things that they will regret having no more.

My spiritual awakening has come gradually in most ways, yet, in some, it was sudden. After identifying my problem, I was soon aware that it was only covering up deeper issues. That awareness helped me be open to all the tools and methods I encountered to delve as deep within myself as I needed to start the healing.

I know that God is, and always has been, right beside me. The Twelve Steps have been crucial to my sobriety, but more than that, they have become the foundation for my entire life. The program has not only saved my life, but also given me a blueprint for a life better than any I could have imagined for myself.

~

I am loved. I am healthy. I am whole. My Higher Power has given me a second lease on life and I have a responsibility to share this miracle with others like me.

March 2

"Gentleness is a different way."
Sex Addicts Anonymous, page 65

Before recovery, shame was a self-perpetuating way of life for me. For years I consciously and deliberately hated myself. I felt I had to hate myself just to keep a lid on my behavior. I feared that if I let up on myself, my life would crash. And I felt I deserved to hate myself. That was just the conscious layers of shame, the ones I was aware of. I was also desperately lonely and terrified of intimacy.

When I started SAA, I was stunned at the love and compassion I received. You told me I was not a bad person, but that I suffered from a disease. You suggested I be gentle with myself and leave my shame behind. As with so many things in recovery, the action comes first and the attitude follows. I started to practice gentleness as I saw it in these rooms, and what better place to start than facing my pain and taking responsibility for my life as I worked the Steps.

As gentleness became an integral part of my recovery process, it slowly entered the rest of my life. I've evolved from never doing housework, to doing it occasionally because it's necessary, to doing it because it gives me a nice place to live. I don't know when the ability to practice gentleness with myself happened, but it happened in SAA. It's not perfect, but continues to evolve as I continue to work this program. Gentleness begets gentleness.

~

Today I will let go of shame and be gentle with myself.

❧

> "We turn our will and our lives over to the care of God because our self-directed thoughts and actions have so often led us to acting out, negative consequences, and despair."
>
> *Sex Addicts Anonymous*, page 29

I struggled to find recovery despite being in the program for more than a year. The problem was that I was doing recovery primarily to save my marriage. Through a series of events, and despite my regular participation in recovery-related activities, my wife separated from me against my will. This drove me to a new low and I was faced with whether to continue pursuing recovery now that my reason for recovering was gone. For some reason, I decided to stay with the program.

I'm realizing that surrender means letting go of people, places and things, and trusting my Higher Power to take care of me and everyone else in the process. Turning my will and my life over to the care of my Higher Power means all of it, not what I pick and choose; and with each bit of surrender, I create room for growth. I must recover for myself, regardless of desired outcomes, circumstances, or any entitlements that I feel are due me.

I had to let go of the most important thing in my life— my marriage—to finally learn that my Higher Power cares for me and wants me to be happy, joyous and free. And I am learning how to have real relationships with real people now.

With each bit of surrender, I create room for growth.

ભ

"We found ourselves isolated and alone,
often gripped with fear and despair."

"Sex Addicts Anonymous: A Pathway to Recovery"

I have a life-stealing, soul-sucking disease. I spent decades isolating, afraid of any but the most superficial interactions with people. There were times I felt I couldn't go on, that life wouldn't get better and didn't seem worth living. At times, suicide seemed like a reasonable path.

I know of others who also believed that. Some took their own lives. They chose to end their lives rather than take the risks of reaching out and asking for help, or feeling the discomfort of self-discovery and acceptance. Maybe they couldn't believe their own recovery was possible. If they tried recovery, it didn't seem to work. If there was progress, it was too slow or was punctuated by setbacks. They gave up.

My own pathway to recovery also seemed slow. I had downs and further downs. I watched others come into recovery through the gift of desperation. They worked the program and the program worked them, yet there I was, still feeling so low. Sometimes I didn't think it would ever work for me.

But I kept coming back to SAA. At my lowest point, I realized I had to do something. I reworked the steps and started to get honest with myself. I realized I had problems I was keeping secret, so I reached out to other sex addicts. Eventually I made connections, internal and external, that have transformed my life. I began to heal. Today, I'm grateful and glad that I'm still here.

~

I am worth it; you are worth it; life is worth it. It really does work if you work it!

☙

> "Sex Addicts Anonymous has no opinion on
> outside issues; hence the SAA name ought
> never be drawn into public controversy. ...
> When we carry our message, or present SAA
> to the public, that is the one subject on which
> we are qualified to provide information."
>
> *Sex Addicts Anonymous*, page 92

Before I got sober, I had an opinion about everything, and I believed my opinions to be the correct ones. Slowly, over time, I am learning to apply this tradition to my own personal life, focusing on my experience rather than throwing around opinions to hear myself talk.

It strikes me as deeply humble for SAA to say we only have one subject on which we are qualified to have an opinion, and I am grateful for this tradition. It means that, at a meeting, I will not be subject to people's political or religious views, or even people's views on something like sex addiction research. These are all outside issues. We are together to share our experience, strength and hope to the still-suffering addict—our unifying message that we can be relieved of our sexual addiction one day at a time, sometimes one moment at a time, by working the Twelve Steps of recovery.

Today I stop sharing so many opinions and focus on how my experience, strength and hope can benefit others.

∞

> "Admitted to God, to ourselves, and to another
> human being the exact nature of our wrongs."
> *Sex Addicts Anonymous*, page 21

When I first looked through the Twelve Steps of SAA, Step Four was the first one that scared the crud out of me. However, when I started working that step several months later, I found it more grueling than frightening.

Moving on to Step Five, I re-found the fear I thought I had lost during Step Four. Writing these things down gets easier the longer I do it. There's nothing easy about saying the things I discovered to another human being. I took comfort in the thought that I should now know my sponsor fairly well, and realized that nothing I say would likely surprise her.

In my case, once I actually got started, after a couple of minutes of reading, it got easier and just kind of flowed. And, true to form, my sponsor stayed with me and offered support throughout the process. When I was done, I felt emotionally drained. That passed after a few days and I was simply glad that I was moving on, one step closer to sanity.

In working the Steps with a sponsor, I get practical training in something I never would have imagined: how to trust the process, my sponsor, my Higher Power, and myself.

~

SAA is a place to practice trust. Grant me the courage to take the leap.

"With anonymity as our foundation,
we dedicate our efforts to something
much greater than any one of us."
Sex Addicts Anonymous, page 96

We have but one primary purpose: carrying the message of recovery to the addict who still suffers. The
Twelfth Tradition lets each of us set aside our personal
identities to focus on the spiritual principles of this
program. Thus, I can perform selfless service, knowing
that my identity is safe and secure. Besides protect-
ing my identity, anonymity allows me to be part of a
process that is far greater than my individual efforts.
Without my personal desires and ambitions on the
agenda, I can contribute my best judgment and experience, and then wait on a loving God to be expressed
in our informed group conscience.

Ironically, letting go of power strengthens my participation in the work of my group. I feel a stronger sense
of purpose when I let go of control. Our deliberations
have a spiritual foundation as we let God guide us to
a higher good. Synergy increases the results of our efforts far better than we could achieve individually.

As I grow spiritually, I grow in recovery. I can set the
example of recovery without letting my "self" get in the
way.

*Today, I thank God for the anonymity that allows me
to perform selfless service with freedom and safety.*

ભ

> "The spirit of unity prevents disagreements from turning into quarrels, factions, or destructive personal conflicts. We cultivate tolerance and good will towards other members, holding the welfare of the group above our own personal preferences, desires, or opinions."
>
> *Sex Addicts Anonymous*, page 78

At times, there are rifts in our fellowship. Perhaps people do not like how a meeting is run, so they start a new meeting. Sometimes there is gossip, judgment, or criticism among our members despite our best efforts to avoid these character defects.

While I cannot control other people, I can and must look at my own behavior. In order for there to be unity, I must do my part. If I find myself in criticism and judgment, I do a quick Tenth Step spot check. I talk to my sponsor and others in the program about my own behavior, not that of others. I surrender my character defects humbly to the God of my understanding and make my best effort to live from the spiritual principles of love, tolerance, and gratitude.

~

My program of recovery makes a difference to our community as a whole. Today I work the best program I can for my own sobriety and the unity of our fellowship.

> "In our addiction, we experienced sex as compulsive. We felt driven, as if by an irresistible force to engage in sexual behavior rather than freely choosing to be sexual."
>
> *Sex Addicts Anonymous*, page 70

An issue that eventually comes up for most addicts is that working an SAA program differs from some other Twelve-Step programs in the fact that we don't want to abstain from sex entirely (unlike drinking in AA). What we are striving to break free from is compulsive, unhealthy, or dangerous sexual behavior.

In my own recovery, I found that sex and love had somehow become separated from each other. This resulted in the odd reality that, because I loved my husband, I didn't want to have sex with him. My husband couldn't grasp the idea, though my brothers and sisters in recovery understood perfectly.

Ultimately, what I'd lost was intimacy. I had lost the ability to connect deeply with anyone—not necessarily in a sexual way, but in a way that I could see another's inner being—who they really were. And, of equal importance, I was unable to let them see the real me.

Finding intimacy again was the key—the intimacy that has nothing to do with sex, the intimacy that allows me to connect deeply with another. Once I discovered that, my sexuality began to look healthy for the very first time. This was not an overnight process but it was worth working for, worth crying for.

~

I finally understand what real intimacy is and, for me, it has nothing to do with sex.

ଔ

"As we let go of old ways of approaching life,
and trust that God will reveal new ways,
many of us begin to have a greater vision
of what our life <u>in recovery</u> could be."
Sex Addicts Anonymous, page 43

My Higher Power recently relieved my character defect of fear of being alone. I was given the strength and courage to end an unhealthy relationship. I am a forty-year-old woman and, for the first time since I was a twelve-year-old girl, I am alone without a boyfriend.

I took some suggestions and wrote down my life goals and aspirations: travel, pay off student loans, help my daughter pay for college, foster healthy female friendships, spend time with family. I was amazed to realize that not one of my aspirations involved a man. My addict's primary goal was to seek acceptance and attention from men no matter the cost.

This new freedom is a gift from my Higher Power from doing the work of recovery. I have moments of weakness, which help remind me that I am still a sex addict. I pray for my Higher Power to remove my shortcomings, and I am now able to focus on my true goals and aspirations.

~

I am willing to do the footwork of recovery so that I will be ready if and when God removes my character defects.

ભ

> "We may have setbacks and difficult times.
> We may suffer the painful consequences of
> past behavior, or experience the pain of new
> growth. It is important that we not give up."
>
> *Sex Addicts Anonymous*, page 66

My life is like a giant wheel. The top of the wheel is in the light and fresh air; the bottom of the wheel is grinding through mud. This wheel represents the ups and downs of life, and the way of life I have learned in SAA is like a snorkel. When I'm on the muddy side of the wheel, when I'm stressed and want to act out, I now have tools and people available to help me breathe as I slog through the mud on to the sunny side.

Now, when I see an opportunity to act out, I can ask my Higher Power for help, call my sponsor, find another activity, or meditate on my recovery. No longer must I hold my breath and suffer through the bottom of the wheel, or worse, try to back up and hide in my addiction. I have come to understand that the low points will happen, that they are just part of life. I have also discovered that, sooner or later, the wheel will again come around to the sunny side. And every time I go through a muddy patch and stay sober, the sunny side is a new experience of life. Today is the day where I am no longer bound by the chains of addiction.

With the tools of SAA, I can keep breathing through the difficult patches and come out on the other side.

&

> "What we gain in this program is a blueprint for
> full and successful living, whatever may come."
>
> *Sex Addicts Anonymous*, page 61

Sex addiction kept me caught up in the high and the lie produced by things like intrigue, obsessing, and acting out. It insulated me from experiencing painful feelings, but ended up numbing me to all feelings. In recovery, I have learned to embrace and open myself up to all of my emotions.

However, it's very difficult for me to stay present to the hurt when people don't treat me respectfully or lovingly. It's easy for me to start carrying resentment or to interpret another's actions to mean something about myself. My inner critic wants to tell me that I'm not worth respecting, or that I somehow deserve to be treated poorly.

Working the Steps on a situation when I feel hurt by others helps me recognize which things I'm powerless over, such as other people's bad behavior, and to own my part in the situation. A phrase I love, "not my circus, not my monkeys," reminds me to leave the issues and problems of someone else where they belong— with that other person. This brings me the precious gift of freedom!

God, help me let go of what isn't mine so I can tend to this precious gift—my life.

ങ

> "We gain not only freedom from our disease,
> but the freedom to be at home in the world."
>
> *Sex Addicts Anonymous*, page 74

I know I am powerless over my sex addiction. I am grateful that SAA has helped me find a power through which I can change and grow. There is another sort of powerlessness I struggle with, and it comes when world events seem to go crazy—natural disasters, human violence, injustice, etc.

My attempts to control my addiction triggered various character defects—self-pity, denial, shame, and resentment, to name a few. My powerlessness over world events triggers defects as well—rage, denial, and cynicism, to name a few. I want to make bad things stop and punish anyone who contributes to them. I am tempted to a bitterness of heart and mind because bitterness seems powerful. Temptations to anger and cynicism, as well as urges to seek power, are natural. However, my history shows that following my natural inclinations almost always leads to trouble. I need to apply the Twelve Steps here, too.

Recovery has taught me that:

- Acting on my character defects only makes things worse.
- My arena for action is always and only right here, right now.
- If I surrender, my Higher Power will guide me to what, if anything, I am supposed to do in the situation.
- When my Higher Power guides me, I can act out of love.
- I am never completely powerless. I can pray for courage, strength, and guidance.

~

Though I am powerless over many things, I always have choices.

ca

"The purpose or goal of our service is
to carry the SAA message: that freedom
from addictive sexual behavior is possible
through the Twelve Steps of SAA."
Sex Addicts Anonymous, page 84

I have had the privilege of twelfth-stepping several newcomers into SAA. This can be a daunting task. Newcomers are often people in crisis. They may have lost a job or a marriage or both. They may be facing arrest or imprisonment. Their friends and family may no longer be speaking to them. Their lives have been shattered; often they are in tears.

What can I say to someone in that situation that will make a difference? Here's where the Fifth Tradition comes to the rescue. I need only have one message for the newcomer in crisis: that no matter how bad things may be, there is hope. Others have been where they are—in fact, I have been where they are now—and have gone on to live healthy, happy lives in recovery. And the vehicle of that hope is the SAA program.

That's not much of a speech to give, but the Fifth Tradition assures us it is all we truly need to get across. It is enough to say.

May I carry the message of SAA in my own heart, so I may readily share it with those who still suffer.

ଔ

> "Diversity of thought and opinion helps
> make our service work vital and creative.
> The First Tradition channels this
> creative energy towards a single goal: the
> welfare of recovering sex addicts."
>
> *Sex Addicts Anonymous*, page 78

At first glance, this tradition may seem clear enough: the principle of unity—being in accord, harmonious, undivided. Yet the connection to music implied by a synonym of unity, namely, harmony, calls to mind not the copy, but rather the sum of many voices, or many parts, joining to create something greater.

In our fellowship, our individual voices can clash with one another when we insist that we have the only right way, and this can become restrictive, disharmonious, or one-note. If we had just one voice, we would not have a vital, ever-growing community of fellowship. Our voices can remain distinct, yet join together to create something complimentary to the broader message, or song, of SAA. As with singing, layering our distinct experiences, strengths, and hopes becomes a beautiful blending that transforms and uplifts our message.

~

How can I have a clear, unique voice in our fellowship that compliments and enriches the wider message of Sex Addicts Anonymous?

ର

> "Whatever method we use, we make ourselves
> available to our Higher Power, opening
> ourselves to whatever insight we may receive."
>
> *Sex Addicts Anonymous*, page 57

I appreciate the Green Book's definitions of prayer and meditation, prayer being simply talking with my Higher Power, which can be both sharing what is going on in my life, my struggles and my challenges, as well as an opportunity to ask for help. Meditation is then about listening, about slowing down and being open to the answers and direction from the God of my understanding.

My core prayer is the Serenity Prayer, and I turn to it regularly for guidance, patience, and courage to live life on life's terms. I also try to start each day with a simple prayer, giving my day to my Higher Power. I try to close each day giving thanks for what has happened.

I am still exploring ways to meditate. I take walks or bike-rides, and simply try to get in tune with the world around me. Sometimes it is finding quiet time at home. And of course, there is my recovery work that pertains to written meditations, both those that I read each day, and those that I write, like this one. The reflection helps me gain new insight into my life and my path.

My spiritual connection is like any other relationship—I need to show up and participate in it to keep it strong, healthy and vibrant. My Higher Power is always there to help me along.

~

More will be revealed if I keep the door open.

଼

> "We are free to discover what works best
> for us; the important thing is the goal of
> maintaining and improving our connection
> to the God of our understanding."
>
> *Sex Addicts Anonymous*, page 57

I had been in SAA over two years when I read a book about hermits who lived in the desert during the third century, and who had practiced habitual prayer by mentally reciting a short prayer over and over.

I thought about it. Could I do that? And then I asked myself, "Why not?" So I started doing it over and over, day and night. After a few days, I thought to myself, "This is crazy. It's cultish. It makes no sense." Then it occurred to me that perhaps that was the point—it made no sense, at least to me at the time.

Then I realized something else. The constant repetition of the prayer was increasing my awareness of the presence of my Higher Power. It was increasing my conscious contact with God as I understand God. It was bringing me back to my center.

Now, twenty-one years later, I am still saying it. I hope I never stop.

~

I took many risks in acting out. I need to take risks in my recovery, even some things that might at first seem crazy.

"Step Three was a problem for me. I didn't know God."

Sex Addicts Anonymous, page 283

I have always had trust issues, especially with authority figures. This meant serious trust issues with the ultimate authority figure: God. I believed that God's grand plan involved dragging me through a briar patch. When it came to Steps Two and Three, my understanding of God really got in the way.

However, there was no real evidence of anything untrustworthy in God's plan for me. I now believe God led me to actions that caused anxiety and even embarrassment, but that proved healing and helpful.

I felt a nudge to speak out at my church about my recovery and to apologize to the women of the church for objectifying them. After a reality check with my sponsor, I asked the pastor and he immediately said yes. When the day came, I was trembling, but was able to forthrightly tell about my Twelve-Step journey. I described my compulsion to objectify and I apologized. I expected stunned, embarrassed silence, but people applauded! I spent the rest of the service hiding in the balcony, shaking and emotionally raw.

Since then, the parents of an alcoholic, and two sex addicts from my church have started Twelve-Step recovery because I was willing to listen to that nudge. My shame was dealt a serious blow. I am coming to believe that a Power greater than myself is lovingly restoring me to sanity. I am slowly turning my will and my life over to God's care.

~

With God's help, I can trust God and find courage to change the things I can.

☙

> "Sex Addicts Anonymous should remain
> forever nonprofessional, but our service
> centers may employ special workers."
>
> *Sex Addicts Anonymous*, page 89

Tradition Eight gives me freedom. In my professional life, I have developed skills, knowledge, and experience. Unfortunately, I have also developed a lot of pride in my work and feel most confident when I am living from that part of myself. My shame led me to hide behind my professionalism, even when I was involved in things that are not part of my work. I bonded much of my identity to my work.

I wanted to hide behind my professionalism in SAA, too. Of course, I had no real experience, knowledge, or skill with recovery at first, so I tried to fake it. I wanted to be a professional SAA recovering person, whatever that is.

Through Tradition Eight, I realized that my approach was wrong. Hiding behind my image actually limited me. I needed to be an SAA rookie and an SAA seeker. I had to be open.

This tradition freed me from the straightjacket of my false pride. It also freed me to live a new way. I can be vulnerable, I can admit that I do not know everything and do not have to, and I can let other people lead. I can let whatever skills, knowledge, and experience I developed serve others rather than serve my ego.

~

The non-professionalism of the program offers me freedom from my false identity and freedom to discover the real me.

ଓ

> "Honesty is the foundation on which
> all further progress is based."
> *Sex Addicts Anonymous*, page 23

Honesty and the truth are things I've struggled with my whole life. Keeping the truth hidden about who and what I really am, even to those closest to me, was something I held onto with great fear. As an addict, I also told lies to impress upon other people that I was a better person then I believed myself to be.

Who is it I long to be? I can choose to become a person of integrity—authentic and honest at all times. I have come far enough to understand that, in order to become this kind of person, I need to have rigorous honesty in my program, my recovery, and my life. First, I need to be honest with my Higher Power and myself, then let the honesty of my true being flow through to those closest to me—a sponsor, friends in recovery, and family.

Without rigorous honesty, I am holding myself back from the will of my Higher Power. When I tell a lie or omit the truth, I fall back into self-hatred and disease, separating myself from God and those closest to me. This is always a result of my will. God's will, however, will lead me to a sense of peace and contentment. The more aware I become of my dishonesty, the more motivated and able I am to work honesty into my life.

~

I can live the saying "the truth shall set you free"—free to become a person of integrity, living God's will, one day at a time.

CR

> "Being fully self-supporting means being
> aware of the responsibility of every
> member for supporting the group."
> *Sex Addicts Anonymous*, page 88

Taking care of myself is vital for the health and welfare of my relationships. From my base of sobriety, I maintain my self worth. From this foundation, I am able to be responsible in my relationships.

In the past I used people to fulfill my selfish wants regardless of the consequences to others or to me. In recovery I have come to recognize I can't go it alone. At the same time, I am responsible for my well-being. I have also recognized the danger in thinking that one individual has the capacity to meet my every need. For example, I am an avid marathoner, while my spouse is a homebody who enjoys gardening and romping with our dogs. Because of our different needs, we have different friends to meet those needs. He has friends through the gardening club, whereas I have friends through the running club. By being responsible for ourselves, we take care to meet our own needs without trampling on the rights of the other.

We are a unit, both standing strong in our recovery, self supporting, neither one in charge. Rather, we're walking side by side, moving in the same direction. There is nothing we must face alone because we are both able to contribute.

~

By taking responsibility for my own welfare, I actually have something to contribute to my relationships—me.

ભ

> "We can only make amends to the best of our
> ability and leave the rest in God's hands."
> *Sex Addicts Anonymous*, page 51

Many of the people closest to me have pushed away the hardest as I work at my recovery. The hurt I dealt to them has been deep, and, in many cases, I have struggled in making direct amends. For now, the best amends I can make is to continue working my program and to live the Twelve Steps each day.

In contrast, those furthest removed are often easier to make amends to—my employer, acquaintances, even some acting out partners. The smaller the emotional connection, the easier it has been for me to relate my story of the harm caused and to seek to make things better. Being honest, focusing on my work while I am at the office, informing people of the risks I put them in, not flirting, and other admissions and changes are all amends that show I am sincere about improving my behavior.

This is also a step where I need to remember myself. Making amends means not only working my program of recovery, but also letting go of my past. I will improve myself by focusing on my outer circle activities, by allowing myself to do things that my addiction took time and energy away from. Restarting hobbies, sports, or other activities are important to keeping me balanced, healthy, and whole.

When "wherever possible" presents itself, I must be ready. In the meantime, I trust that my Higher Power will present the right opportunities for me to meet with those my addiction has affected.

> "I finally learned that I did not have to give up
> my self, my identity, my sexuality, or my money
> to have the love and acceptance I had sought for
> so long, in so many painful and isolating ways."
>
> *Sex Addicts Anonymous*, page 157

At one of the first telemeetings I attended, the secretary said, "We're here to love and support one another." The thought popped into my head, "You mean
without having to give sex?" Part of me didn't know
this was possible. My eyes misted up as I entertained
the possibility.

After hearing tons of program people speak, I know
I'm not alone in this. It seems that many of us were
taught that we had to give sex, or something else, in
order to be loved. I'm not sure how different we are
from non-addicts in this regard, but this message, often served with a helping of sexual or physical abuse
or neglect, seems like it came out louder and stronger
for me. What I received when I sacrificed my true self
was never love.

When I became sober and found recovery, I found
I could receive love just for being me. In meetings, I
have experienced unconditional love that I never knew
before. SAA is full of the support and friendship that I
have always craved.

I've also learned to give that same love back to others
to the best of my ability. That ability continues to grow.

*Today I can be loved as I am, and I can love others as
they are.*

ℭ

**"Many of us come into recovery feeling
unlovable <u>and</u> unworthy."**

Sex Addicts Anonymous, page 14

Early in recovery, my subconscious version of Step Two was that God would restore me to sanity once I proved myself worthy. I believed that I had no inherent value as a person, and that I had to prove I was loveable. In other words, I thought I had to fix myself before I could ask God to help me.

In recovery, I allowed a seed to be planted when I first asked for help, and God has lovingly watered the ground and shone life-giving light on me since. I've been growing as a result of God's care, care that I allow in, a little at a time, as I work the Steps.

But I'm not done growing yet. It's not fair of me to expect I will look like a full-grown plant before I've grown to that point. I am exactly where I should be in my progress. My Higher Power wants to nourish me as I grow, not shame me for failing to be something I'm not, yet.

I don't have to earn God's love or approval. God knows me and tenderly helps me grow. Today I will rejoice in the progress I've made and accept myself right where I am on my journey.

God will meet me right where I am.

CR

> "In taking the Fourth Step, we begin to
> know ourselves _for who we really are._"
>
> _Sex Addicts Anonymous_, page 31

In my addiction, I lied to everybody about everything. I used sex to escape the pain in my life and then lied to protect that lie. I am a good person with good values, but the behaviors I developed to protect me from pain resulted in my losing connection with that good person. Through years of dishonesty and avoiding problems and pain in my life, I grew farther and farther from my true self.

In recovery, I have been given a second chance to live in congruence with the self my Higher Power wants me to be. My first action toward being more authentic was to discover my defects of character. I wanted to be thorough and honest, so I joined with other sex addicts to work the Fourth Step together. As I explored my resentments, my fears, and the harm I had caused, I began to see specific behaviors that caused many of my problems.

While understanding my part in my problems was helpful, the real key was using my newfound knowledge going forward. Spotting my defects indicates disconnection with myself. For example, after an argument, I can go back to my Fourth Step inventory and ask which defect might have contributed to the argument. Owning my part in the problem gives me new power—the power to be the person I was meant to be.

By honestly acknowledging and owning my defects, I advance in the journey to recover my true self.

ଦ

> "We do not have to obsess about the past
> or worry about the future. We can turn our
> attention to the present, where we really
> live, and become open to new solutions."
>
> *Sex Addicts Anonymous*, page 29

Someone admitted at a meeting, "I'm having trouble letting go of my desire for a better past."

What do I do when something triggers a painful memory, a regret that arises unbidden like a cloud covering the sun? Sometimes I have to admit that my own thoughts are one of the things I'm powerless over.

Instead of trying to distract myself, or becoming overwhelmed by such thoughts, I can look at them from a program perspective. Is it something I can turn over to my Higher Power? Do I need to take some action? Have I dealt with this before in my First or Fourth Step? Are there amends that need to be made?

Many of our pasts are full of things that can be embarrassing or even shameful to remember. Working our program cannot change the past, but it can offer a way of living in the present, unshackled from old encumbrances. If our feelings haven't caught up to our new way of life, our sponsor or our friends in the fellowship can remind us of the changes they've seen.

I don't have to change my past—I can't. Help me remember that I'm living in a better place—in recovery, in the present.

ଔ

> "Cultivating self-acceptance along the
> way is an important tool in recovery."
>
> *Tools of Recovery*, page 31

I want more sobriety. I want to be a big shot. I want to be liked. I want more money. I want things to go my way. I want it now. Look at all of these "I" thoughts with me in the center of the universe!

Acceptance leads me to serenity and allows me to be peaceful, not lustful or greedy. Impatience is a selfish act. Wanting things to be different—that is an illusion.

What is the cost of doing things my way or imposing my will on people and situations? What is the cost of not looking out for myself, of giving into fear, or creating a test I cannot pass?

Today I take care of myself. I care about my suffering and other people's suffering. I won't believe in the lies of the past that defined me as bad or good. I trust my Higher Power to show me the way.

~

I pray to connect with my source, and may patience and acceptance fill my heart.

> "This profound surrender of old beliefs,
> habits, and behaviors is something
> we learn to renew every day."

Sex Addicts Anonymous, page 30

Step Three is an affirmation of the radical faith I believe is necessary to flourish in my recovery. There was so much negativity in my past—abuse, neglect, abandonment—which sparked my addictive patterns and forced me to go into a survival mode. But with the Third Step, I learned to trust again. I try to remember that the means by which I protected myself in the past, which manifested as addiction, never really worked and no longer apply to my present.

I am not always sure how or where to find comfort in the absence of acting out, and so I turn to my Higher Power, who is love and understanding. I sometimes become jittery or angry or triggered in situations that challenge my intellect or emotions. But when I take a breath and reach out to my Higher Power, I can find calm in the storm. I surrender the desire to will myself out of or into a situation, or to control outcomes. Instead, I give that impulse up to God, and trust that all will be well as more is revealed to me. When I accept that I do not have to see all the answers to the challenges I face, the challenges themselves shrink and become manageable instead of overwhelming.

I rest assured that, whatever the outcome, my challenges are better met with faith than with white-knuckled self will.

> "We may say a prayer to call upon our
> Higher Power for help, or we may reach out
> to another addict. Calling someone on the
> phone, even if no one is there to answer
> the call, is a powerful act of surrender."

Sex Addicts Anonymous, page 68

I know some of the things that trigger me, and I can be aware of these triggers and set appropriate boundaries so I'm not exposed to them. For example, I realized it was triggering for me to go to the gym, so I've found other ways to exercise. I avoid past acting-out partners and parts of town where I acted out.

Sometimes, I can be triggered by a smell or a sound or a summer day, so I can't completely isolate myself from all potential triggers. If I sat alone in a dark room, I could still be triggered by fantasies. I've realized that, for me, the trigger is in my head.

My defense against triggers is to maintain fit spiritual condition. I need to have close contact with my Higher Power, other recovering addicts, and the SAA program. I need to take care of myself, and I need to practice spiritual principles to the best of my ability in all areas of my life. In other words, I need to live in my outer circle. Then the triggers in my head don't set off very loud reports.

Conscious contact and personal contact defend me against triggers—external or internal.

ରଷ

> "We may have only been ready to
> face certain truths about ourselves
> when we first worked the step."
>
> *Sex Addicts Anonymous*, page 36

Sometimes, newcomers get the idea that one thorough Fourth-Step inventory will cover all their character defects for all time. That did not work for me. In my twenty-plus years of active addiction, I developed many false beliefs about myself that only gradually yielded to recovery. In no small part, this was because they were layered and interlocking.

As I worked the Steps, discovering and releasing a defect would eventually reveal another trait that didn't work too well, either. The layers were all false, shame-based beliefs I developed in trying to cope with other false beliefs. After years of recovery work, I found the origin of all this was in having been molested as a toddler. It started with elemental pain and fear.

I did not make this mess overnight, and I have not recovered in one glorious flash of insight. I have to be patient, work the program, and let the program work me. It means working the Steps multiple times, and seeking help from multiple sources. I gradually teased out the false beliefs that permeated my life. Along the way, I got strength, assurance, and an ocean of love and support from my partners in recovery. For the first time in my life, I'm not alone!

~

The complexity of my addiction is no match for the simple honesty and love of the program when I live it, one day at a time.

ભ

"From this simple beginning, belief in a Higher Power can grow."
Sex Addicts Anonymous, page 27

Many people get stuck at Step Two for one of two reasons. Some never believed and find it doubly difficult now after all the misery their addiction caused. Others, like me, were sincere believers, but the God I thought I knew did not fix my addiction. My image of God was corrupted by my addiction. Relying on my old God was like asking my addiction to provide recovery. I looked for a new God, but kept finding the same old one.

In desperation, I tried a simple, practical approach: I collected spiritual data for thirty days. I wrote down evidence of the program or of a Higher Power at work in my life, and in others in the program. I noted data points like a day clean without urges to act out, doing something different in response to an old stimulus, or a new opportunity to grow or help. I noted improvements in the lives of people in recovery. I did not read my notes; I just collected.

After thirty days, I sat down with the notes and my sponsor. The general path of addiction is downward. The data showed something different, something bigger at work in my life and in the lives of people around me. I started to see that my Higher Power had been there all the time.

~

Evidence for a Higher Power is all around me. If I open my eyes and heart, I just might find it.

CR

> "We also tried to hide our addiction
> from ourselves—by working hard, being
> perfectionists, or perhaps being very religious."
>
> *Sex Addicts Anonymous*, page 6

I was a devout practitioner of my religion before I got into recovery. I went to religious schools, participated in religious services each week, prayed daily, and received a degree from a seminary. When I got into SAA, I thought this spirituality thing would be easy, and I could just transfer everything I had learned in my religion.

At first, in fact, I resisted the spirituality of the program, preferring my own version. Then a friend in the program crushed my defenses with one comment: "If your religious practices are so great, they would have worked on your addiction, and you wouldn't need SAA now." I had to admit he was right.

In truth, much of my religious practice was unhealthy. I was self-righteous, rigid, and intolerant of others who were not as devout. I tried to bargain with God when I prayed. I hid behind my faith instead of facing difficult situations. When it came to my addiction, I wanted God to fix my problems without my having to lift a finger.

Spirituality does not require religion. I have needed many passes through the Steps, learning to let my Higher Power rid me of my rigid opinions and expectations. As I have worked the spiritual program of SAA, my religious life has slowly changed and deepened.

This program makes every dimension of my life healthier.

ભ

> "We have found it helpful to ask ourselves,
> 'Am I willing to go to any length to stay
> sexually sober <u>and</u> to recover?'"
>
> "Sexual Sobriety and the Internet"

I had finally had an acting-out experience that was demoralizing enough to get me to a meeting. I knew of two meetings and attended one a few days later. Later, looking at the meeting schedule, I was distressed to learn how far the meetings were from where I lived. I had just moved, and none were close. Some were as far as fifteen miles away.

After a meeting, I was complaining to somebody about the distance and expressed doubt as to whether the program was really for me. After all, had I been led to the program before I chose to move, I would have been closer to the meetings. He replied with some of the wisest words I had ever heard: "How far did you go to act out?"

My most recent acting-out experience was about forty miles from home. Also, because I had anticipated that it would be the perfect experience, I had spent significant time arranging for it, and hoped I might repeat it many times.

On the other hand, the meetings, as far away as they were, were simply there for the asking. I needed no special arrangements other than gas in the tank. I became a regular attendee very quickly and now I have a circle of friends and support I could never have imagined.

~

If I make my sobriety a priority, I open the door for recovery and change.

"When we are free from self-importance, we can recognize that we have <u>much</u> to be grateful for."

Sex Addicts Anonymous, page 45

I am in an exam room at our local ER. I ran a drill-bit through my thumb. Within twenty minutes of arriving, I was admitted, interviewed, x-rayed, and shown to the exam room. That was two hours ago. This room is cold. It's way past suppertime, and my thumb really hurts. But mostly, I am grateful.

After an hour, I stuck my head out to see if they had forgotten me. They were gracious and apologetic, assuring me that they would see me as soon as possible. Then I looked around. Every room had someone in it, and they looked worse-off than me. Quick visit from the doctor. He apologized, telling me of heart attacks and strokes among other patients.

Second round in this room alone. I am still cold and hungry, and my thumb hurts, but in a while, I get to go to my loving home, eat a nice supper, and sleep in my own bed. I may be the luckiest person in this ER. I used this time to call program friends and family, and even did some creative writing. Good news from the x-ray: no bone or metal fragments, so they won't have to dig anything out. A tetanus shot, a prescription, a few simple instructions, and I can go home.

Not my best day, but, thanks to the program of Sex Addicts Anonymous, I was able to be gracious, and found many reasons to be grateful.

~

I always have something to be grateful for.

ॐ

> "With small but significant actions, we
> can work Step Three by establishing
> a commitment to the program."
> *Sex Addicts Anonymous*, page 30

I have found that faith is not so much a feeling as an action. Faith is certainly dependant upon action. My recovery is like walking upward on a downward-moving escalator. Every minute of every day I'm granted the serenity and strength to abstain from my addictive behaviors as long as I keep climbing by being vigilant and working this program. If I practice the principles I'm learning in recovery, I'm given power.

I know that my own actions aren't keeping me sober; God is. But the things I do—reading SAA literature, talking with my sponsor, working steps, making outreach calls, praying and meditating—are avenues to my Higher Power that give serenity and power to stay sober. If I take time to connect with God, I provide opportunities for my Higher Power to communicate and to help me.

When I make choices that disconnect me from my Higher Power or isolate me from others, I'm not as able to sense God's will or influence. The downward escalator of addiction will then carry me back into unmanageability pretty quickly. I can't demand God's power, but I can open my mind and heart, and invite God to help and strengthen me.

May I make the time and effort to invite God's power and love into my life.

ଓଃ

> "Eventually, discomfort gives way to a
> sense of belonging and feeling of relief
> that there are others like us."
>
> *Sex Addicts Anonymous*, page 12

I was at my wits' end. My daily need for porn at work had destroyed my career and was about to do the same to my marriage and family. I was summarily dismissed after my employer investigated my computer at work. I now had to explain to my family why our income and lifestyle would end, and I considered ending my life rather than facing my spouse.

Fortunately, I found SAA online and contacted the local group secretary. He talked me out of doing anything rash, and invited me to visit the group that evening before going home. At my first meeting, I immediately had hope that I could overcome my addiction and rebuild my life. Other members understood my shame and pain. I received guidance on how to approach my family and friends.

During my three years in the program, my family has supported my recovery and the rebuilding of my life. People I love depend on me, and I have much to live for. Most important was discovering that I am not alone. Others in the fellowship have experienced problems similar to mine, and they offer hope.

God, thank you for letting me find that I am not alone.

> "An attitude of humility and sincere regret for
> the harms we have done will carry us far."
>
> *Sex Addicts Anonymous*, page 49

In Step Nine, my toughest amends went to my family, who suffered mightily when I was arrested for acting out. In our small community, my business was destroyed, my income went to zero in thirty days, and my children bore the brunt of our loss. They suffered a lower standard of living, and their mother had to go back to work to support the family.

In anger, my wife left me, and I did not see my children for six years. The separation hurt badly, and I missed the teenage years of my two sons. My desire to reunite with my family provided added incentive to stop my acting out behaviors. My sponsor guided me through the Twelve Steps, which changed my life. However, in my first Ninth Step, I could only make indirect amends to my family members. I remembered them in my prayers, and their memory motivated me in my new way of life.

Over the course of those years, my new life gradually and visibly showed that my work in SAA was sincere and had taken hold. When they saw my living amends, my children slowly reentered my life. I had become accountable for my behavior and had become a better person—the kind of father they wanted to claim!

God, thank you for showing me how to make living amends to my family, to my friends, and to myself.

☙

> "Keeping our attention in today helps
> us to show up and be present for our
> own lives, while resting in the faith that
> God's care is sufficient for the future."
>
> *Sex Addicts Anonymous*, page 65

How much freedom we would feel, how liberated from anxiety and shame we would be, if only we could keep our focus on the present moment! As addicts, we often become so wrapped up in trying to escape our past or control our future that we pay little attention to simply doing the next right thing. Yet visions of past and future are just thoughts. This very moment is all that is real.

I use my daily meditation time as a way to focus in on what's happening right now, letting go of the past and the future. In this way, I learn to encounter my Higher Power moment by moment. By daily practice, I acquire, develop, and maintain the skill of staying in the present moment. When I am in the present moment, I find it easier to turn things over when difficulties arise.

~

Today I will deepen my conscious contact with my Higher Power by turning my attention to the present, where I really live.

ぺ

> "A growing sense of community within the
> SAA fellowship, and a newfound ability to
> live in the moment under God's care, gives
> us the courage to go forward in recovery."

Sex Addicts Anonymous, page 31

I was feeling selfish and disconnected for a few days this week. I was not accepting of things the way they are. I wanted to be in a different place in a different time. That is not helpful to my recovery. Thinking too much, I get lost and flood myself with thoughts such as, "The negative behaviors don't seem so bad."

My serenity and recovery are the good stuff. Focusing on negativity or avoiding problems has never been a solution. When I am quiet and still, clarity and honesty seem to surface. May I open my heart to love and find my outer circle. Thank you for a few quiet moments. The hush of heaven holds my heart today. Thank you very much. Amen.

When I remove myself from the center of the universe and look for the good, I can find serenity.

> "Unable to stop, we stayed at the computer looking for one more jolt of excitement."

"Sexual Sobriety and the Internet"

Isolated and alone, seeking validation and relief from myself in a series of zeros and ones displayed in the form of an image, I wasted hours and money numbing my soul. While the Internet consistently delivered what my addict assured me that it would, it never delivered what I was truly seeking. So I would promise once again "I will never do that again," only to return time and time again to that reliable "old friend."

As I entered the program of SAA and began to work the Steps, I found that, with the measure I surrendered, I could measure the relief I received from my compulsive sexual behaviors. As the light of honesty was shined on my behaviors, that light also revealed a beautiful soul longing for freedom. The light was no longer emitted from some monitor in a dark empty room, but from within as a reflection of my Higher Power.

I am grateful that the light of my recovery has drowned out the light of that monitor in the corner. I am hopeful that the light of my recovery will help the addict who still suffers to shine a light upon the beautiful soul that lies within.

Instead of the light of my monitor, I will turn to the light of my Higher Power.

ଔ

> "Tradition Five states that no other purpose
> can be greater than, or equal to, that of
> carrying the message of recovery."
>
> *Sex Addicts Anonymous*, page 84

Seven months ago, after serving twelve years of a fifteen-year sentence, I was detained due to the state filing a petition to have me committed as a sexually violent predator. Few ever win their freedom, and less than eleven percent of those committed are ever released.

SAA has been a vital part of my thriving in this stage of life's journey. I help in every way I can to fulfill the primary purpose—carrying the message to the sex addict who still suffers. Is there a better place to be of service than where I am?

I carry the message by living a life of sobriety that's attractive enough that other sex addicts want what I have. I try to conduct myself in a way that lets everyone know I am committed to recovery. I work to keep my priorities straight and be of service to those who still suffer. In maintaining my own sobriety, and by giving away what I was freely given, I am, in turn, being inspired.

Amazingly, my life has never been better. I've never been a better person, had better friends, or had a greater purpose. As I surrender my will and my life to the care of God as I understand God, trusting in God's divine plan, and living a life of service one day at a time, my life has purpose and meaning.

~

To be inspired, be inspirational.

ଔ

"For sex addicts, resentment is one of the most stubborn obstacles to our spiritual growth."

Sex Addicts Anonymous, page 34

I nursed a sullen, bitter resentment towards my father for decades. He took up three pages of my Fourth Step the first time through it. He had been a rageaholic, with an explosive temper. He likely belonged in our club, having had serial affairs with my mother's friends.

For this last offense I painted him the villain and swore that I would never be like him. As I became more and more like him through my own addiction, I began to feel compassion for him. Through my recovery in SAA, I began to see our linked patterns and, perhaps more importantly, how my resentment and silence towards him had driven my life and blinded me. In the subsequent steps, I began to let go. On my second time through the Fourth Step, my father did not even make it on the list!

I am grateful for the miracles of recovery.

"Wanting our lives to change is not the
same as being actually ready for change.
The negative patterns uncovered in our
inventory represent a lifetime of ingrained
beliefs, attitudes, and habits of behavior."

Sex Addicts Anonymous, page 40

It took me a while to understand the significance
of the Sixth Step. Being ready to have my defects removed requires the admittance that I have flaws. While
I created an inventory in my Fourth Step and admitted
the nature of my wrongs in my Fifth, it was not until
this step that I realized I had to truly accept that there
were parts of me that were not as healthy as I'd like to
believe.

This is also a gentle step in that it only requires my
willingness to have my Higher Power remove these
flaws. It is very similar in nature to the Second Step,
an acknowledging that God has the power to help me
in this task and then readying myself to try it out. It is
a preparatory step for the work that is to follow.

This step for me was another level of surrender, relinquishing the idea that I have the control or ability to change certain things in my life. It was a time
for me to let go of even more of the reins of my life
and open myself to following the will of the God of my
understanding.

~

*I am flawed, but that is part of being human. I can
accept this and ready myself to let my Higher Power
remove all these defects of character so I can become a
healthier person.*

 og

> "For the first time I felt that I had a home
> and a family who supported me, understood
> me, and let me unload all my shame."
>
> *Sex Addicts Anonymous*, page 213

I'm as sick as my secrets. Many times I heard it and said it. However, I couldn't tell anyone my secrets; they were too shameful. I thought if I did, people would surely reject me.

After I got into SAA and started working the Steps, I heard that I had to develop rigorous honesty and "rat out my addict." Slowly I started reaching out to others in the program and telling the truth about what I was thinking and doing. It has transformed my life.

When I started talking honestly with others, especially on the phone between meetings, a surprising thing happened: people didn't reject me. In fact, people said they admired my courage, that they could relate to what I said, or that they had the same problem. People thanked me for sharing—the exact opposite of what I expected. This tool has had a profound impact on the effectiveness of my step work.

My shame is like a vampire. It sucks the life out of me and keeps me in the shadows. But importantly, it cannot tolerate the light of day. My disease was lying when it told me I had to keep my secrets. Perhaps it knew that bringing them into the light of day would kill its power over me.

~

I am as sick as I am secret. My shame withers when I open up.

○3

> "Some of us write a history of our sex addiction,
> from as far back as we can remember up to
> the present, trying to leave nothing out."
> *Sex Addicts Anonymous*, page 23

I was afraid to face the history of my addiction. I felt it would be a compilation of the ugliest facts about a human being ever written. Yet, that was exactly what my sponsor and group were encouraging me to do.

I protested, squirmed, and prepared to explode from shame. Finally, I started writing. I calculated approximately how many times I had acted out. My guess was 1,000, but the actual number was 12,000–15,000. Other statistics were equally telling. I wrote until I covered all twenty years of my active addiction. Then I experienced three surprises.

First, my history was not a list of humanity's worst, nor did I explode when I read it. In fact, it was somewhat boring. Second, I assumed that a compilation of the facts would tempt me to act out. In fact, it brought relief from addictive thoughts and behavior. Third, when I reluctantly shared my history with my group at a meeting, they did not reject me. They applauded me, supported me, and thanked me for my honesty. It was the first time I felt like I belonged to the group, or any group, for that matter.

When they said, "The truth shall set you free," I had no idea they meant freedom from acting out, self-condemnation, and isolation. I received these gifts from writing and sharing my sexual history.

Through a little courage, my load got a lot lighter.

ᗉᗆ

"We learned that our First Step was both
an event and an ongoing process."
"First Step To Recovery"

Being a sex addict requires a certain wariness. There
are times when my addiction seems to go into remis-
sion. I'm free from inappropriate sexual urges. I think
that maybe all that work I've done on the Steps and on
myself and all the therapy has healed me. I begin to
feel that I can go to meetings, but I don't have to worry
about a slip.

Invariably, something comes along that triggers me
and I'm proved wrong. It's disappointing, but it's okay.
I'm a sex addict.

But there is a safeguard against this disease. I have to
acknowledge on a daily basis that I'm a sex addict, and
surrender my addiction to my Higher Power. I have
found that it is easiest to do at the beginning of my day
when I wake, before I pick up my cell phone or turn
on my computer. Sometimes I visualize wrapping my
addiction up and handing it to my Higher Power. My
prayer is that my day will be sober and not controlled
by my addiction. For me this reprieve lasts one day.
My life will become unmanageable if I think otherwise.

At day's end, I review my day and gratefully discover
that my prayer has been answered.

～

*I acknowledge that I'm a sex addict, asking my Higher
Power to help me stay sober, today.*

"And as we grow in recovery, many of us
choose to integrate our sexuality with our
spirituality. When we are sexual with love,
gratitude, and generosity, sex can be an
expression of our highest spiritual ideals."

Sex Addicts Anonymous, page 73

I spent many years trying to control my sexuality in
one way or another. When I realized I was being ruled
by addictive behaviors, I tried to stifle, bury, or run
from sexual feelings, and I shamed myself for having
passions. I had no clear concept of what healthy sexuality was, and I was afraid of being used or of using others. I didn't view sex as anything spiritual. I
couldn't even use the words "God" and "sex" in the
same sentence, much less invite my Higher Power to
help me experience the spiritual side of sexuality.

But in recovery, I have come to believe that sexuality is a God-given part of who I am. As I surrendered
my addiction, I saw the need to surrender control over
other areas of my sexual behavior. I started putting my
sexual life in the care of a loving God. I am learning
to include Higher Power in my sexuality, channeling
that energy into behaviors that promote intimacy and
connection with my partner. When my sexuality isn't
being used to control someone else, nor controlling
me, when I allow God into my sexuality; it becomes a
powerful gift that both my partner and I can enjoy—
physically, emotionally, and spiritually.

*Higher Power, help me use my sexuality to express
love, appreciation, and faith.*

> "Most of us know that we caused harm in one
> way or another, but in the past we chose to
> feel guilty without doing anything about it."
>
> *Sex Addicts Anonymous*, page 45

For centuries, doctors the world over took the Hippocratic Oath. In modern times, the surgeon Thomas Inman is reported to have encouraged a version of the oath distilled by a surgeon several centuries before: primum non nocere, "First, do no harm." It seems to me that this idea is embodied in the Twelve Steps.

It starts in Step One when we finally decide to get off the merry-go-round and stop destroying our lives and the lives of others. First, do no harm. In Steps Four and Five, we look at the painful areas in our lives with an eye toward gleaning our part in creating the pain. From there we take steps to stop contributing to the cycle of pain. First, do no harm.

In Steps Eight and Nine, we become willing to make amends to anyone we have harmed, and then make amends directly whenever possible. But, we must not make direct amends to people we have harmed if it could injure them or others. First, do no harm.

In the Tenth Step, we continue to take inventory, and when wrong, promptly admit it. We take this inventory because we are still addicts, boundaries are not our strong suit, and we will make mistakes that can injure relationships. This step allows us to repair any possible harm that might have occurred. First, do no harm.

First, do no harm. Is there a better way to inform my actions?

> "The danger in playing the victim is that we
> might develop a sense of entitlement to act out."
>
> *Sex Addicts Anonymous*, page 65

I had always had a vaunted attitude of responsibility.
I thought I was superior to others in being well-man-
nered and having high-minded ideals. The problem in
being what I thought was morally upright all the time
is that I was often left out of fun and interesting activities with other people. I found myself lonely, frustrated, and resentful, and I used these emotions to rationalize engaging in questionable behavior. I had to steal
what I thought I needed to survive.

I am now taking more responsibility for my life. My
deprivation was the result of a narrow, distorted view
of the world. I am letting go of blame and I am learning
to take in love and support. I no longer have a score to
settle. I need not take advantage of others; they don't
owe me anything. My Higher Power and the program
are showing me how to meet my needs.

*I pray for the courage to let go of old attitudes and
embrace new ones that are loving of all, including me.*

&

> "Autonomy also means that each group
> has the freedom to make mistakes and
> learn from them at its own pace."
>
> *Sex Addicts Anonymous*, page 83

I come with baggage. As I reflect on Tradition Four, I realize I am a part of a larger whole—something greater than myself. My behaviors and decisions affect my spouse, friends, family, and community. Nowadays, I behave in a way that brings openness and a sense of honor, not just to myself, but also to those who know and associate with me. This has not always been an easy process. When my addiction was active, I lashed out, pushed people away, even stole from them. My behavior was atrocious. I fled in terror from every mistake, only to repeat it.

As I started down the road of recovery, I fell on my face more often than not. My sponsor would gently suggest solutions. Needless to say, I always tried my way first, usually to the detriment of myself and others. My sponsor, honoring his and my autonomy, said I was free to make mistakes. He also said that, if I stayed sober, the pain of doing it my way would get great enough, and I would be open to learning from others.

That's the great gift of sobriety and recovery—when I get miserable enough from trying it my way, I have tools and support to actually learn from my mistakes. Over time, and mistakes, I learned how to let go of the self-centeredness that fueled my addiction, and how to connect with others without fear of driving them away.

Mistakes are inevitable. Now, I can learn from them.

ଔ

"And it takes gentleness in the form of self-care.
By completing this step we show a commitment
to our recovery and to living in reality."

Sex Addicts Anonymous, page 37

The Fourth Step was the first step that scared me.
Even with the support of my sponsor, step group,
and the fellowship, I didn't feel ready to delve into the
depths and examine all my faults. I procrastinated because of two fears until a couple messages finally sank
in. First, I thought I had to produce a perfect inventory. Nope, no way, no how. Like everything in the program, it is meant to be done to the best of my ability at
the time. I will have plenty of chances to do it again, to
learn more the next time.

Secondly, I feared that focusing on all those negative parts would just pile on the shame and pull me
back into my addictive thinking. Fortunately, the step
workbook our group had chosen deliberately alternat-
ed between negative and positive aspects, allowing me
a more comprehensive picture of myself.

In the end, the exercise is not about judging myself.
This task is about risking awareness—truly seeing
who I am, warts and beauty spots alike. It's only by
gaining this insight that I can claim a starting point
for change.

Taking stock of who I am gives me perspective, not
just on those parts that dominated my life and pro-
pelled my addiction, shame, and loneliness, but on the
complete package. As the song goes, to know me is to
love me.

~

In this honest look, I will begin to heal.

ଓ

> "For too long most of us found it familiar,
> almost comfortable to remain in the
> cycle of acting out, feeling demoralized,
> swearing off, and <u>then</u> acting out again."
> "Three Circles"

I had established my circles before sobriety and found that I spent far more time in my middle circle than my inner circle. If I could just stay in my middle circle, I thought, I might not feel so demoralized. At least my sobriety date would be intact. But the middle circle heads in one direction.

A favorite acting-out place was thirty miles from home. I often headed there around eleven o'clock at night. I would feel physical changes from anticipation. My car had a mind of its own, and I was just along for the ride.

I told myself I would stay only until a certain time, but before I knew it, it would be six o'clock in the morning and I would rush home and back to work with another sleepless night. I would tell myself never again, yet, after a few hours' rest that evening, I was back in the cycle.

Awareness of my circles had an effect, however, and I began going home earlier. Then one night, driving to act out, in a flash of clarity, I said, "I don't really want to do this." I turned around and headed home. My car and my fledgling recovery had both reached a turning point. A well-defined middle circle helped me spot the cycle, and eventually steer clear of my inner circle.

When I use them, these tools work wonders. What circle am I in right now?

ଔ

"We are sex addicts."
Sex Addicts Anonymous, page 1

As I read this stark, bold, introductory statement at the beginning of each meeting, I am both exposed and empowered. I want to stop after that first sentence and reflect, then perhaps pray... grant me the serenity to accept that I am a sex addict, that I cannot change this fact. Recently, while taking inventory, I realized I still had some pride in my sexual conquests, the same ones that brought pain, humiliation, shame, and destruction. I search my attitude even now as I read that sentence—may I never again delight in harmful behavior and attitudes.

Yet, do I feel intense shame, that somehow I am too broken and worthless because of this reality? No, this program moves me from shame to grace. So where is the grace in this statement?

I find grace in "we"—I am not alone. I am known and accepted. There are finally others in the world who get me. "We are"—I am who I am. I am human with limitations which happen to include sex addiction and associated character defects. I can accept myself as I am.

"Sex"—is a powerful aspect of my humanity. It can help me see my deepest needs and desires, connecting me to my spirituality.

"Addicts"—I am not in control. I need a Power greater than myself. I also need help from my fellow addicts. to make beautiful life music. I make the world better by practicing my daily recovery plan.

～

I find serenity to accept my reality today. I experience grace in this fellowship of sex addicts.

જી

> "We found in each other what we
> could find nowhere else: people who
> knew the depth of our pain."

Sex Addicts Anonymous, page 2

How could anyone possibly understand the pain of wanting with all my heart to be with my family and friends and yet repeating the sexual behaviors that destroy my relationships? Or the pain of feeling like a pervert? Or the pain of withdrawal during early recovery?

Simply put, only a fellow sex addict knows. And helping each other pass through such pain into a better life creates a bond that I, quite frankly, rarely find outside our fellowship. Whether it's the knowing nods as I speak the truth of my pain in meetings, the sighs of recognition from old-timers as they listen to a first step, or the one-on-one phone conversations between struggling addicts, our common pain binds us in a community that sets us free.

~

With the support of those who know the depth of my pain, I can accept that pain as a valuable teacher.

"Made a decision to turn our will and our lives
over to the care of God as we understood God."
Sex Addicts Anonymous, page 28

God, for me, appeals to all people, spiritual beliefs
and practices. My understanding of God is that God
is everywhere: in the majestic sky at night, in every
animal and plant, in every grain of sand on the beach.
God is in me. Everything is God—God is one.

Concerning sex addiction—for me, it was only possible to act out when I lost track of the concept that
God is nurturing, like a bird who takes me under her
wing. I did not care. I just wanted that quick fix, that
rush. It had nothing to do with patience or good will. I
abandoned God.

How do I turn my will and life over to the care of God?
By taking that leap of faith that God is in control, that
things are working out in God's time, in his or her
manner, not mine. I am part of God's world but that
world does not revolve around me. After the Third
Step, I can look at myself as a part of one—God is one.

~

*My understanding is that God is forever. I put my life
in the care of God.*

"While physical exercise is clearly an outer-
· circle activity, we feel it deserves special
attention because so many have found it to be
a valuable support for maintaining sobriety."

Tools of Recovery, page 40

Sometimes I can't identify my feelings, or I feel too overwhelmed to talk to anyone without being toxic and regretting my words. Other times I feel drained, numb, flat.

Moving my body can help break the stalemate in my mind. I don't have to be an athlete to use this tool. Just getting outside to walk or put my feet in the grass is often a quick way for me to get unstuck. Seeing the vast sky or hearing birds can instantly remind me that there is much, much more to this life than the old tapes that clamor to frighten and debilitate me. Also, doing something with my hands like puttering in the garage, tending the garden, doing some housework, or making something can help break the cycle.

Any physical action can be meditative. As I move, my mind slows to a manageable pace. I can recall and repeat a program slogan, affirmation, prayer, or mantra. I can explore my feelings and create space between my thoughts and actions. Beneath the shell of chaos, I often discover hurt, loneliness, or vulnerability.

I can ask myself what I need. Perhaps I'll call a sponsor or friend, go to a meeting, or write in my journal. Maybe I will prepare some wonderful food or do something creative. Maybe I will simply relax and enjoy the beauty of this day.

When my mind gets stuck, moving my body can change the view.

❧

> "We may experience abstinence from our
> inner-circle sexual behaviors as a gift from
> our Higher Power rather than as the result
> of our own white-knuckled efforts."
>
> *Sex Addicts Anonymous*, page 31

I know it's tempting for some to put off committing fully to the program until they have a better understanding of it, but I've found I don't have to know it all perfectly before I act. In fact, I can't.

The founders of twelve-step recovery and our own Green Book both say that, in order to progress, we need to be willing to do whatever it takes to be sober. This spiritual program asks me to start walking forward even when I don't know where I'm going or how I will get there. I can only choose to trust my Higher Power and those who've gone down this road, those who understand that it's through the exercise of willingness and faith that we gain strength to grow beyond what we presently are.

Abstinence from addictive sexual behaviors allowed my body to reset, and eventually made it possible for my thinking to become clearer. One day at a time, in willingness and faith, I am given the strength to abstain from my inner circle behaviors.

Today I choose to trust my Higher Power and the experience of those who have paved the way for me.

"Sexuality is part of who we are, a part that
became lost and distorted through our addiction.
When we reclaim the possibility of healthier
sexuality, we regain a vital aspect of our being."

Sex Addicts Anonymous, page 72

I am a sex addict and a sexual anorexic. After decades of sexual acting out, I entered a year-long period of sexual anorexia before I found SAA. During that
year I starved myself of not only healthy sexuality with
my husband, but even non-sexual physical affection
and connectedness in all my relationships. I felt like
an asexual, emotionless robot that was dead from the
neck down.

As I started working the Twelve Steps of SAA around
my sexual anorexia, my body came alive again. In the
past, I had always acted out on those feelings, so I
didn't know what to do with them. This terrified me,
and I prayed for my Higher Power to remove my sexual
feelings.

Soon, my Higher Power spoke to me very clearly.
Those feelings are a natural part of being human. Like
other dimensions of my being, they are not there to be
denied or abused; they are there to be nourished and
nurtured. Over the years, the emotions and associa-
tions I had with those feelings had been warped and
perverted from their original purpose and from the joy
and connection they could provide. The path of healing starts by being emotionally connected with myself,
then by moving in the belief that my sexuality can be
part of a greater connection with my partner and with
life.

~

*Please teach me how to nourish my sexuality in a
healthy way.*

ॐ

"In SAA, we learn to be accountable for our
own feelings and behaviors, and to let go
of unhealthy responsibility for others."

"A Special Welcome to the Woman Newcomer"

Today, through my prayer and meditation time, a
women's telemeeting, and my outreach calls, I realized
that I am carrying burdens that my Higher Power never meant me to have. I am working Step Three, and the
invitation is right before me to turn these over to the
God of my understanding. Great! So, I've turned them
over, right? No. Why is it so hard to let go, especially
of the sense that I am responsible for the feelings and
behaviors of others?

As a woman, I think such burden-bearing is a particular liability. Cultural and familial pressures encourage it. I have been relieved, though, to find that I
do not get that message from people, especially men,
in recovery. They don't blame me or other women for
their reactions to us.

To me, recovery is an artistic gift to the world. It allows me to make beautiful life music. I make the world
better by practicing my daily recovery plan.

But I need to take responsibility for my actions in
meetings—it is no place for exhibitionism, flirting, at-
tention-seeking, or games. Early on, a few men called
me on my inappropriateness after meetings when I
tried to fit in by making sexual jokes. I was surprised
and hadn't even realized what I was doing. Yet I appreciated the respectful feedback. I actually felt safer and
more accepted because of their openness and honesty.
I am learning to trust recovering men and women, and
to be more trustworthy.

*I take responsibility for my reactions, feelings and
behaviors. I let go of unhealthy responsibility for
others. I let go and let God.*

∽

"I had to take responsibility for my past
actions to be able to live with myself."

Sex Addicts Anonymous, page 325

I have no idea where many of the people on my Eighth
Step list are. They are no longer in my life. I am willing
to make amends to them, as suggested by the Ninth
Step, but how can I make amends to people if I don't
know where they are?

One of my compulsive sexual behaviors is objecti-
fication, in my case, of women. It makes people uncomfortable, earns me looks of disgust, but usually
that's all in terms of immediate consequences. I don't
know about the long-term consequences. There are so
many people in this category. What is an appropriate
amends?

A form of amends for me is service to the type of person I objectified. If I can be of service to others in that
same group, it's at least a start toward balancing the
taking I did all those years.

I volunteer to answer calls to the local hotline and
e-mails through the local website. Some of them are
from women. I let them know that recovery from sex
addiction is possible, and I make a special effort to tell
them that they would be welcome in the local fellowship. When one of them responds positively, I rejoice.
When a woman newcomer attends one of my meetings,
I make a point to gently and safely welcome her.

∼

I can make living amends by acts of service.

ↁ

"Seek a temporary or permanent sponsor as
soon as possible to guide you in getting started."

"Sex Addicts Anonymous: A Pathway To Recovery"

I spent my whole life essentially alone. I had one or
two friends over the years, but those relationships
were unsatisfactory. I normally and subconsciously
chose people with whom I could have dysfunctional,
isolating relationships, mirroring my life growing up.

So when I came into SAA, I resisted suggestions that
involved other people, such as making telephone calls,
getting a sponsor, or even going out for coffee. I was
more attracted to those aspects of the program that I
could do in isolation, such as reading program literature. True to form, I tried to work the program in the
same solitary way I had acted out in my addiction.

Even though I let my sponsor nominally help me with
the First Step, I essentially did it alone. As a result, I
wasn't happy with the outcome, and I left the program
looking for my real bottom. I found it.

After a year, I came back and jumped at the opportunity to find a sponsor. Though it was difficult at first, I
started relying on that sponsor. Making daily program
calls and being pleasantly surprised that most members actually called me back reinforced the idea that,
together with my sponsor and others, I could actually work the program and get better. I would never go
back to trying this alone.

*I can't do this alone. Thank you, God, for my sponsor
and friends in recovery.*

"The only requirement for SAA membership is
a desire to stop addictive sexual behavior."
Sex Addicts Anonymous, page 77

I often have a difficult time believing that other people
will accept me as I am. That's because I have a difficult
time accepting myself as I am. These beliefs make it
easy for me to feel shame and to prefer isolation—the
very things that fuel my sex addiction.

I believe that SAA meetings are the primary way my
Higher Power teaches me to give and to receive acceptance. The Third Tradition throws the doors wide
open, welcoming all sex addicts regardless of gender,
race, class, sexual orientation, or religious beliefs. It
particularly welcomes those who have not yet established sexual sobriety and those who have slipped or
relapsed. Absolutely anyone who wants freedom from
acting out, no matter what they have done, has a place
at our table.

Before I went to my first SAA meeting, I was afraid of
some of the people I might meet. I drew a sharp dis-
tinction between my own acting out, which was "normal" or at least not so bad, and the sexual behavior of
others. Yet as I listen to the stories of my SAA brothers
and sisters, I recognize myself in them. This recognition naturally gives rise to compassion and to acceptance. And as I feel warmth and acceptance toward my
fellow sex addicts, it gradually dawns on me that I can
accept myself, too.

~

*No matter where I am in my sex addiction, I can
always find support and acceptance at an SAA
meeting.*

ରେ

> "Recovery from sex addiction rarely
> happens overnight. It takes patience—a
> quality often in <u>short</u> supply for us."
>
> *Tools of Recovery*, page 11

Of all the useful slogans I've learned in SAA recovery, "One Day At A Time" has been both the most useful and the most difficult one for me to apply to my life.

When, at the age of 66, I finally became aware that I had been a sex addict for most of my life, I was eager to get as far into my recovery as soon as possible. Nothing was going to hold me back.

But then the reality of Step One pulled me up short—I really had to struggle to accept my powerlessness and unmanageability. Days and weeks went by as I read, prayed, meditated, attended meetings, and met with my sponsor. Fortunately, my sponsor set the pace, held me accountable, and wouldn't let me rush through Step One or the steps that followed.

I came to accept my powerlessness, and with that acceptance, the realization that my recovery was a daily, if not hourly, task. Each day I must recommit to every aspect of my recovery. In matters of recovery, tomorrow doesn't exist. Living one day at a time is a challenge for me, but my recovery depends on my learning to be patient.

~

Today is the only day that matters to my recovery.
Help me to make it a good one.

> "Accepting our sex addiction brings hope
> by acknowledging the truth and begins the
> spiritual journey of Twelve Step recovery."
>
> *Getting Started*, page 8

Early into SAA, I tried thinking my way through the First Step. I saw the evidence of my powerlessness and unmanageability, and believed recognition would suffice. However, I wasn't getting clean. Then an old-timer explained that "admitted" means more than just thinking. It means that I engage my whole self in the truth about my addiction.

"Admitting" happened for me when I finally let down my defenses and felt guilt for what I had done. I was on the floor, sobbing non-stop for an hour. I was raw and felt the full weight of my addiction. After I was all cried out, a voice inside said, "Stay in touch with these feelings."

Each day I tried to return to those feelings by praying, listening to music, journaling, reading—anything that helped. Two amazing things happened. First, the compulsion to act out left; second, I found myself being lifted out of that pit a little more each day. After twenty years of acting out, my Higher Power was rebuilding me without my addiction. Now, with decades of abstinence, I am still growing.

Someone said: "Name it, claim it, and let it go." I had to claim it, to hit bottom emotionally devastated, and stay in touch with it, so my Higher Power could free me and rebuild me. It hurt, and it still hurts a little, but my new life is worth every ounce of pain.

Hitting bottom is the doorway to my new life in recovery.

> "Each group has but one primary
> purpose—to carry its message to the
> sex addict who still suffers."
>
> *Sex Addicts Anonymous*, page 84

As I travel through my own recovery, it is easy to forget our primary purpose. There are days when my middle-circle behaviors beckon me like a siren's song to slip into the inner-circle abyss—enticing me to act out. There are also days when I get wrapped up in my duties as secretary of my home group. Other days find me involved in intergroup activities and projects.

I get so self-absorbed in my own recovery or daily activities that I miss the primary purpose—to carry the message to the sex addict who still suffers. I would never want another addict to endure the devastation that tied up my life for years.

I have heard it said in meetings that the newcomer is the most important person in the room. Periodically I need to stop and ask myself if I am making the SAA message of recovery understandable and accessible to newcomers. I also need to provide a welcoming atmosphere that makes members want to stay, share, return each week, work the steps with a sponsor, and commit to their own recovery.

What can I do today to reach out to other sex addicts who seek help?

ଔ

> "If we are continuing to act out as a pattern,
> it is possible that we aren't fully willing to
> admit powerlessness over our addiction."
>
> *Sex Addicts Anonymous*, page 69

For years I continued to act out then go to meetings and say I wanted to be sober. Continued relapse brought me hopelessness and self-pity. There were times when I was ready to call it quits on the program. This disconnect was finally reconciled when I admitted I didn't know if I wanted to be sober. In truth, I was unwilling to admit that I am powerless. In the back of my mind, I still thought I could someday, somehow be able to control this acting out.

The beauty of the Twelve Steps is that, if I have the desire to stop acting out, I can begin recovery anew today. The beauty of the Twelve Traditions is that, as long as I have the desire, I can belong to this fellowship. My Higher Power decides when the compulsion is lifted, but it's up to me to apply action to my desire for recovery. Only I can admit that I am powerless over this compulsion and then surrender any thoughts of control. From there, I can begin the journey to a new life through the Steps, sponsorship, meetings, fellowship, prayer, service, and outer circle activities.

Victory can begin now with my complete surrender.

ଔ

"Working the Fifth Step helps relieve us of
the burden of our secrets, break through
our isolation, and face ourselves honestly
in a way we cannot do alone. With the
Fifth Step, we come out into the open."

Sex Addicts Anonymous, page 37

The Fifth Step was big challenge. Having the discussion with my Higher Power about the exact nature of my wrongs, the underlying issues and drivers, took a good deal of courage and insight into my past and present behaviors. But in that process, I gained more awareness about myself, and was also able to start putting my wrongs into a healthier perspective. This started loosening the power and control they had to keep me shackled to my addiction.

Sharing this story with another person was something akin to giving a First Step, but with more depth and more varied emotions. It was a reasonably lengthy conversation, spanning several hours. At the end of it all, another huge weight was lifted from my shoulders, and I know I laid the foundation for forgiving myself in that process.

I view the Fifth Step as a cleaning of the slate, an opportunity to let go of many hurts and wrongs that kept me tied to the past. It enables me to spring forward with renewed energy and focus in my recovery.

~

In voicing the nature of my wrongs and the anger, resentment, and pain of my past, I will give up those burdens that keep me locked in my addictive ways.

"As a fellowship, our commitment is to the
common welfare of recovering sex addicts
everywhere. The First Tradition makes it
clear that each member's recovery depends
on the strength of that commitment."

Sex Addicts Anonymous, page 79

I love and hate this tradition, just as I have a love-hate relationship with recovery. I love that my addiction is bringing me into a new way of living, with the promise of spiritual transformation, yet I hate that I am powerless over, and limited by my addiction. I hate that I cannot recover alone, yet I love experiencing unity in this program. If I could do it alone, I would never have the privilege and power of sharing in that unity. And I can experience that unity at every meeting when we pray together.

We are united by a common problem, for a common goal, and in a common faith that a Power greater than ourselves can restore us to sanity. In the rich diversity of experience, beliefs, opinions, values, and preferences in our fellowship, I find a powerful spiritual principle in the unity of this program. This tradition reminds me that my individual welfare depends upon our common welfare. My commitment must be to "cultivate tolerance and good will," to let a spirit of unity oversee disagreements. Without this unity, I will lose recovery, and I will find myself "isolated and alone... spiritually empty." Been there, done that.

I need us so I can find a new life. May I be mindful of what we share.

ॐ

> "Our disease kept us from being fully
> present when we were sexual....Many of
> us recognize healthier sexuality when
> we experience something very different
> from what we knew in our addiction."
>
> *Sex Addicts Anonymous*, page 71

When I eat a piece of bread, I don't usually think about who grew the wheat, what it took for the wheat to become bread, or how many hands it passed through before landing in mine. I'm disconnected from that whole series of events, and I don't feel much gratitude and appreciation for what I've been given.

Likewise, I missed out on so much when I was caught up in my disease. I missed out on true connection with my partner by not being present during sex. Like the attitudes modeled in sexually explicit media, I was disconnected from the deeper meaning of those interactions, leaving nothing but a mere shadow of actual intimacy. Those behaviors don't serve me.

In recovery I practice being present by being still and observing what my senses tell me. I allow myself to experience my emotions without judging them, denying them, or burying them. I am starting to accept my partner's loving affection, and to allow myself to both give and receive sexual nurturing while being fully in the moment. This brings deeper meaning and connection in our relationship, and greater satisfaction in our sexual experiences. Being present allows any moment to open up in rich and rewarding ways whether I'm eating toast or connecting with my partner.

Higher Power, please help me be present and mindful in all I do today.

> "To hit bottom is to reach such a low point—
> mentally, physically, emotionally, and
> spiritually—that we break through our denial."
>
> *Sex Addicts Anonymous*, page 8

A founder of Twelve Step programs reportedly told addicts to remember their bottom every day. As simple as this guidance is, the particulars vary from person to person. For many, it is the painful consequences—relationship and job losses, arrests, diseases, or public humiliations—that result from addictive behavior. For me, the landmarks were more internal.

When I hit bottom, I was flying high in my job, had bought a new house and a new car, just had a new baby, and was getting lots of public approval. Everything on the outside looked good. Inside, though, I was crashing. I was lonely and desperate, terrified of getting caught, and being crushed by the shame of my addiction. I was a lie, a good-looking disaster. Why would I want to remember that?

Every one of the Steps, from facing my powerlessness to carrying the message, leads me to revisit my low points. By remembering, I not only face the facts, I re-experience the emotions of those times, and I become more emotionally and spiritually vulnerable and available. This openness seems to create room for my Higher Power to work in me. The gifts of surrender—another day of abstinence, a little more spiritual growth, a means to be of service, an ever-deepening gratitude for my life—now flow from this remembering.

When I remember what brought me here, it becomes a channel through which my Higher Power delivers hope and strength.

ॐ

> "Many find it beneficial to do a personal
> sexual history, including an exploration
> of sexuality in their family of origin."

"First Step to Recovery"

When I was young, my brother touched me in ways that felt tingly and warm. When I protested, he would hold me down and continue. I knew it was wrong. I tried to tell my mom, but the words would not leave my mouth. Then one day, he stopped. I felt shame for wanting him again. I felt abandoned. I hated him for years.

When I wrote my Fourth Step, I realized that I had to include the word molest. That was hard for me to acknowledge, even to my sponsor. I hated that my brother took my innocence. I had a lot of unanswered questions. However, I moved forward, and eventually it was time for Step Nine.

My first amends was to my mom. We got on the subject of my brother, and she told me that he had been abused by a woman who had told him to practice at home. He practiced on me and then went to my sister when she started puberty. That's why he abandoned me.

Although it sickened me to hear this, it changed my heart. I felt sorry for my brother and my sister. I had compassion and empathy for my abuser! Later, I was able to make amends for things I had done to him. My burden was lifted. It was painful to explore this chapter in my past, but it was worth it. My serenity is worth it.

~

Serenity is a choice I can make at any time.

> "Slippery behaviors are things we do that
> expose us to triggers. They may not be sexual
> themselves, but they put us at risk to
> act out."
> "Abstinence"

When I drive through the section of town where I used to act out, I need to focus on my legitimate business there or avoid going altogether. My sponsor recommended "geographical creativity" in planning my travels so that I avoid those areas of acting out. I devised other routes to travel to business destinations.

I have discovered new neighborhoods in town that I heretofore had missed. Serendipitously, I even found a coffee shop on one of the new routes across town where they have a unique dark roast coffee that I have come to love. Now, I go out of my way to use the new path. I am convinced that God rewarded me because I chose an alternate route—a route that is even more desirable than the slippery routes.

~

Today I ask my Higher Power to guide me to non-slippery paths, which turn out to be more pleasant than the slippery paths of the past.

ભ

"We loosen the grip on our old destructive
patterns, perhaps not knowing yet what
will replace them, but in the faith that
something better will be revealed."
Sex Addicts Anonymous, page 28

Step Three is one of conscious surrender and commitment. It is a small but measurable action to change my ways. This is where I take the risk to put my faith and trust in something else—not my addiction, not myself, not my friends or family. This is the humble pledge that asks that my Higher Power's will, not my own, be done. It is the difficult task of letting go of the wheel. One member sums up the first three steps as: I have a problem and there is help, if I am willing to ask for it.

Step Three is where I consciously admit that I want guidance from someone or somewhere else to steer me down a better path. Many struggle with the notion of a God of their understanding, but this program asks and allows each of us to discover a Higher Power that works in our lives. It can take many forms, including the group conscience, nature, the universe, and good orderly direction. The program allows for all these and more.

What matters is that we believe, in no matter what infinitesimal amount, that something beyond ourselves has a better idea of where our road should lead.

~

If I can accept that perhaps I am not the master of my destiny, and surrender what I cannot control, my life can head in a different and more positive direction.

> "But the steps are more than a series of
> exercises. They provide basic principles
> for living. Most of us find opportunities on
> a daily basis to apply one or more of the
> steps to some challenge in our life."
>
> *Sex Addicts Anonymous*, page 22

Walking up a steep hill to his new home, a friend of mine was disappointed to find himself gasping, his leg muscles burning, while his housemate scurried up the hill, seemingly without effort.

"This hill will always be steep," his friend said, "but you will get stronger."

This is a great metaphor for my recovery. Being sexually sober doesn't mean my life will always be smooth and fun. However, I have access to a Power greater than me that helps me through difficult moments and shows me how to respond to challenges in new and healthy ways. I will still have problems, the hill may still be steep, but living life according to spiritual principles transforms my difficulties into strength-training exercises and opportunities for discovery.

God, help me see my stumbling blocks as stepping stones, as the opportunities that they are.

ॐ

"The middle circle is <u>not</u> a place to hang out."
Tools of Recovery, page 8

In recovery, my new computer became my source for information, news, entertainment, and even dating. I began to spend more time on dating sites. The sites I visited allowed all types of pictures in the profiles. Each time I visited those sites, I was triggered and got the hit I wanted. After a while, the pretense of looking for a date fell away; I was going there just to look at pictures.

Going to these sites produced an unanticipated effect—I wanted more. I began to search for sites that would get me even closer to my addiction. I withheld more from my sponsor and my friends in recovery. Eventually, hanging out in my middle circle led me to my inner circle and relapse.

The road back from relapse taught me that the middle circle is a safety net, not a place to park and hide. Identifying my middle circle provides a landmark where I can stop and turn back to my outer circle. Regularly talking to my sponsor about specifics of my middle-circle behavior helps me recognize and move out of it. I check in about the sites I go to, exactly what I see, how much time I spend, and what I do. Sharing in meetings about my middle-circle experiences frees me from worrying about my image, allowing me to stand openly in the light of day.

Staying out of my middle circle leaves more time for my outer circle and for life.

ॐ

"We also discover that our character defects
can become useful in God's hands."

Sex Addicts Anonymous, page 45

As an active addict, I have found myself powerless around strong feelings such as rage and fear, and around actions such as lying. I have been saddled with bottled anger or fear which, over time, turned into resentment, then complacency, dishonesty and delusion. Often, I am at multiple points in this process at the same time!

As a recovering addict, I recognize and acknowledge to myself the character defects I have. Rage, fear, dishonesty, and resentment are only some of the character defects I unearthed. More often, these defects are the signposts that point to the real work and the real me. Only when I embrace these feelings and am honest with myself about what I am feeling deep inside my heart do I begin to experience the miracle. This is the miracle that converts my anger into a discovery of my real feelings behind the anger. Perhaps the underlying feeling is fear because my boundaries were violated or that I felt unworthy.

When I use fear as an indicator of an opportunity underneath, I am surprised to find a courage that is driven by reason. Very slowly, but surely, my character defects become my allies, helping me forward on life's path. I feel blessed to be who I am, blessed to have lived the life I have so far, and I look forward to the rest of it.

~

I will remember that my character defects are not my enemies. When I embrace them, real change begins. Before I know it, my defects will turn into assets.

ॐ

"For our group purpose there is but one
ultimate authority—a loving God as expressed
in our group conscience. Our leaders are
but trusted servants; they do not govern."

Sex Addicts Anonymous, page 79

Taking on my first service position taught me humility. I was impatient about waiting on the group conscience because God may have been moving too slowly for me in a few instances. When I focused on spiritual principles and let go of personal needs and desires, I found a loving God available to guide my group to a more powerful decision and a more all-embracing solution that appealed to the entire group.

The group conscience met the group's needs and desires and satisfied me in a way that no authoritative decision could have. It was not a matter of right or wrong; rather, it was a matter of letting God's guidance and time lead us toward a decision that transcended mere agreement. I still work to seek the will of my God in my life and in my group experience. I practice surrender as I take on service positions. As I surrender, the circle of trust grows.

~

Group conscience produces better group decisions because they occur on God's time, not necessarily my time.

> "Any small effort we make to slow down and listen is a step towards connecting with our Higher Power, and will bear fruit in time."
>
> *Sex Addicts Anonymous*, page 57

I have often tried, and found I could not find my Higher Power. No one in the past could tell me where or what it was. I knew I would never find it outside myself.

I started praying long before I began meditating, so praying was easy. Did I have to know where the prayers were going? Not so much.

It took awhile to understand that the only place to find the God of my understanding was in the moment. The gateway to the moment was stillness of mind and body.

Sitting in a quiet place, gently breathing in and out, watching my thoughts and emotions, at first like an action movie, slowly drifting into melodrama, and ending with a love story. And then just quiet stillness.

Living neither in the past nor the future, I let myself be where I am.

"When we show up, we help create a place where
others can pass on the message of recovery,
even if we don't say anything ourselves."

Sex Addicts Anonymous, page 60

I have a hard time believing that my presence counts
for anything. As far back as infancy, my parents
thought of me as a doll, rather than as a real person. I'm not alone. Many addicts I know were given
that same message in various ways: through physical, sexual, or emotional abuse; or through neglect or
abandonment.

When I was acting out, I didn't believe my actions
actually affected other people. After all, it wasn't really
who I was. Like others in the program, I considered
myself a sane and good person, in spite of behaviors
that would indicate otherwise. I made the addict-part
of me invisible, even to myself.

The truth is, I'm always visible. All my actions, and
even my energy, do count. They have an effect on other people, whether I know it or not. I am not God; I
cannot control what others may do or think. But I
am a precious child of God; my presence always matters. This is particularly true at meetings. Everyone
who shows up creates a vessel, week after week, that
people can rely on. My sitting there silently may help
another addict stay sober for one more day. When I
attend a meeting, it is an act of service to others, even
while I'm helping myself.

*Today I remember that my presence and my actions
always matter.*

ରେ

> "We also learn specific tools to help us change
> our behavior and disrupt the compulsive
> cycle of sexual acting out and despair."
> *Sex Addicts Anonymous*, page 12

Many newcomers ask how long they have to work this program before they're fixed. The old-timers smile and nod and tell the newcomer to keep coming back. My experience also supports the notion that the disease of addiction is incurable. There's one more thing: I am always in motion.

One mark of addiction is a steady, downward spiral where nothing ever improves. I've watched friends who are practicing addicts directly or indirectly report that their lives are: "Same stuff, different day." I still have problems, but they're new, improved problems.

Recovery means change. If I'm sober and showing up for my life, my spiritual, emotional, psychological, intellectual self is constantly changing, adapting, adopting, growing, reacting, acting, and sometimes learning. Every decision I make and action I take sets other events in motion. There is no destination; it's all a journey. The question then becomes: in which direction do I want to move?

My definition of the outer circle is simple: it is any action that takes me further away from acting out. It can be almost anything: prayer, service, cooking good food, holding the door for somebody, doing my job, giving myself a break or a treat, folding laundry, playing music, walking my dog, enjoying the company of friends or a beautiful day or a powerful storm, or the very difficult acts of practicing restraint and courage.

~

I always have options. Which direction am I heading right now?

ଓ

> "A newfound ability to live in the
> moment under God's care gives us the
> courage to go <u>forward</u> in recovery."
>
> *Sex Addicts Anonymous*, page 31

"You have no keel. You need to develop one to face the vicissitudes of life without capsizing and sinking." That was my evaluation? Stunned and enraged, I dismissed the professional's metaphor; he didn't know the real me! That was nine months ago. Now, I am in SAA, working Step Three with my sponsor. Looking back, I see that the assessment was generous and gracious.

I researched keels and was dismayed. The keel is the part of the boat around which the rest is built. It provides stability, converting lateral forces of wind and waves into forward movement. My 'boat' had been built with self-reliance; my mantra from early childhood had never changed—I can do it myself. Clearly, I cannot. But how does one build a keel once the boat is built? How do I find a center after years in the devastating wake of my addiction?

Keels are usually made of heavy, strong material, which speaks of spiritual substance to me. In Step Two we came to believe that a Power greater than ourselves could restore us to sanity—perhaps, lay the keel? Now, my challenge in Step Three is to decide to turn my life and will, my boat, over to the care of God. Only a spiritual solution, weighty and eternal, is sufficient. Only a loving, caring God is safe for me to trust with such a life-transforming process.

~

Thank you, God, for the new course my life is taking.

ભ

> "Obtaining and maintaining abstinence
> from inner circle compulsions is the
> bedrock foundation of all the personal
> growth which <u>will</u> surely follow."
> "Three Circles"

The only requirement for SAA membership is a desire to stop acting out. However, the reason I joined Sex Addicts Anonymous was to actually stop the acting out. In early days, I, like many others, had a number of slips. However, as time went on, I achieved abstinence from my inner circle through the Twelve Steps of SAA.

The phrase "progress not perfection" refers to my spiritual growth through the Steps. It is not a way for me to rationalize occasionally acting out over the years. Being gentle with myself does not mean deluding myself. Long-term abstinence is achievable, a day at a time, through the Twelve Steps of SAA. Without this abstinence I have no foundation—I am a still-suffering sex addict waiting to start recovery.

Having worked the Twelve Steps, I know a freedom and security I could never have imagined. For me, this would have been impossible without the bedrock I have been given by obtaining and maintaining abstinence from my inner-circle compulsions.

~

Am I being honest with myself about Step One? Do I admit that I am powerless over my acting out and have to give it up for good, a day at a time? Or am I deluding myself that somehow, someday, I may be able to get away with acting out one more time?

> "We would often put our addiction
> first and everything else second."
>
> *Sex Addicts Anonymous*, page 25

God has always been my Higher Power of choice. I had come to an understanding in my adolescence that God was not exactly like any religion had led me to believe, and that understanding was something uniquely my own. Yet it took a while after I came to the program for me to realize that, even though I had this core belief, my spiritual higher power for many years, decades even, had been my addiction.

As I began to work the Steps and see how they applied to my own life, I saw how my addict had worked very hard to cover up the existence of my true Higher Power. The key part of Step Two has always been "could restore us to sanity." My other higher powers professed and possessed the ability to do many things, but they kept me crazy, lost, and sick.

While I have made reasonable progress reconnecting to my spiritual center, I know I have many miles still to travel. I am not alone and do not need to face the challenges of life without support. The experience, strenght, and hope of my fellow brothers and sisters add to my journey. I am more willing to surrender because my personal experience has demonstrated that letting go is the only way I gain the power to overcome my disease.

~

I know by trusting in a Power greater than myself, that I can find a new, better way to face life.

"We choose to keep the company of people
who respect us, care for us, and treat
us well. We start to see life in terms of
growth, change, and transformation."

Sex Addicts Anonymous, page 59

My SAA journey has been, despite its many struggles and apparent setbacks, a rediscovery of faith and
hope. The truth is that I, who gave up on a benevolent,
personal god long ago, now believe in both the promise
and power of miraculous redemption.

Before I joined the SAA fellowship, I judged sexual
predators mercilessly. They deserved, I felt, only the
most harsh and absolute punishment. Then one evening, a man—a gentleman in every sense of the word—
who handed out sobriety chips at my SAA meeting,
shared that he had systematically molested his daughter. My jaw dropped. This man, whom I'd come to ad-
mire as sort of my SAA grandfather was now loved and
admired by that daughter—and by me. At that moment I came to believe that redemption and even miracles are possible.

I later learned that such fantastical stories of growth
and transformation are commonplace in SAA. In fact,
another former sex offender is a member of my weekly feedback group. He is my mentor and my friend. If
such miracles and redemption are possible for others,
then maybe they are possible for me, too. I am amazed
by, and oh so grateful for, the company I now keep.

~

*Today I can believe in miracles and redemption. The
evidence is in the company I keep.*

"By God's grace I don't have to fall
into my old pattern of thinking."
Sex Addicts Anonymous, page 284

For too long, anyway.

I can get tired of being a responsible adult. I want to give up making decisions for myself and others. I want someone else to tell me what to do. It's not that anything is wrong. I just get tired. And then, I may fall into a hole. But I am a sex addict, and when I fall into that hole, my addict gets energized. I start fantasizing, overeating, losing my spiritual focus, and cutting back on program calls and step work.

In the hole, I am tempted to use willpower to force myself out, but it doesn't work. I just fall back in. I had to learn to surrender and let my Higher Power lead me out.

Surrender starts with accepting myself for being tired of adulthood (surrendering my self-judgment). Then I acknowledge my hole-y emotions: sadness, loneliness, hopelessness, and fear (surrendering my self-avoidance). Finally, I ask my Higher Power to teach me and lead me through this hole (surrendering my self-management). I then become right-sized, and adulthood soon returns.

The holes are opportunities for my Higher Power to teach and re-teach me lessons about surrender, lessons that I have passed on to others in recovery.

Even if I fall into a hole, it can be a passage to learning and healing.

ભ

> "Change occurs in <u>God's</u> time, not ours."
> *Sex Addicts Anonymous*, page 44

Just completing Step Six, I stood there with my list of character defects in my hand—glaring at me as though they were poison that I couldn't be rid of quick enough. I got down on my knees and asked my Higher Power to remove these defects. I asked them to be removed so that I could be of service to others. I got up from my knees and went about my day.

The next morning, I again prayed to have these defects removed, and continued to repeat the process daily. Within a week, I noticed some character defects were not a struggle, while others still plagued me on an almost daily basis. Soon, I began to doubt how I could be of service while struggling so much with my character defects. Why wasn't my Higher Power removing all of them?

Then one day, I honestly shared with a sponsee about these struggles. This opened up the conversation to some very vulnerable dialog. I learned a very important lesson. I can carry the message by working my program and remaining sober. But sometimes I am of service because of my struggles—not because I overcame them.

~

Today, I can admit my successes and my struggles so that I may truly be of service to others.

> "Changing old routines that are
> associated with our addiction is an
> important tool for staying sober."

Tools of Recovery, page 13

Once I begin to act out, I'm in the reptilian part of my brain—the selfish part that only wants what it wants. It's impossible to stop. Before I start, however, I still have a chance. In that moment, I need to acknowledge the lie that acting out will give me what I want. The truth is that I won't enjoy the act, or I'll deeply regret it later, or both.

When first sober, I practiced remembering how bad acting out made me feel. Usually, the first thing I'd do before acting out was to close the Venetian blinds, so I practiced doing that while I thought about the negative effects of my addiction. Eventually pairing those two activities paid off. As soon as I'd think about closing the blinds, I'd recall the effects of my acting out.

It's not a cure, but it's a tool. It buys a precious moment of clarity before a potentially mindless and dangerous move. The desire to act out may show up for the rest of my life. I don't have control over the thoughts that pop up into my brain, but I have a choice as to whether or not I believe or entertain those thoughts.

Today I no longer believe the addict's voice in my head. Instead I turn to my Higher Power, my friends in the program, and my own wisdom.

"Our circles are not set in stone for all time."
Sex Addicts Anonymous, page 16

Once, while praying and sitting quietly awaiting some kind of reply, I noticed I was uneasy with what message I might get. My prayer was about behaviors that were becoming a problem in my life and the shift of focus I might need in my recovery to address them.

I had gone through my circles with my sponsor. It seemed odd that they might need to be revised. My emotional reaction to the idea was resistance—this might require work.

Early in recovery, I was willing to make the changes that would get me out of the immediate pain I was feeling. The worst consequences of my addiction dropped off when I became abstinent from my inner-circle behaviors, but without the impending catastrophes that motivated my early changes, I became complacent. As my awareness grew, behaviors that I hadn't put in my inner circle started to become questionable in light of the effect they were having.

My first action was to name the behavior and acknowledge that it, at least, raises questions. I prayed about it and then took it to my sponsor as we reviewed my circles. Reviewing my circles with my sponsor is a way I can get direction on behaviors I question, and the process brings them out into the light of day.

I will be honest with my sponsor. I will share behaviors that I question.

☙

"When evaluating our program, we are ultimately
asking if recovery is our highest priority."

Sex Addicts Anonymous, page 68

We need not wait for a relapse to re-evaluate our program. At any time, complacency can settle in like a cloud, leaving our minds to wander. Perhaps we get busy with the daily grind and lose sight of what enables us to be productive.

In either case, making the slightest attempt at becoming centered and grateful, while asking the God of our understanding what we have to do today to continue improving our recovery, will always lead us back to a place where God and our program are our highest priority.

~

Today I will honestly ask my Higher Power if I am making my program my highest priority and I will wait for the loving and honest response.

"To look within and embrace the many parts
(sometimes fragments) of myself rather than
looking for my definition in others has been an
important process. I know that I am on track
spiritually when I am able to be honest with
myself and be present both with my feelings
and with the moment at hand, no matter
what it is. At these times my thoughts toward
myself are like those of a loving friend."

Sex Addicts Anonymous, page 130

Step Eleven encourages us to meditate. There are
many ways to meditate, but those who meditate tell us
that it is a foundation for spiritual health and the path
to true peace and happiness.

To meditate means to be connected to, and present
in, an immediate reality. No fantasies, please. No gran-
diose delusions about how powerful I am. No self-judg-
ing conclusions about the shamefulness of acting out.

Meditation is a practice, a behavior. Its power comes
not from what I do, but from being still and open to
what is—a world far removed from the beliefs and
fears that drove my addiction. And they're right; I can
find peace.

*Addiction is mindless action. Meditation is meaningful
stillness.*

ରୀ

> "Without needing to completely understand
> our Higher Power, we can accept and use
> this Power in order to find freedom from our
> addiction. Our belief that recovery is possible
> gives us the strength to take action."
>
> *Sex Addicts Anonymous*, page 28

When I first encountered the notion of sanity in Step Two, I was skeptical. I could not grasp the idea that I could be restored to something I was pretty sure I never had and could not define.

Working Step Two formally, several times (after every relapse), and practicing this step regularly, have shown me that what I thought was complicated and improbable is really very simple when I accept the following as true:

1) God actually exists.

2) God really cares about me.

3) God is capable of restoring me to sanity.

4) God wants to restore me to sanity.

5) Sanity is possible in this world.

6) I am worth being restored to sanity.

7) I am willing to believe and willing to be restored to sanity.

I am grateful today. I am still a work in progress, but because of Step Two, I am being restored to sanity by a loving Higher Power.

I have reason to be grateful today.

☙

> "When this happens, I stop, take a deep
> breath, and think, 'Oh yeah, that's right,
> it's not about me.' In this way, I can start
> my day over any time I want to."
>
> *Sex Addicts Anonymous*, page 326

Before I even got on my knees this morning, I realized I had already been off to the races—off and running on the old racetrack of my mind. In the time it took to fix some coffee, let the dog out, and start my prayer, I had used the three-second rule twice, rehearsed the events of yesterday, and started obsessing. I was already self-focused—my problems, my ego, my way.

Gently, I heard God calling me back to the starting line. Okay, a false start. Let's try again. I prayed, "Help me fix my eyes on you. Help me run this race called life according to your will and not mine. Put the things that matter uppermost on my mind and heart. Let love be my fuel today." I became "open to making new choices...in the light of my Higher Power's transforming love and care...a way of gentleness and compassion."

I then asked how to do that today. The message was simply to be more present with the person I was with. I read a familiar passage on love, which reminded me of the Fourth Step inventory. Although I wasn't there yet, I knew that my Higher Power was already beginning to lead me on this new, off-track race—a long distance, endurance run, not a sprint—something far better than anything I could imagine. By Grace, I could run it today. I drank in the love for fuel, and I was off and running.

～

God, in the race set before me today, show me how to run it your way, the way of love.

ଓ

"Sex Addiction is a disease affecting the
mind, body, and spirit. It is progressive,
with the behavior and its consequences
usually becoming <u>more</u> severe over time."

Sex Addicts Anonymous, page 2

Every morning I try to count my blessings and think
about what I have to be grateful for in this life. Near
the top of the list you'll always find SAA and sexual
sobriety. My sobriety is a gift of opportunity—the opportunity to live a normal life. However, my gratitude
for my abstinence goes deeper than this. For, even as
my sexual sobriety contains the seeds of a normal and
even joyful life, so my acting out contained the seeds
of its progressive nature. Had I not stopped when I did,
who knows where my disease would have progressed.

I am one of the lucky ones. I found SAA and have giv-
en myself to this simple program. Without it, I would
be an isolated, probably suicidal individual, on the
edges of society and hating myself for what I had become, with a sick spirit and mind, and perhaps a sick
body. But the paradox of SAA is that, from complete
defeat can come victory, thanks to Step One and the
eleven following steps. Just as my disease would have
progressed, so my gratitude can now progress. Each
year I move further away from the person I became—
the only requirement is to try and apply a few simple
spiritual principles.

*Help me remember that abstinence is a gift from my
Higher Power and all I need to do is surrender. Help
me be grateful that I am sexually sober just for today.*

ॐ

> "As sex addicts, we are especially
> prone to isolating. Many of us
> acted out alone or in secret."
>
> *Sex Addicts Anonymous*, page 11

I was asked many times by my wife, "Why don't you have any friends?" The answer was to misdirect her to the fact that my friends didn't live close. They were my college friends from twenty years ago. They lived on different continents or on islands in the Pacific or I had lost track of them. My proof was in the Christmas cards or calendars that some of them sent.

The truth was that I was more comfortable being alone or with my dog. In my recovery, I began to notice that I was declining invitations from others to do things that we had in common like going on a photography daytrip. When my wife planned a family event, I found that I was full of anxiety and didn't want to go with her. On reflection, I asked myself if I had lost the ability to form new friendships.

As I started to recover, part of me woke up from the coma of isolation. I started longing to create friendships, to get out of the house and away from the hypnosis of the TV. At first it was awkward and uncomfortable for me to try these new behaviors, but, thanks to the loving fellowship of SAA and the tools they taught me, I now have new friends.

～

One of the results of my recovery is the reversing of isolation. This unexpected benefit brings me joy and serenity because I can now share my life with others.

✆

"With this step, we recognize that we have a
disease, not a mere weakness or character flaw,
and that we are powerless to change this fact."

Sex Addicts Anonymous, page 23

Shame tells me that I have the power to control my
addiction, but that I don't use that power because I'm
a bad person, guaranteeing the cycle will continue.

Step One is the beginning of the end for my shame.
Admitting powerlessness undoes the lie that I could
control my sexual urges if only I were a better person.
Powerlessness allows me to see the truth—my addiction is a progressive disease, affecting my mind, body,
and spirit. I cannot control this disease with willpower
any more than a person with cancer or Parkinson's.
No one judges them for not succeeding. My disease
takes away my power of choice when it comes to sexual thoughts, feelings, and behaviors.

Powerlessness allows a paradigm shift from me being
a bad person who needs to be good, to being a sick
person who is getting well through the Twelve Steps
of Sex Addicts Anonymous. The disease is never removed, but, one day at a time, the symptoms—harmful sexual behaviors—are lifted and I can begin to live
a life with meaning, a life where I am no longer alone.

I am not a bad, unworthy, or weak person; I am just
a human being with an illness. SAA offers a remedy for
that illness if I'm willing to use it.

The medicine is right here.

> "It is a proven practice, handed down
> through generations, that recovery from
> addiction can only <u>take</u> place with others."
>
> "Getting a Sponsor"

In recovery, I have learned that sudden, flaring emotions are seldom about the present. Something now is triggering a past hurt. There have also been times when protective action was warranted, but my radar didn't detect it. Fortunately, I'm in recovery and learning from experience.

Last month, a coworker said something disparaging and false about me at a team meeting. I was shocked but said nothing. I knew it reflected more on him than me, but my pain and anger did not subside. When he left for the day, I started following him to the parking lot. After only twenty steps or so, the voice of reason chimed, "Nothing you do out there will end well. Stop!"

I immediately recognized its truth. I turned around, went back to the office, waited, went home, and called my sponsor. My sponsor provided an active solution. It was nothing I would have chosen if I had been able to think of it, but it was appropriate and gave everyone involved a chance to be a decent grownup. The result was more healing than I could have imagined.

Many of my emotions belong to the wounded child in me. If I act on them, I may well be acting childishly. When I act as an adult, I provide a safe place for that child to heal. For me, that usually requires outside assistance.

I thank God for my sponsor and the generations of sponsors that make life with dignity possible for me.

> "Many of us have found that automatic
> interventions are better than trying to
> evaluate whether we are at risk for a
> relapse. We can make a phone call whenever
> we are exposed to a trigger, regardless
> of whether we feel like acting out."
>
> *Sex Addicts Anonymous*, page 68

Making a habit of staying connected through regular use of the telephone can be a tremendous asset in my recovery toolbox. With a consistent pattern of telephone calls to a few recovering members, I develop the framework of support I need in my recovered life. During challenging situations I will be more inclined to pick up the phone, make a call and reach out for the support I need in order to keep me from moving into addictive behavior as the result of a triggering situation.

Today I will commit to making three phone calls to members of the fellowship.

"Rather than struggling with our life's
challenges as if we are alone and need to
'figure it out' ourselves, we share our thoughts
and feelings with our Higher Power."

Sex Addicts Anonymous, page 56

Sometimes we may be hindered in accepting and carrying out God's will for us because we feel unworthy, ashamed, or defective. Our addictive behavior strengthened our sense of shame and unworthiness. In turn, these negative beliefs made us more vulnerable to slips or relapse.

I am prone to shame and have spent much time kicking myself for my mistakes. Other people tell me I'm talented and that they see me as a good person, but I find their words hard to accept.

It's easier for me to hand over these negative thoughts and beliefs about myself when I bring them into prayer. Since these beliefs are deeply rooted and laden with emotion, I try to go slowly, one belief at a time. For example, "God, I have come to believe that I'm defective and can never measure up to others. Is this true? What would you have me know?"

Sometimes nothing comes to me. If thoughts come, I try to write them down without analyzing or judging them. As I re-read what I have written, it becomes clearer if my thoughts have come from my Higher Power, from myself, or some mix of each. Often I'm surprised and uplifted by what I write and find myself going back to these words in times of discouragement.

Today I will allow God to speak the truth to some area of my negative thinking.

ଓଃ

> "The response of any particular person,
> positive or negative, is not a measure of how
> well we make our amends. The success of
> our amends depends only on how honestly
> and thoroughly we make them."

Sex Addicts Anonymous, page 49

I received a letter from my folks today. It's a miracle that my folks and I communicate at all, as my childhood was filled with rampant sexual, spiritual, and physical abuse. I went a decade without speaking to them. Needless to say, I had to face and let go of my resentments and fears. Even now I am still blamed for breaking the family secret, for shaming the family. I am pigeonholed as the proverbial black sheep.

As I actively work the Twelve Steps, I continually make living amends. As a boy I watched men build a bridge spanning the Ohio River. Over a six-month period I watched in wonder as two crews on opposite sides built up dirt ramps, poured the pylons, and ever so skillfully met in the middle to complete the bridge.

Amends are like that for me. I am only responsible for building my half of the bridge. Then I continually maintain my half whether the other person ever builds their half or not. I think it's my responsibility to keep my half of the bridge sparkling, so that, if they ever consider starting their half, they will know it wasn't just words from me. They'll know I meant it because I am living it.

Am I building my side of the bridge or waiting for others to pour the first pylon?

> "But if we can honestly face our problems and are willing to change, the Twelve Steps of SAA will lead to an awakening that allows us to live a new way of life according to spiritual principles."
>
> *Sex Addicts Anonymous*, page 20

Willingness is an essential factor for the addict seeking recovery. Typically born of desperation on the one hand and hope on the other, willingness must precede the actions suggested by the Twelve Steps.

We may be motivated to take certain actions, but we may be unwilling to do so because of fear, anticipated cost, or other factors. Willingness is the energizing force that moves us from idea, concept, desire, or intention into action. It fuels the admissions, the beliefs, the decisions, and the actions that we take working the Twelve Steps in our quest for recovery.

The Twelve Step program of recovery may be envisioned as having two sides—an input side and an output side. Willingness is the gateway to the input side. It fuels our actions. It is the driver behind what we must do to experience recovery.

The second is the output side. It is the transformation that only God can give us. We can be willing. We can work the Steps. But it is in trusting God for the outcome that we find the spiritual awakening that ushers in true recovery.

When I am willing to go to any length—to do what I can do—God will do for me what I cannot do for myself.

ଓଃ

"What is important is that we get honest
about our addiction, and let go of the idea of
controlling our behavior with our willpower
or managing our lives without help."

Sex Addicts Anonymous, page 25

Once, after a meeting, a person said to me, "Do you
have any sense of sobriety at all?" This came as a
shock, like a cold slap in the face, yet it was completely
accurate. For weeks I had been acting out, under the
delusion that I was fooling everyone and not hurting
anyone. Of course, this belief is part of the illness.

When the statement was made, I realized I wasn't
fooling anyone. People knew what I was doing even
though I was careful about covering my tracks. And
I knew. I began to realize that the greatest deception
was to myself. The lies I told myself were the basis of
the destruction around me.

I think back to this conversation often, and I am
deeply grateful to that person. It could not have been
easy to say, and I realize it was said out of love. A good
friend is a person who gives that wakeup call, who
makes that bold statement, who removes the glasses
of deception. I'm so fortunate to be part of an organization that offers unconditional support, which can include uncomfortable honesty. Tough love is not a new
concept, and it is vital to my recovery.

One of the gifts of attending meetings is that I get to
witness honesty and, in turn, start to practice honesty
in my life.

If I can be honest, I'm headed in the right direction.

ଏଠ

> "Asking for help releases us from the toxic
> isolation that drives our addiction."
>
> *Sex Addicts Anonymous*, page 25

I was on my knees in a treatment facility, sobbing into my hands the painful words "I am so alone" when I realized how bereft I was of meaningful human contact. Sure, I had my acting out—a series of images that kept me isolated in endless shame, more extreme by the day. The insanity of doing the same things with the hollow oath "it will be better this time" ringing in my ears led me to hopelessness culminating in attempted suicide.

That day I made a commitment to reach out to others. I called and texted people. I asked people out for supper before the meeting or coffee after. I live an hour and forty minutes from the nearest face-to-face meeting. This requires a level of commitment and planning that I was not prepared to give to my recovery before. Other members noticed this commitment. They started to approach and talk to me. I was rarely touched as a child, and the hugs I was given really impacted me.

I now have numerous sponsees. I put time and effort into using the tools of recovery, and I have opened my heart to the wonderful communion that I can have with my Higher Power and with another human being. I have even learned to connect with myself. I have love to offer and I offer it. I am learning to accept love when it is offered to me.

~

I have love to offer. I will offer love today.

ଔ

> "We learn not to use half-truths to
> manipulate others. We accept responsibility
> for our actions and our lives."
>
> *Sex Addicts Anonymous*, page 63

Before joining SAA, I sincerely believed I was honest. I worked through Step Seven and had a long list of character defects, but dishonesty was not among them. It took a slip and several days of not disclosing it to my sponsor before I realized that dishonesty was my most deeply rooted character defect. It was the character defect I relied upon when I was most at risk, particularly when I feared the anger of others and when I needed to protect my acting out behavior. When I admitted the slip to my sponsor, I said that I now recognize dishonesty as a character defect.

I began to include the question, "Was I dishonest today?" in my evening inventory. How do I recognize my dishonesty on a daily basis? It's easy—where am I anxious? There I often find dishonesty in the mix. I have been amazed at the many forms dishonesty takes in my behavior: withholding information, delaying communication on something important but difficult, and especially, being almost honest as a way of covering up something that I fear would threaten my safety.

Recognizing my dishonesty is a gift. It is a landmark where I can drop my shame and head down a path of honesty, a path along which I find my Higher Power and others in recovery.

~

Grant me the courage to stop, look, and listen. I can drop my shame and choose a better road.

☙

"Taking the Third Step means acting on
our belief that a Higher Power can relieve
our addiction and restore us to sanity."

Sex Addicts Anonymous, page 28

I thought that if I just stopped acting out sexually I'd
be okay. But, when I stopped my addictive sexual behavior, that's when the real fun began! I was still left
with me. I had to begin my Third Step journey with the
understanding that, in a way, my problem was really
my insane thinking.

Science has reported that the mind of an addict is actually mapped differently. But science has not figured
out a way to re-program my pathways of thought. In
my experience, only God can restore my mind to right
thinking.

Part of my daily prayers to God include asking for
freedom from the bondage of my broken thinking.
Today, I know the problem isn't sex; the problem is
me. With God's help, I'm getting better!

～

*I think I will let a Power greater than myself manage
my thoughts—just for today.*

ભ

> "We learn many new solutions to old problems.
> Central to these are the Twelve Steps, a
> spiritual program of recovery. Following these
> steps leads to freedom from addictive sexual
> behaviors and to the healing of our minds,
> bodies, spirits, relationships, and sexuality."
>
> *Sex Addicts Anonymous*, page 2

I first came to SAA seeking a solution, but not really sure what I was looking for. At first I sought identification, empathising with the acting-out of other sex addicts. I stopped acting out, but the obsession remained. Eventually, after much frustration, I accepted I was powerless over acting out, and I realised I had to try and apply the principles of all of the Twelve Steps to my sex addition. I did so and placed myself at the service of newcomers and Sex Addicts Anonymous.

To my immense gratitude I found a vision for my future through the Twelve Steps of SAA: freedom from acting out in body and mind, a tool for drastically reducing fear and resentment in Step Ten, a Higher Power which I grow closer to through Step Eleven, and a freedom culminating in the practicing of the Twelfth Step—working with other sex addicts. Suddenly, what was originally for me a secret and shameful problem became the heart of a solution I could offer to others desperate enough to want to stop. The Twelve Steps changed my life and gave me a future.

If it feels like there is something missing in my recovery, I can ask myself, "Am I trying to grow in practicing all the principles of the Twelve Steps?"

ॐ

"And yet to let go of control, even a little,
struck fear in <u>many</u> of our hearts."

"Recovery from Compulsive Sexual Avoidance"

Thank you for sharing. I truly heard you when you said, "I was sitting on the floor with the phonebook open to the counseling pages, unable to call for help." I too looked through the Yellow Pages but could not call. Why yellow? Maybe to reflect my fear of what might happen if I told the truth to anyone, let alone myself.

I even walked past meetings. I saw people out front and knew we were connected at a deep level. I saw where I belonged, but I could not join. I could not ask for help. That was too hard—impossible pride. I used fear, anger, cowardice, and shame to stay imprisoned, far away from my true self.

It was easier to chase the thrill that promised release if only for a moment. Once again I surrendered my freedom for a meaningless moment, and too soon the burden was back. I then returned to the seclusion of my shame, heavier than the phone I could not pick up.

Thank God for the desperate, unguarded moment when I could bear this pain no longer, yet somehow knew I deserved to live—the moment I finally asked for help.

~

Could you ever have imagined that we would all be here together at this time?

ભ

> "One of the most dangerous aspects of our addiction is our inability to see it for what it is."

Sex Addicts Anonymous, page 8

At age twenty-nine, my life felt torn apart by the sudden death of my father from a heart attack. He died when our relationship was still superficial and unresolved from his alcoholism and my teen rebellion.

I didn't know how to handle, or even recognize, my grief. Within a few months of my father's death, I turned from my wife and two young children to a one-night stand and then to an affair with someone else at work. That grew into multiple affairs and one-night stands. I put my own family in the addiction blender and broke their hearts one by one. However, I couldn't see that I had fallen into the pit of my own addiction—sex addiction. I was putting my family through the same hell that my father's addiction had put me through.

When I finally begged God for relief, I found SAA. In my first meeting, I heard and saw how the Twelve Step program had helped others achieve recovery from compulsive sexual behavior. This knowledge took thirty years for me to discover, yet the sweetness of my recovery has eclipsed those years.

I no longer blame my father's death for my years of acting out. That was my choice in how to medicate the pain of both losing him, and of not having the chance to reconcile our relationship.

~

Running, hiding, and self-medicating never worked. Thank God, all I have to do is stop and ask for help.

ભ

> "Working [Step Ten] allows us to let go of
> both perfectionism <u>and</u> grandiosity."
> *Sex Addicts Anonymous*, page 55

My ego has a difficult time taking a wide view of my
strengths and weaknesses, my challenges and successes. My ego has no perspective. It thinks any single
action by me will be the only factor that determines
whether I am a good person or a bad person. This
leads to paralyzing perfectionism. The Tenth Step reminds us that we will be wrong on a regular basis;
therefore, there is nothing wrong with being wrong.
The SAA program teaches us what to do when we're
wrong. We examine our part, we promptly admit our
part, and we make amends when called for.

When I turn to my Higher Power, being wrong is not
a sum total accounting of my self-worth. It is merely a normal occurrence in the life of a human being.
This perspective allows me to relax and gives a sense
of freedom to my life. I have been wrong in the past,
I will be wrong in the future, and I have the tools to
clean up my mess when I need to.

If I keep growing in my recovery and in my life, I will
continue to make mistakes because I will continue
to do new things. Because I am now sober in recovery, I have every chance of actually learning from my
mistakes.

~

Mistakes can be a sign that I'm growing and learning.

૭

"Over time, the spiritual principles in
the steps become integrated into our
thoughts, feelings, and behavior."
Sex Addicts Anonymous, page 22

I spent my childhood hiding from an abusive, alcoholic father. As a result, I didn't develop any healthy tools and behaviors to prepare me for, or assist me with, the uncomfortable situations I would face in adult life. Because I didn't know what to do with anxious and uneasy feelings, I turned to sexual acting out to numb them. At first, I thought I could control the sexual activities I used to deaden these feelings, but I was soon out of control. The behaviors became more frequent and dangerous, as did the shame and incomprehensible demoralization from this behavior. To whom could I turn?

The Twelve Steps of Sex Addicts Anonymous provided me a roadmap to a healthy, sane, and productive life. From that paramount, first admission that I am a sex addict beckoned in Step One, to having had a beautiful, spiritual awakening predicted in Step Twelve, the spiritual principles in the Steps are now a part of me. And when I find myself in uncomfortable feelings, I can call on the powerful spiritual principles of honesty, willingness, courage, humility, forgiveness, responsibility, gratitude, and faith to restore me to sanity. As a result, I can walk soberly through, rather than around, difficult feelings.

～

Today, through my Higher Power and the spiritual principles of the Twelve Steps, I can face any anxious or unpleasant feelings that may arise.

ભ

"We chose sex and romantic obsession
over those things we cherished the most—
including friends, family, and career."

Sex Addicts Anonymous, page 4

My father was in the hospital, having spent a month in ICU recovering from a heart attack. He needed me to pick up tax returns at his accountant's office so he could review and sign them. It was late on a Saturday night and I was caught in my obsession, wanting to go act out. Driven by my compulsion, I was impatient while my father took his time reviewing the documents. I was caught in what SAA describes as the bubble, wanting him to hurry up and sign the tax returns so I could go act out. I had no idea that my father's health would take a turn within the month and that I would be by his side again, this time as he took his last breath. I wish I could go back and spend a little extra time with him that night. My relationship with him is far more important than any brief encounter I ever had acting out.

That's what addiction does. It takes me away from those people, places, and things that are most important, in my case, trading anonymous meaningless sex for quality time at my father's bedside during the last month of his life. That was a heavy price to pay, but it helped me find the willingness to change.

~

What are some of the costs I've paid in exchange for fleeting moments of acting out?

ର

> ## "Our focus remains on the solution,
> rather than the problem."
>
> *Sex Addicts Anonymous*, page 12

This phrase made no sense to me when I first started attending SAA meetings. I was in treatment and was clueless about the solution. I barely got the problem. Weren't we meeting to focus on sex addiction? And wasn't that the problem?

Over time, I've heard members sharing their experience, strength, and hope. I've read the literature. I hear that each of us still has problems, and we're all still sex addicts, but we face problems squarely. Yet I hear members describing real change— not only maintaining sexual sobriety, but also responding to and experiencing life in new ways. Invariably, the solution is in the Twelve Steps, applying one or more to a specific problem, along with the gradual changes that come from applying the principles of this program to our lives.

Today I faced an ongoing problem in a relationship. I prayed and listened, and my Higher Power guided me to think differently about the issue. That allowed me to respond differently the next time we interacted. It is a small beginning, yet it is a change, and it is part of the solution.

~

Today, I will face my problems, but focus on my recovery and live in the solution.

"The phone is a central tool of
recovery for many addicts."
Tools of Recovery, page 9

Although I had been attending SAA regularly for two
years, sexual sobriety had been hard for me to maintain. I would be sober for a couple weeks then return
to my inner circle behaviors. I called my sponsor regularly; we worked the Steps together; I attended meetings regularly and shared at them; I took on service
commitments; yet I continued to slip.

At my home-group meeting one night the topic was
"using the telephone." I had heard this before, but early in recovery I had decided it was not for me. I did not
want to "bother people," people who I truly thought
would not want to hear from me.

In the discussion that night, I heard myself sharing
how happy I was when people in SAA called me. Then
it occurred to me that others might feel the same way
to hear from me—and that I deserved to reach out in
this way. The next day I decided to finally give this tool
a serious try. On a regular basis, I began connecting
with others outside the meeting in a new and deeper
way, and I began developing closer relationships with
others in the fellowship. I believe today that the willingness to finally try this particular tool helped contribute enormously to the sexual sobriety I enjoy today, one day at a time.

*Why wouldn't others be as happy to receive my phone
calls as I am to receive theirs?*

ca

"With the Twelfth Step we seek to consciously
practice these principles in our lives, not only
as ways to keep us sexually sober, although
that will always remain important, but as
lights to guide us in everything we do."

Sex Addicts Anonymous, page 61

I've heard the Twelve Steps described as progressive surrender. Early on, I struggled with the concept of surrender. I liked the slogan "Let Go And Let God," I wanted to experience conscious contact with the Higher Power of my understanding, but I couldn't figure out how to control my spirit or push the surrender button. I felt like an infant, kicking and flailing without knowing what's wrong.

Through sobriety and the Steps, I learned to apply spiritual principles in any situation. When I'm disturbed, I reach out to others, especially my sponsor, and ask for help working steps applicable to the issue. I ask myself, what am I powerless over in this situation? I reaffirm my belief that my Higher Power can lead me to clarity and peace, and I demonstrate trust in that Power by owning my part. When my character weaknesses are highlighted, I humbly ask for willingness to let them go and ask God to remove them. I make amends if needed. I often share my circumstances with fellow travellers and my sponsor, borrowing their clear-headed thoughts and listening to their experience, strength, and hope.

When I work the Twelve Steps, I demonstrate willingness to align my life with a power greater than me. Through practicing these principles, I now look forward to surrender.

For today, God, open me to spiritual principles.

☙

> "When we make a decision to turn our
> will and our lives over to the care of the
> God of our understanding, we begin to
> notice signs of growth and transition,
> evidence that the program is working."
>
> *Sex Addicts Anonymous*, page 31

When I first came into the program, to imagine a life of honesty and openness seemed all but impossible. The maintenance of my secret life required the exact opposite of honesty and openness. But by becoming willing to make small changes in my life, I found first relief and then serenity in small doses.

Keeping in mind the idea of treating my addiction as a disease helps with my willingness as well. Maintaining my spiritual condition continues in much the same ways that my diabetic friends maintain their health, with choices and small actions throughout the day and throughout life.

Working the spiritual program of SAA continues to provide hope and experience in being restored to sanity in my life. Though not every day is sunny, I can be grateful for many things in my new life in recovery.

～

My willingness can begin with small choices leading to small actions. Honesty with a sponsor and being open to my own new ideas about the God of my understanding are a great start.

☙

> "I would wallow in self-pity and exaggerate problems in order to manipulate the object of my infatuation to give me more attention."
>
> *Sex Addicts Anonymous*, page 228

Amongst addicts, I have found a common fear that we will end up homeless and destitute. A couple months into the Steps, I was driving down the freeway awash in this fear. I contacted a friend with decades of Twelve Step experience. I sobbed that, "I'm afraid I'm going to be homeless and live under a bridge someday." She responded, "What makes you think you'll have a bridge?"

Her response snapped me out of my self-pity. In reality, at that moment, I was driving home from work. I had no reason to believe I would ever be homeless. I have found that, when I call a program friend to sob about my fears, I am not looking for a solution. I am hoping they will join me in my pity party, and I am miles from an attitude of gratitude. The best response is like the one I received above.

On the other hand, if I admit to a program friend that I am struggling with self-pity and ask for help, help will be given. I can then be open to and led by my Higher Power to help me see the reality of the situation. I can always start by looking at my present circumstances and building a gratitude list.

~

Today I am grateful for the experience, strength, and hope of my friends in the fellowship. They prevent me from buying into self-pity and help me keep in fit spiritual condition.

> "Humility is a result of the self-honesty
> we have gained through working the
> preceding steps. It comes from a realistic
> view of ourselves, a knowledge of both
> our strengths and limitations."
>
> *Sex Addicts Anonymous*, page 43

Enumerating my character defects could easily descend into self-flagellation, but humility isn't about beating myself up, it's about accepting that I am nothing more and nothing less than human. In my active addiction, I set god-like standards for myself, and when I inevitably fell short of these delusional goals, I would swing to the other extreme and think I was utterly worthless. But as I journeyed through the Twelve Steps, I realized that I am not super-human or sub-human, I'm just plain human, and that's okay. God loves me no matter what, and I don't have to be perfect to be good enough.

This attitude of compassion toward myself soon broadened to the people around me and the world at large, and I gradually became less judgmental of everything and everyone. I have found that as long as I am in judgment of another, I am not at peace with myself. Once I let go of judgment, I can begin to appreciate the people God has put in my life and the abundant gifts and blessings they bring. With the realistic perspective of humility, I can learn to love myself and others the way God already loves me.

~

Instead of finding fault in myself and others today, I can just let us all be human together. I can let go of harsh judgment and find peace through humility.

ભ

> "We report how we are taking care of
> ourselves and what positive risks we are
> taking to challenge ourselves and grow."
> *Sex Addicts Anonymous*, page 53

Rather than viewing Step Ten as a "maintenance step," my sponsor explained to me that it is a growth step. Doing a written Tenth Step everyday certainly has aided me in my spiritual growth. For me, it is necessary to do a written Tenth Step.

One of the many things I look at is positive risks I am taking to challenge myself and grow. When I first started working this step, I didn't feel comfortable taking any risks and I actually resented this question on my Tenth Step form! It seemed enough to stay sober daily and begin to rebuild my life. Looking back, I see that I was taking healthy risks at the time, and just was not aware of it. After some years of sobriety, I am more open to taking healthy risks. These risks may take the form of investigating potential friendships, learning about healthy dating, different levels of service work, or doing something in my outer circle that I haven't done recently or perhaps ever. These are risks that help me grow in recovery, and have a fuller, richer life than I ever had before.

If I feel afraid, I can always call upon my Higher Power and support network; talking about my feelings and sharing honestly helps me to put things in perspective and to know whether the risk is a healthy one.

~

I am grateful for the opportunity to grow in recovery by being open to healthy risks. I have a Higher Power and people in the program supporting me. I am not alone.

ଔ

> "These outer-circle behaviors are clearly
> the antithesis of our old way of life, and
> it is the practice of these actions which
> will lift our obsessions and compulsions
> and bring us serenity and joy."
>
> "Three Circles"

As my experience working the SAA program taught me to value myself, it also taught me to value my outer-circle activities. At first, going to a meeting was the only action that could lift me from compulsive and obsessive thinking. Over time, like leaves on a tree, my outer-circle activities multiplied and became my way to absorb the nourishing sunlight of my Higher Power.

From helping others in the program, to cooking a good meal, volunteering for a worthy cause, or just taking care of myself, today my outer-circle behaviors make recovery not only possible but worthwhile.

~

Do I have enough outer-circle leaves to support the trunk of my recovery tree?

❧

> "We keep everything as simple as possible,
> and this helps us focus on recovery."
>
> *Sex Addicts Anonymous*, page 90

Sometimes doing the business required to success-fully navigate day-to-day life can feel overwhelming to this addict. I cannot stand beside a curling ocean wave and command it to stop. Like that wave, sometimes my feelings feel like they can and will consume me.

Sometimes a compulsive thought or scheme arises. At these times of seemingly disorganised, messy feel-ings, I know that my best course of action may be to relax and do nothing.

In participating in the business of such a fast-grow-ing fellowship as SAA, I operate similarly. When I am not sure what step is the next right thing, I can wait, and do nothing. I can reason things out with others or just trust the process.

~

All I have to be is authentic. If the next move is not clear, or if the noise is too loud—internal or external—I can relax, trust the process, and wait on clarity.

"By practicing the principle of surrender,
we can trust that God's guidance, as
expressed in our group conscience, will
take us right where we need to be."
Sex Addicts Anonymous, page 80

What is my Higher Power's will for my life? Simply put, God's will is that I do the next right thing. At times I have no idea what the next right thing may be. At these times I remind myself of what I do know. I know it's not God's will for me to yell, scream, abuse, or belittle anyone. This helps me be aware of old character defects where I attempted to use power over others in hopes of manipulating the situation to my desires.

With so many options before me, how do I know what to do? For me it's a matter of doing the work. God can only work with what I give him. The more I do, the more God has to work with. Over time, God's will for my life is revealed through others and by having the work I've done bear fruit. This concept is similar to group conscience applied on a personal level—God expressing his will for my life through people.

As I turn my will and my life over to God, knowing I've done my part, I can rest assured that whatever comes my way is truly God's perfect will for my life at this moment in time.

෬

"We find now that we have to take the First Step
daily in order to keep current or centered."

"First Step to Recovery"

The First Step contains a paradox. In admitting I was
powerless, I gained release from my addictive behavior. In admitting my life was unmanageable, my life
became more manageable.

Whether I must surrender my addiction to sexual behavior, or surrender behaviors that I start to uncov-
er through working the Steps, it is a daily process.
Admitting my behaviors and feelings is essential for
creating awareness—the starting point for recovering.
Sometimes the process of surrender happens hour-
by-hour or minute-by-minute. For example, instead of
yelling at God or anyone else when I have a flat tire,
the best course of action is to accept that fact and
change the flat tire. This not only gets the job done, I
don't get wrapped up in emotional baggage and I don't
owe anybody amends.

It is only when I realize surrender is a practice, not a
one-time event, that I become more centered and serene. For the First Step paradox to become a reality,
I must practice it regularly and be part of the process
of recovery.

～

*Just for today, help me remember to surrender, take
the First Step, and acknowledge my reality.*

☊

> "For many of us, prayer simply
> means talking with God."
>
> *Sex Addicts Anonymous*, page 56

I am in constant contact with my Higher Power whether I am conscious of it or not. Conscious contact means I am aware of the contact. Any time I make a point to notice my Higher Power in my life, I am being conscious. I can consciously connect by talking openly and honestly to my Higher Power throughout the day. I don't censure or censor the words, thoughts, ideas or feelings.

For me, intimacy starts with being open and honest. As I practiced talking openly with God, I began developing internal intimacy and intimacy with my Higher Power. This building of intimacy created the conscious contact that the Steps refer to.

Once I found the connection to my Higher Power and felt safe to just talk, I was able to start opening up to the people in my life. I began trusting that, no matter what, I would be okay. This was the beginning of building intimacy with others. What a beautiful journey, and it began just by being willing to talk with God! Three prayers I often return to are help, thanks, and wow!

~

Conscious contact can start with a single word.

"Our leap of faith into the unknown in Step Two may have felt like jumping from the deck of a familiar, but sinking, ship...Although we may have flailed at first, as our panic passed, we found ourselves floating in the company of others who had made the same leap."

"Recovery from Compulsive Sexual Avoidance"

I feel concerned when friends say they're isolating to focus on their relationship with their Higher Power. While I applaud efforts to strengthen relationships with God, it was by learning to open up and connect with others that I started feeling and recognizing God's love and will for me. I can't see or touch God, but I can see and touch my friends. Hearing the empathy in their voices or seeing the love in their eyes are ways I experience God.

I once heard that only an addict would think the solution to loneliness and insecurity is to isolate. In beginning recovery, I had to disengage from unhealthy relationships and spend time getting to know myself, but isolation is part of the path of misery. Forming friendships with sober people who offered their experience, strength, and hope as I grew and changed was a vital part of my recovery. In time, I was able to offer that same support to others.

～

I will ask my Higher Power whom I should reach out to today, and I will take action.

> "If you think you are beating the system, you misunderstand the nature of the system. It is not in the nature of systems to be beaten."
>
> *Sex Addicts Anonymous*, page 122

When I was in my addiction, I thought I could get away with anything: lying, cheating, stealing. I thought I was entitled to behave this way. I justified those behaviors because I thought I was better than others and therefore didn't require the social norms that everyone else had to observe—norms like honesty, kindness, generosity, and respect for others. I could take shortcuts without fear of consequences because I was immune.

Of course, I couldn't escape these social norms. The moral and spiritual support system they provide for humanity endures for one simple reason: it works. Something that works cannot be beaten.

When I first came to the program, I didn't give it a chance. I took shortcuts or made no effort at all. True, I attended one meeting a week, but I did not get a sponsor, try to work the Steps, or try to grow spiritually. The fruits of this were exactly what the wise pioneers said they would be—nil.

Much like life itself, the program of recovery endures because it works. Now, I do my best to rely on my Higher Power and follow the structure, experience, and discipline of the program exactly the way it is, not the way I would like it to be. Experience has shown me there are no shortcuts.

The program endures because it works. I pray for the willingness to give an honest effort.

> "At this point in our program, we are
> simply willing to move forward. We decide
> to make a commitment to recovery,
> and to our spiritual growth."
>
> *Sex Addicts Anonymous*, page 29

In another Twelve-Step program I learned, and loved to tell, the story about three frogs sitting on a log that ends with the query, "How many were left after one of them made a decision to jump off?" The answer is, "Three, because the frog had only made a decision."

My problem was that I didn't know what action should follow the decision in Step Three. So I made up an answer, namely that there was a missing step, which I liked to call Step Three-A: Turned our will and our lives over to the care of God as we understood God.

One day, someone who is older and wiser—well, wiser anyway—told me that my answer was wrong. There was a much simpler answer that didn't involve rewriting the Steps. After I got over my initial resentment for being corrected, I pondered it with an open mind and realized that she was absolutely right: I make the decision in Step Three, and then actually start turning my will and life over in Steps Four through Twelve. The action is not a single thing I do, but rather, the way I live my life from then on.

May I live this day as an expression of my decision to turn my will and life over to the care of my Higher Power.

ଓଃ

> "My best friends belong to the
> fellowship, men and women."
> *Sex Addicts Anonymous*, page 153

I spent years in isolation, sure that people would reject me if they knew me, especially women. In recovery I made progress at being myself, but only with other men. I was too fearful to approach women. Then my Higher Power intervened.

My therapist asked me for local contact info so a female client could find a meeting. I was shocked to learn that half his sex-addicted clients were women—a ratio not reflected in our local groups. A light bulb went on in my head. I felt a nudge: "Do something!" I believe my Higher Power was whispering to me to move forward in my recovery. This prompt to reach out and offer healing to the female addict sparked a new direction.

At first it went badly, but I knew I was supposed to do this. Over several years, with persistence, I developed some good recovery friendships with women. My fear-induced obsession decreased markedly. I learned to offer safety and encouragement to the women I befriended, and I received something priceless in return—their acceptance. This, I believe, is what my Higher Power had wanted all along.

I am slowly learning to be myself and to support others in being themselves. I am breaking free of my shackles, and I am growing up. It is a sometimes scary but ever-beautiful experience.

~

With God's help, I can be myself with the entire human race.

"Disagreements are a natural part of any healthy community."
Sex Addicts Anonymous, page 78

I'm only half kidding when I say I want to start a Twelve-Step fellowship called Conflict Avoiders Anonymous. Growing up, my brothers and I cowered in terror while my drunken father verbally abused my mother, often, it seemed, over something I had done. I grew up fearful of discord and without good conflict-management skills. Sometimes during disagreements, I would physically shake with fear. This fear seriously impaired my ability to be intimate, adding fuel to my sex addiction.

Conflict is part of any healthy relationship. I want healthy relationships, so I need to face my fear and learn healthy, mature ways to manage disagreements. In other words, I have to change. This change has been particularly difficult for me; however, I now have a program.

I admit powerlessness over my childhood and its effects on me, and recognize the need for a power greater than me to restore me to sanity. I decide to face this with the help of my Higher Power. I inventory conflicts and my fears around them and share this with my sponsor and program friends. I am rigorously honest here–scary in and of itself! I become ready for God to remove this fear, then ask God to lift it and to grant me wisdom. I seek outside help as necessary. I practice this in all my relationships, and I inventory and promptly admit it if it goes poorly.

Every time I face a fear and use these tools, I gain confidence and strength.

I may feel apprehensive, but I now have tools that work.

> "In Step Three we listened closely for the
> still, quiet voice of our Higher Power, and
> learned to distinguish it from the din of our
> ego or the voice of <u>our</u> internal self-critic."
>
> "Recovery from Compulsive Sexual Avoidance"

I've heard it said that humility is an open channel for
the power of God to flow through, and I've wondered
why that is. One thought is that, with humility, we're
open to God because our ego isn't getting in the way.
For example, when I'm acting on self-centered character defects, they block my connection and receptivity
to my Higher Power.

Another thought, though, is that humility isn't just
recognizing and admitting our character defects. It is
also being open to our own abilities, and knowing that
we deserve the flow of a Higher Power in our life.

As an active addict, I thought I wasn't worthy of good
things from a Higher Power. It was pointed out to me
in my early recovery that it's actually a form of arrogance to believe that other people are worthy and I'm
not. I'm not a special case for whom the rules don't
apply. Neither am I a nobody without rights or consid-
erations. In other words, I'm no better or worse than
any other addict or human being on the planet. We all
deserve goodness from our Higher Power, and humility
allows me to be open to my Higher Power and allows
my Higher Power to work through me.

*For today, may I be open to the loving direction of my
Higher Power.*

> "The middle circle can be seen as a safety
> net, allowing us to walk the tightrope of
> abstinence without having to fear that a false
> step would necessarily be disastrous."

Sex Addicts Anonymous, page 19

I have a long history of sexual acting out, but I came to SAA in extreme sexual anorexia. It was killing my well-being and my marriage. I soon learned that sexual addiction and anorexia are symptoms of a single, deeper issue—intimacy avoidance with others, my Higher Power, and myself.

In defining my three circles, I took great care to capture all of my intimacy-avoiding behaviors. Being honest and thorough is necessary for recovery, but I took it into perfectionism. My inner circle included watching more than one episode of television at a time, surfing social media for more than five minutes, eating or shopping compulsively, etc.

This meant at least a weekly relapse in my SAA recovery through these other behaviors. I eventually realized that this rigidity was setting me up for failure. Instead of focusing on abstinence from sexual acting-in and -out behaviors, I was distracted by focusing on these other behaviors, which led me to feel ashamed. Ironically, that shame helped lead me back to sexual acting-in behaviors more than once.

With my sponsor's help, I moved those non-addictive behaviors into my middle circle. They aren't healthy, self-loving activities, and I must address them, but I need to focus on my sexual recovery as I work the steps in SAA, and treat myself with compassion and understanding as I brave this difficult but healing journey.

For today I will let go of perfectionism and embrace self-compassion.

"To work this step, we only need to be open-
minded enough to try something new. For most
of us, *coming to believe* is a gradual process.
We don't need to believe in any particular
concept of a Higher Power in order to begin."

Sex Addicts Anonymous, page 26

I considered myself an atheist, and when I saw
"God" mentioned in the Steps, I thought this program
wouldn't work for me. I voiced my skepticism in meetings. Others shared having had similar reservations
but finding a way to make it work for them. I was relieved to learn that I didn't need to accept any particular concept of God, and I'm grateful that no one tried
to push any personal religion on me. I was able to lower my defenses and take a fresh look at spirituality. I
saw that I had been prejudiced and arrogant, and had
closed my mind on the subject.

To take Step Two, I had to accept that maybe I didn't
have it all figured out. I focused on the word "could" in
the step—"that a Power greater than ourselves could
restore us to sanity," meaning it was possible, that just
maybe there was something to all this spiritual stuff.
I didn't have to instantly believe in God, I just had to
be open to the possibility. When I stopped fighting and
opened up to the idea, it got much easier. I didn't have
to figure it all out, I just had to keep coming back, keep
an open mind, and be willing to let the program work.

*I may or may not understand what "God" means,
but today I will keep an open mind and believe it is
possible for that Power to help me.*

ॐ

"As active sex addicts, we hid who we
were and what we were doing—from
others, but also from ourselves."
Sex Addicts Anonymous, page 37

The process of developing self-honesty has been one
of a willingness to share openly with trusted members
in my support circles. When I am willing to trust in a
Power greater than myself and bring that trust into
the process of sharing with others, I feel a sense of
freedom from self-imposed shame and a level of healing only available to me when I connect with others
honestly.

~

*Today I will trust that I am perfect in my imperfections,
and that sharing openly is a form of self-acceptance
and key to healthy recovery.*

಴

> "We have come to realize that both
> extremes represent symptoms of the same
> disease. Whether we were acting out or
> not being sexual at all, our addiction
> involved being emotionally unavailable."
>
> *Sex Addicts Anonymous*, page 6

Before recovery, I found it easy to be sexual with strangers, and difficult or impossible to be sexual with my intimate partners.

I didn't understand how I could be a sex addict and a sexual anorexic at the same time. The paradox is that when I am sexually acting out, I am avoiding true intimacy. When I am being sexually avoidant, I am also avoiding true intimacy. In both cases, I am not available, to myself, to God or my partner.

Today in recovery, I look for the ways I may be avoiding being present. Only when I am available to myself and my Higher Power can I be truly available to others.

~

I cannot be in a loving intimate relationship with anyone without being available to myself and my Higher Power first.

℞

"We learn to turn uncomfortable feelings
about others into opportunities to practice
keeping our focus on our own lives."

Tools of Recovery, page 33

Years ago, I was taking a break, sitting alone in a room with all the slogans in plaques on the wall. My eyes came to rest on "Live And Let Live." My sense of it had always been that I am to allow others to be. As I just stared, blankly, a light-bomb went off in my head. The slogan isn't "Let Live;" it's "Live And Let Live." The first order of business is to get a life. Wow.

After years in recovery, this understanding holds up. If I am neglecting my sobriety, my recovery, my health, my spirituality, my life, I am much more likely to be victimized by what others do, say, don't do, don't say, etc.

The Steps, sponsorship, fellowship, service, and developing my outer circle lay the foundation. If I am engaged in and responsible for my own life, making it as rich and loving as I can with my Higher Power's guidance and the time I have, I am better able to let other people have their lives. I am better able to engage with the lives of others in ways that enrich and ennoble us all.

All I ever have is this precious, present moment. This is my opportunity to turn it over and make a life I want to live and be a person I want to be.

~

I am responsible for the gift of my life, right here, right now.

ଓଃ

> "The Seventh Tradition ensures that every
> SAA group takes full responsibility for its
> own needs and expenses. As addicts, we were
> often all to ready to shirk responsibility and
> allow others to take care of us, clean up our
> messes, and attend to the necessities of life."

Sex Addicts Anonymous, page 87

When I was acting out sexually, I avoided responsibility for who I was and what I was becoming. My sponsor taught me that I was ultimately responsible for my recovery. Consequently, I had to start growing up if I wanted the freedom that this program offered. Recovery is a challenging process. It is easy to want others to take care of me. However, I am doing myself a disservice because spiritual growth begins when I take responsibility for my life and my sobriety. I am not helpless, and it is gratifying to know that I can take action to help myself change. Being responsible helps me become who I always was but never allowed myself to be.

I do not expect someone to do what I am capable of doing and need to do. This also applies to the SAA groups I attend. We pay rent, provide a safe haven for all sex addicts, and have business meetings. We are all in this together and, the more the group succeeds, the more likely the individual sex addicts will succeed in staying sober. I need the groups to succeed so this individual can survive and recover.

~

Am I being responsible, not only for my sobriety, but for the welfare of the groups I attend?

"We may see, for example, that our
expectations of others have led to
disappointment <u>and</u> resentment."

Sex Addicts Anonymous, page 41

The first time I went on a date with my partner, I had
a sense of hopeful anticipation for what the evening
and the person would be. It was a brand new experience, and I was open to whatever might happen.

A few months later, however, familiarity had set in,
and I had come to have expectations of that person.
These expectations helped me to develop the relationship by building on what I learned—a map, of sorts, to
our interactions. This was very useful in anticipating,
for example, how she wanted her coffee or other small
ways to be of service.

But this map also became an obstacle. As I moved
from curiosity to expectations, my expectations set
limits, creating disappointments when not met. What's
more, my imagination began to enhance the map, adding my own hopes and fantasies about the relationship
to my list of expectations, eventually creating a yawn-
ing gulf between daydream and reality. The inevitable
result was frustration, resentment, and isolation.

Living with expectations may be unavoidable, but releasing others from their obligations to meet my expectations is a step towards freedom for them and for me.
Learning to live with open awareness and a little wide-
eyed, hopeful wonder can dissolve barriers and unlock
choices. I can pray for the willingness, then practice
being a loving partner, and let the consequences be
what they will.

~

*Just for today, help me be open to the opportunities for
life that await me.*

ભ

"Meetings are the heart of the SAA fellowship."
Sex Addicts Anonymous, page 10

When I first started the Twelve Steps I was not sure it was for me. I still wanted to act out after meetings. I would feel alone, crazy, and helpless, making calls to act out rather than reach out. But I kept coming back and found that, over time, if I kept to regular meetings, I had less crazy, unhealthy thoughts. Things people said would surface later in times of need.

One day I came home tired, wanting to act out, and I remembered someone talking about connecting to their Higher Power through nature and observing a strong wind. At the same moment, I observed through my window the wind blowing the trees, and I felt the presence of a Higher Power. I relaxed and no longer felt like acting out.

~

I can now see that perseverance brings truth to the saying, "Keep coming back—it works and we are worth it."

"We find our serenity growing as we
align our will with God's in each new
area that is revealed to us."

Sex Addicts Anonymous, page 58

Much of my life I lived without understanding the
healing and transformative power that God's love could
have in my life. Confused and turned off by my early
religious teachings, I rejected those ideas about God,
instead turning to others and to selfishness for my
identity. "When the going gets tough, the tough get going" was my motto. Fear and insecurity were constant
companions, leading me further into my addictive life
with ever greater pain, hopelessness, and shame.

Today I realize that God was there all the time, waiting and watching for me to find the willingness to ask
for and accept help. Desperation was my motivation
and the Twelve Steps were the key to opening myself
to a new understanding of God, one that continues to
unfold and to empower my life.

I understand the healing power that God's will can
have for me, but I am in charge of making that conscious contact first. Like a TV signal that is always
present, God waits patiently for me to turn on the set
and tune in the channel to receive the colorful messages. God delivers love and acceptance that I always
wanted and needed.

*Today I trust that my prayers will be answered, but I
must open the channel.*

CR

> "In taking the Eleventh Step, we
> dedicate ourselves to an increasing
> spiritual awareness and a greater
> connection with our Higher Power."

Sex Addicts Anonymous, page 55

It was time to start meditating. I already had an image and a sense of my Higher Power, but now I felt like I needed a feeling, too. I searched for a safety, a comfort. I thought about a good friend, and what it felt like to sit next to him and lean into him physically. I had felt safe and protected, but now he'd moved away. What or who could I lean into instead?

I have a fleece blanket with my favorite cartoon character on it. I got out the blanket and draped it across my shoulders, enfolding myself in it. Suddenly, I felt warm, cared for, and satisfied. For the next two years I wrapped up in the blanket whenever I meditated, drawing closer to God through a manmade piece of material. And it was good.

~

I draw closer to my Higher Power in a way that feels good to me.

> "But if we are patient and open-minded,
> we will discover an understanding of
> a Higher Power that is unique to us,
> and that we are comfortable with."
>
> *Sex Addicts Anonymous*, page 27

The focus on spirituality was a problem when I started recovery. I just figured I would find a way to work around it. Fortunately, I also heard something that made sense: spiritual fitness, like physical fitness, requires exercise and time. My spiritual self had pretty much withered from neglect.

My sponsor emphasized that the Second and Third Steps could be a journey to finding a Higher Power that I connected with. The idea of a personal Higher Power started to become more important, interesting, and exciting. Then I started to hear the great diversity of spiritual approaches that my fellows in the program have, and that was, at least, interesting.

One day, a member described how she connected to her Higher Power through an element of nature. Wow! I had always felt a deep connection with this same element. Hearing her allowed me to see how personal and meaningful a Higher Power could be. I now listened more carefully in meetings, read spiritual works, and worked on my Second and Third Steps. Gradually, with exercise and time, the notion of a Higher Power and a working relationship with that power, that is, spirituality, emerged. The journey towards a Higher Power and to greater spiritual fitness has been the cornerstone of my recovery, and a gift I never imagined I would receive.

If I start with an open mind and a little willingness, my Higher Power can do a lot.

03

> "We can then admit our part and prepare
> to do whatever is needed to set things
> right, whether it is making direct amends,
> adjusting our attitude, or simply letting go."
>
> *Sex Addicts Anonymous*, page 54

One evening, I realized I owed amends for something I had done that day. I was embarrassed and wanted to contact the person, take ownership, and clear the wreckage. But it was late and that person might already be asleep. Yet, I was racked with guilt and wanted this off my chest.

I'm not sure where it came from (wink), but something told me that Step Ten is a daily application of Steps Four through Nine. Step Nine states, "except when to do so would injure them or others." Calling at this hour might well apply.

Step Eight held the key, though: "became willing to make amends to them all." Was I willing to make amends? Yes. OK, that was enough for now. I committed to my Higher Power that I would make amends the next day. I was able to let go of the guilt, and got a good night's sleep. The next day, I made the amends.

This event encapsulates my experience with amends. A great gift of amends is the unburdening and liberation of my conscience, but that is the by-product. The real purpose is to make right what I have done wrong, to live with honor and responsibility, and to do the right thing, just because. There is a gift in this that I may never be able to describe.

I thank God for these tools that allow me to truly live.

"We need patience to work the Seventh Step,
and trust that our Higher Power can help us."
Sex Addicts Anonymous, page 44

It is said that the only constant is change. As a sex addict, change was initially a scary proposition for me. I've lived so long with my addiction that I've come to rely on it as I would a faithful friend. While working the program of Sex Addicts Anonymous, I tended to want those positive changes to occur according to my expectations, to my calculations, to my timetable. God had other ideas.

Impatience can be an obstacle to my recovery, a set-up for me to act out. The temptation for me is to buy in to the lies by convincing myself that good things are not happening fast enough, or, "I stopped acting out, so why aren't things going better now?" I have found that the changes I have experienced as a result of working this program, more often than not, come gradually rather than instantly.

I believe in the miracle of recovery, while trusting the guidance and timing of God. As much as I'd like to, I can't predict the future. In developing a recovery partnership with God, I'm cultivating an attitude of patient expectation, as I am convinced there are more things for me to learn. I utilize this waiting time creatively by celebrating the changes that do occur in my life, by attending meetings, sponsoring and being sponsored, and being of whatever help I can to the sex addict who still suffers.

If I continue to work for it, the miracle will happen—in God's time, not mine.

ॐ

> "When we sense what God would have us do,
> we also ask for the <u>power</u> to carry that out."
>
> *Sex Addicts Anonymous*, page 58

When I'm feeling overwhelmed, it's usually because I'm doing things on my own. Old habits of trying to measure up or prove that I'm of value through my actions may be surfacing. Or I may be so excited about giving Twelfth-Step service that I take on more than I can handle. Sometimes, I allow schedule changes to get in the way of practices like prayer and meditation that keep me connected with my Higher Power.

I've heard that recovery has a shelf life of about twenty-four hours, and it has proven true for me. If I get lax with daily conscious contact, the connection wavers, and I start feeling confused, fearful, unsteady, or irritable. There are times, though, when I have been consistently spending time with God, that I still feel like life is too much for me to handle. When this happens, I'm probably doing my best to know God's will and carry it out, but forgetting to pray for power to do it.

My experience has been that, when I've thought to ask for strength, wisdom, and ability, I have been able to accomplish much more than I ever could have alone. God has helped me prioritize and manage my time. I've been able to remember things. Doors have opened. Supporting friends have appeared. Miracles great and small have happened. And I trust it will continue if I remember to ask.

~

May I remember to look to the source of power today and ask for help.

ଓ

> "We may work a Fourth Step again when
> we have new challenges to face or when we
> need to examine ourselves more closely."
>
> *Sex Addicts Anonymous*, page 37

After some years in recovery, I began another Fourth Step inventory by making a list of people I'd known in my life. Looking through old photo albums and journals, I saw my past through new eyes. I saw behaviors and thought patterns indicating sex addiction and intimacy avoidance throughout my life.

It was clear I had problems back then. However, nobody could have known the exact nature of my illness. Understanding of the problem and its solution were still being developed by the pioneers of this fellowship.

Like a person diagnosed with a learning disability later in life, I now look back on my life with dawning understanding. I had a disease! As I see my past self more clearly, my compassion grows. This compassion is most evident as I continue to discover past wrongs that require amends. I can now look on that broken child of God, not with shame and revulsion but with compassion as I take responsibility for my life.

I did not ask to be sick. I was doing the best I could with what I had. However, I have now been blessed with tools like a Higher Power of my understanding, the Steps, Traditions, and slogans. With the support of fellow recovering addicts, I don't have to remain stuck in the past.

~

No longer bound by it, I can view my past with acceptance, love, and compassion.

◌◌

> "In SAA meetings, we try to share from our
> own experience, rather than giving advice."
> *Sex Addicts Anonymous*, page 94

I believe Tradition Eleven applies to my interpersonal life as well, and I recently had a dramatic lesson in its wisdom. I reach out to people in our group and sometimes run into my character defect of trying to force solutions. This can show up as believing I know what is best for someone and wanting to ensure they get it, whether they want it or not!

Some months ago, I tried to engage with someone in our group, offering "help" for a problem I have experience with. They demurred, and I was crushed. I started beating myself up for my high-handed tactics, which I "should know better" than to use. My compulsiveness had temporarily won out, and I paid a heavy emotional price for some time afterwards.

Then, at a recent check-in, I shared a particular aspect of my fear of intimacy, and that same person asked a clarifying question afterwards. When I shared openly how this particular fear plays out in my primary relationship, they said, "I am so glad I can come to a place where I relate so well to what people are saying!" That same person called me out of the blue the next day and we had a great conversation.

I have heard it said that, the more I think you need a meeting, the more I need a meeting.

~

All I ever have is my own experience, strength, and hope. I only know what worked for me. Thank God it's enough!

---

*"Our emotions have often been a source of pain
and confusion in our lives, and they frequently
triggered our addictive sexual behavior."*
Sex Addicts Anonymous, page 34

I recently had an uncomfortable exchange with a
sponsee. We had met and had a good discussion, and
what I said was apparently well received. Nevertheless,
I felt uncomfortable afterwards. Although I had no direct evidence that anything had bothered my sponsee,
I sent a text asking for feedback.

A quick response assured me there had been nothing.
Nevertheless uncomfortable feelings remained, but
now the internal dialog shifted to, "Why had I asked
for that feedback? Was it just to quiet feelings caused
by my fears and insecurities?" Interestingly, I soon got
an e-mail from my sponsee, voicing frustration with
my pattern of feedback requests. I was assured that, if
anything were amiss, my sponsee would take responsibility and let me know. So now, I had uncomfortable
feelings caused by my earlier responses to my uncomfortable feelings! Talk about emotional insobriety.

This exchange and other experiences are teaching me
that I shouldn't act on every uncomfortable feeling. I
can sit with them and ask for my Higher Power to help
me see the truth. I can share them with my sponsor or
a program friend. Sometimes these feelings are indi-
cators that some action needs to be taken, but sometimes they are an indication that I need growth and
healing in a particular area.

*"Don't just do something—sit there!" Sometimes I don't
need to act on uncomfortable feelings.*

"While the inner circle relates to behaviors that
keep us in isolation and fantasy, the outer
circle refers to behaviors that help keep us
engaged with other <u>people</u> and with reality."

Tools of Recovery, page 7

I have always been interested in painting, writing,
designing, and decorating. But I always felt guilty for
doing those things; like I had more important things
I should do with my time. In the past, I briefly entertained the idea of being a creative professional, but
economic insecurity and some conception of practical-
ity stifled those dreams. I realized in SAA that I often starve myself of creative outlets in the same way
I starve myself of healthy sexuality and intimacy with
God, others, and myself.

Learning about the outer circle kick-started a re-
awakening of my creativity. Within a few months I was
writing again, and I enrolled in an interior design cer-
tification course. I started designing furniture with my
husband, which also helped us connect on a much
deeper level. I realize now that, for me at least, creativity is not a luxury but a necessity—one of the most important reasons that I exist. My Higher Power created
me, and as a creation, I am designed to co-create with
God, myself, and others.

All my time and energy spent in fantasy, sexual or
otherwise, was simply a misuse of my divinely implant-
ed creative energy. I am learning to direct that creative
energy toward beauty, and to share it with others.

~

*God, for today, help me honor the creative intelligence
that is within me and within you.*

"Having only one primary purpose in our service activities keeps everything simple and focused."

Sex Addicts Anonymous, page 84

On my bookshelf I have dictionaries and grammars for many languages: Latin, Spanish, Yiddish, Hebrew, and Esperanto. I have books on linguistics, history, philosophy, psychology, comparative religions, politics, and do-it-yourself spirituality. I am interested in so many things that I can't focus on any one thing. I aimlessly flitter from one topic to the next, alighting on whatever catches my fancy in the moment. I'm so interested in so many things that neither I nor anyone else knows what primarily motivates me. Neither I nor others know what I want to accomplish in this world. This lack of focus means I've never learned any one skill or knowledge to any degree of expertise.

What would Sex Addicts Anonymous look like if it were as complicated and unfocused as me? Thankfully, I do not have to answer that question. Since coming to the fellowship of Sex Addicts Anonymous, I have received a consistent, focused message: the Twelve Steps and Twelve Traditions of Sex Addicts Anonymous. In the meetings I've attended, I've never heard the message of another program. When I attend meetings of Sex Addicts Anonymous, I'm never confused as to what fellowship I'm attending. Further, because Sex Addicts Anonymous sticks to its message and purpose, it has a level of expertise I've come to trust.

Our singleness of purpose binds us.

ः

> "Often the key to this kind of meditation
> is concentrating on something simple,
> such as one's breath. Or we may just
> sit quietly, turning our attention to our
> Higher Power, allowing ourselves to be
> open to God's grace and wisdom."
>
> *Sex Addicts Anonymous*, page 57

I had tried a little yoga as a kid, but I had never really practiced any spiritual discipline, so meditation was new to me. I started by simply lighting a candle in the morning, sitting in front of it for one minute, and just breathing. I knew I could sit still for one minute, anyway.

After doing one minute each day for a week, it was no problem to do two minutes. In two weeks I was up to three to four minutes, and soon, five to ten minutes of meditation each day was no big deal. I didn't have to go to a mountaintop or a temple or anything; I just lit a candle in my little garret and sat still for a minute.

To me, recovery is an artistic gift to the world. It allows me to make beautiful life music. I make the world better by practicing my daily recovery plan.

The main thing was to start, and then build the habit by doing it every day. By keeping it simple and small-scale, I was able to stick to it, and my ability and awareness gradually expanded, a minute at a time.

~

Today, I will take one minute to be still and feel present with the spirit of the universe.

CB

> "The Third Step invites us to turn our will and
> our lives over to the care of God, not the control
> of God. We are not abandoning ourselves to
> the direction of some powerful taskmaster
> forcing us to do things that are not of our own
> choosing. Instead, we become open to making
> new choices for ourselves in the light of a
> Higher Power's transforming love and care."
>
> *Sex Addicts Anonymous*, page 29

How many times in my addiction did I hear only voices of judgment and criticism? I seemed boxed in by these powerful taskmasters, and I believed I had no choices. I felt compelled to act out in my addiction. I heard no whispers of compassion.

But then I found the seeds of hope in the members of the fellowship. I heard and saw others recovering from sexual addiction and I began to believe that recovery was possible for each of us. I began to see the possibility of a gentle, caring God working in and through the fellowship.

As I stayed sober and my life changed, I began to feel the presence of a loving, compassionate Higher Power. I realized, maybe for the first time, that I was loved unconditionally. Having felt the love of the fellowship, in the Third Step, I gave my life over to the care of the God of my understanding. In my Higher Power's loving care, I began to find different choices in my life—loving choices that had seemed inconceivable before, but that now were transforming me.

How may I care for myself this day in my recovery as the God of my understanding cares for me? Am I developing a sense of trust that new solutions are possible for me?

∞

> "In our groups, there is a collective
> wisdom that has grown and been handed
> down over the years. We learn many
> new solutions to old problems."
>
> *Sex Addicts Anonymous*, page 2

In meetings I heard people share that they were taught to do this or that for their recovery. I wondered how they got such great instruction. No one was instructing me about all these clever ways to be sober. I wanted a manual and I wanted someone to care enough about me to give it to me. Over time I came to understand that the teaching is going on at every meeting. All I needed to do was listen and observe.

Over and over people shared their challenges, hardships, and victories. In every story was information about what tools of the program they used, what experience, strength and hope they received from sponsors and others, and how they resolved their challenges using the program. I was being taught by people who loved me. I only needed to listen.

~

Our solution is available in every meeting. I will take the solutions and leave the rest.

"Listening more attentively to others
is part of my recovery."
Sex Addicts Anonymous, page 193

I could feel a tinge of excitement growing inside me. I was going out to dinner with another member of my SAA group. We had both come to the same convention, and now we were going to eat and relax together. I had known him for over a year and had admired his recovery. Now I was hoping to get to know him better. But the twist in the conversation that startled me, as we began to eat and converse, was that I wanted to hear his story, instead of me wanting to share mine. What was so startling about that?

Well you see, I'm a recovering sex addict, and most of my life has been spent gratifying my needs, manipulating and seducing others to give me pleasure, focusing on myself, and neglecting or ignoring others. This has left me detached and disconnected, unable to experience emotional intimacy, self-centered and self-absorbed. But now I found myself concerned about the other person. What was he going through? How was he doing? What has his journey been like? I asked him if he would share with me how he got started in his business, and that led into him sharing his story. He was entrusting me with the most painful and personal events of his life. What a gift! What a privilege! What an honor!

Most of my shortcomings center around me. When God removes these, I have more of me to share with others.

Today I am grateful for the gift of emotional intimacy. I look forward to being enriched by the closeness that comes from focusing on others instead of myself.

જી

"Some of us who rushed into the First Step
later discovered this might be another
expression of our need to control things
and work the "perfect" program."

"First Step to Recovery"

I had only been in therapy for about six weeks when
my counselor handed me two books about sexual addiction. Over the following weekend, the literature
confirmed that I am a sex addict. The next week, I
discovered a closed men's meeting in my town, and
I began attending weekly meetings. In one month's
time, without a sponsor, I had scheduled my First Step
on the group calendar. Fortunately, someone in the
group took me aside and explained the process. It was
a wake-up call.

As with everything else in my life and addiction, I was
trying to take control. I began to understand how per-
vasively my addiction had taken over my life. It also
made me realize how critical it is to rely on the help of
my fellow addicts, and, more importantly, my Higher
Power. After that night, I began to take the Twelve
Steps more seriously. My First Step would take much
more time, and that was OK.

*Recovery and sobriety are only possible when I accept
my powerlessness and accept help.*

> "We start by admitting that we are
> completely powerless to stop our addictive
> sexual behaviors on our own. We admit
> that our lives are out of our control."
>
> *Sex Addicts Anonymous*, page 23

For many of us who have experienced abuse, we are familiar with being powerless. Often this came from people we saw as authority figures or from those we were convinced we should trust. Powerlessness can be overwhelming and destructive. Some of us chose a re-action that went, "I will never be powerless again." We became bullies, or we repeated the patterns of abuse, believing that this was the best we could hope for.

In recovery, admitting powerlessness is a way of truthfully stating that, as a consequence of trying to control life by myself, my life is unmanageable. One of the paradoxes of recovery is that, by relinquishing control, I began to take responsibility for my life. In developing a relationship with my Higher Power and working with a sponsor, I learn to practice trusting with those who deserve my trust. This opens a door for something I would never have thought possible—safe, loving relationships. And now, I am even becoming a person that others can trust!

Learning to take responsibility for my life is a long process, and there are many things I must act on, but none of it is possible without first admitting to my innermost self that I cannot control this disease, or my life, on my own.

By admitting my powerlessness, I begin to take responsibility for this precious gift—my life.

> "[Humility] means that we are not too proud or
> ashamed to believe that we can be helped."
>
> *Sex Addicts Anonymous*, page 43

Humiliation was the attitude I brought to my first SAA meeting. I was ashamed of my acting out behaviors and was afraid of the possible consequences. I had grown up with a perfectionist religion and family structure and knew that shaming, rejection, and punishment were to be expected. I was fearful and wanted to avoid those reactions. In my meeting, I found caring and humble people who were also seeking help and who were willing to accept me in spite of my imperfections. Finding that acceptance was very healing. It helped me learn to trust my program friends, and to discover and trust my Higher Power.

I feared but did not know what reactions I would receive in response to disclosure of my character defects. First, I had to let go of my expectations of abuse and rejection. In many cases, I discovered more compassion and forgiveness than I had given myself.

I found that my fears were attempts to protect myself, and they were ineffective in doing so. Humility has helped me to become more teachable, vulnerable and open. My pride and my fears have kept me in a prison of my own making. Letting go of those fears and pride are showing me that I can be loved, I can be helped, I can become a healthier person, and I can show the same to others.

I can be loved, I can be helped, I can become a
healthier person, and I can show the same to others.

୧

"The miracle of recovery from sex addiction becomes a reality we experience every day."
Sex Addicts Anonymous, page 66

During fellowship after a phone meeting, I commented that each of the callers in our small group had reported doing something miraculous that week. Someone who'd joined the meeting late asked for a brief recap of what each person did that was so miraculous. Caught off guard, there was stunned silence for a beat or two, and then I shared about my last week. I explained that even though I'm struggling with something in my life, I'm not trying to escape the emotional pain by acting out. I'm asking others for support through outreach calls instead of isolating as I did before. I'm working the Steps around my challenges instead of being overwhelmed into inactivity, as I used to. And I'm giving it to my Higher Power instead of trying to figure it out or control it, as I would have done in the past. For me, this is miraculous!

Many times I fail to see the miracle of my recovery because I'm looking for evidence of progress in a place different than where it's manifesting itself. I may wish I were farther along the path or able to do something that someone else is doing, but comparing myself to others doesn't serve me. Comparing myself with my past self and recognizing the changes and growth fills me with a sense of wonder and appreciation.

I will take a moment to inventory my progress, and to recognize, in joy and gratitude, my recovery as the miracle it truly is.

~

I am living a miracle.

ल्ड

> "We may consider entering into a co-
> sponsorship relationship with a program
> friend for <u>mutual</u> support."
>
> *Sex Addicts Anonymous*, page 14

After I had been in SAA a while, my original sponsor went absent. This brought up feelings of abandonment, anger, and confusion. After a month of this, I started reaching out to my SAA home group and utilizing the phone list.

I soon began forming stronger relationships with friends in the program. This led to group step-study, making outreach phone calls to three friends a day, and most importantly, carpooling to SAA meetings I had never attended before. I had lost my pillar, but found a huge safety net in the process.

It is nonetheless vital that I have a sponsor. A sponsor is one appropriate person with whom I begin to practice trust, a person who guides me through the Steps and who can catch me when I'm fooling myself or others. I eventually found a new sponsor, but if it hadn't been for establishing co-sponsorships with new friends in recovery, I would have been vulnerable to my inner circle during that period.

I learned a lot from this experience. I learned that my sponsor is not here to keep me sober; that responsibility is between me and my Higher Power. I also learned that I cannot do this alone, and when I reached out, I found love and support.

Today, I will reach out to at least one other addict in love and support.

> "We listen respectfully to what others
> have to say and share our experience
> as it seems appropriate."
>
> *Sex Addicts Anonymous*, page 11

Before recovery, I was an advice giver. I gave advice without being asked. Many saw it as telling them what to do, and they were probably right. When others wouldn't take my advice, I would be angry and that would begin a resentment.

After some time in the program and considerable step work with my sponsor, I received a Father's Day card from my daughter, a college freshman. She mentioned seeing changes in me over the last few months, and that she especially appreciated advice I had recently given her. I had not shared that I was in recovery, so the fact that she had noticed changes meant a lot to me.

The irony, however, was that I had actually stopped giving her advice! I now simply shared my own experience with whatever problem she faced and left out the "I think you should try the same thing" advice. Through sharing my own experience, strength, and hope, and not giving advice, she was now benefitting from our relationship.

I continue to practice this principle in my life. I simply share my own experience, strength, and hope, and only when asked. For me, that means when there is at least a question mark at the end of their sentence. This practice allows me to be of maximum service to others, and keeps me focused on my Higher Power's will rather than my own. And now I have actual, mutual relationships with the wonderful people in my life!

Today I will listen first and share my own experience when asked.

> "If we relapse, it is important that we get right back into recovery immediately. We need not turn a mistake into a self-destructive binge."

Sex Addicts Anonymous, page 67

I've relapsed—again! I feel soiled and ashamed. I don't want to go back to my group and tell them that I've failed—again! Maybe I'll take some time off...

Or maybe I could admit that I am powerless over my addictive behavior. Relapse is not uncommon during recovery from addiction. I can decide, again, to turn it over to my Higher Power. I can be honest with my sponsor and my friends in the program, and review what I was thinking and feeling, what I was saying to myself just before I slipped and fell again.

I can go to a meeting, knowing that there I will find someone who understands. I can listen to the experience of others, not to judge myself as better or worse, but to hear how other addicts dealt with a similar situation. I will find acceptance and encouragement from my sisters and brothers in the program.

I will go to an SAA meeting. I will be welcome there.

> "We share our program so that we can gain a
> balanced recovery and we do this by directly
> showing our three circles to our sponsor and
> to people in our group. Without this clarity
> we can continue to act out, because we are
> confused about what sobriety is for us."
>
> "Three Circles"

On realizing that I am a sex addict and that I am also sexually avoidant, I was confused over how to develop my three circles. Praying about it, I came to understand that I couldn't separate the two extremes of my addiction. For me, they're too intertwined. I spent years bouncing back and forth from extremes of acting out to acting in and back again—a cycle I believe originated in childhood sexual abuse.

Hearing other avoidants share that some behaviors were in all three of their circles helped clarify the issue for me. Some of my behaviors belong in multiple circles. It all depends on the context, the effect, my intent, and whether I'm compulsive or abusive about it.

Thanks to a sponsor who understands both dimensions and to others sharing their experience, I established three circles that are honest, comprehensive, and workable.

And only two days after reviewing my circles with my sponsor, I realized that, because I was abstaining from all of my inner-circle behaviors, I now had a sobriety date!

My three circles evolve as I do.

ca

> "Working Step Nine brings us many gifts: true empathy for those we have harmed, compassion, self-respect, and respect for the humanity of others."
>
> *Sex Addicts Anonymous*, page 52

I was making amends, with my sponsor's help, to the people I harmed. I had made several amends already when I had an opportunity to make one to a friend of my father. I had stolen from him as a teenager. I was terrified but I kept praying as I approached him. I made the amends. At that moment, my world opened up and I realized I had harmed not only him, but my father indirectly.

My father's friend did not want the money I offered him, but instead shared his troubles about his own son. I had known his son from growing up. He talked with me for about twenty minutes and since then we have connected on a deeper level. God put me there at that time not only to make things right but also as a servant to comfort another who was suffering.

～

I do not know what God has planned for me today, but if I am able and willing to do the work, I become connected to the people and the world around me.

ca

"Rigorous honesty...includes...willingness to
be honest about what we need to do to stay
sober, such as setting healthy boundaries
around specific people and places."

Tools of Recovery, Page 29

Setting my personal boundaries around acting
out was straightforward. Much came from defining
my three circles with the help of my sponsor. These
boundaries gave me enough short-term abstinence for
primary spiritual benefits to kick in, providing clarity
and direction in subsequent step work.

I realized that healthy boundaries govern all my relationships. Who is it safe to interact with, and to what
extent? What am I reasonably expected to give, and
when is it appropriate to use self-care and say no? Is
someone trying to take advantage of me, or am I trying
to take advantage of someone?

My Higher Power does not want me to be a bully or a
doormat. Now when I interact with others, I check my
motives. Am I aligned with my Higher Power, or am I
seeking status and the accolades of others? Am I being
selfish in any way? Do I need to step up and assert my
own needs? Am I isolating?

I have abundant resources to aid me in this journey:
the Twelve Steps, my sponsor, prayer, friends in the
program and their experience, and meditation. I also
have plenty of opportunities to practice healthy boundaries. Day by day, I am slowly but steadily learning to
recognize and set healthy boundaries.

*For today, help me recognize and honor my boundaries
and those of the people in my life.*

> "Having accepted both the reality of our
> disease and the possibility that a Higher
> Power can help us where our own efforts
> have failed, we make a leap of faith,
> turning to that Power for assistance."

Sex Addicts Anonymous, page 28

It was time to take the leap of faith!

As a new person in recovery, with residual guilt and shame from growing up gay in a strict church in a small conservative town, my understanding of God had been tainted with condemnation, judgment, shame, hypocrisy, and long suffering. I had lost the pure light of compassion and unconditional love that, as a child, I knew my God to be. I had traded it in for the condemning, jealous, authoritarian God that others had convinced me of, as if I even deserved to have a God at all after choosing to be my authentic self.

When it came to the Third Step, I had heard someone share the idea of keeping a "God Box" as a way to turn my will over. I felt a strong tugging from my inner child saying, "I wanna trunk so that I can fit in it, hide, and be safe." As an amends to my kid self, I decorated my God Trunk with of images of color and light and beauty and connection and boundless love—all the things that my kid had known, but I had forgotten. Thank you, SAA, for letting me remember.

~

Choosing to be who and what I was created to be has led me back to God as I understood God.

"Just as there was no question that the behaviors listed in our inner circle were compulsive, addictive, and therefore dangerous and destructive, so there is no question that the behaviors we list in our 'outer circle' bring recovery and are to be encouraged, praised and practiced."

"Three Circles"

I heard that it takes twenty-one days to establish a new habit or to break an old habit. I must be slow because it took me several years to establish the habits of recovery, and I must focus daily to stay on my recovery path.

I had one of my most difficult times in recovery trying to identify behaviors for my outer circle. I knew what belonged in my inner circle, the destructive behaviors that damaged my life, my health, and my relationship. But finding the behaviors to replace my addiction was a new challenge. These are the behaviors that will improve and affirm my life. In my addiction I did not feel worthy of anything that would improve my life.

At first, I had to deliberately program outer-circle behaviors into my daily activities. When I practice outer-circle behaviors, I know that someone else's life is better, even if it is just mine. I take care of myself with daily exercise, prayer, meditation, and family time. I serve the fellowship in my local group and intergroup. When I come from service, I have no time for acting out and those destructive thoughts are less likely to cross my mind.

Today, still one day at a time, I am filling my life and my outer circle with behaviors and activities that strengthen my recovery.

> "An inventory allows us to go over our lives
> methodically and objectively, reevaluating
> assumptions, beliefs, and feelings that
> we have held onto for years but perhaps
> never examined or questioned."

Sex Addicts Anonymous, page 32

For as long as I remember, I have loved garage sales. The process enchanted me: finding a rare gem, then determining if I wanted to pay to call it mine.

When working Steps Four through Six, I had an epiphany: instead of looking at this task as something to be dreaded (as so many people do), what if I looked at it as my recovery garage sale? I did just that. I carefully, fearlessly, and spiritually turned every stone in my mind. Who or what was I angry with? Why? How did it hurt me? What was my part? Most importantly, was the feeling of value to me, or was it better off sold to the universe? I also discovered some awesome things I owned.

In Step Five, my sponsor helped me sort through this garage full of stuff. She helped me identify, label, and better understand many of the items. In the process, we contemplated, laughed, and cried.

In Step Six, I became willing, sooner or later, to let these items go, like the mental macramé owl that somebody gave me way back when. In Step Seven, I gave these to my Higher Power because they were too heavy for me to lift. I also did this in the faith that something better would come to replace it.

~

The Steps are an adventure that clears the clutter, reveals hidden treasure, and opens up space for even better things.

> "As our recovery progresses, and we gain
> new understanding about ourselves and our
> addiction, we are free to add or delete behaviors,
> or move them from one circle to another, in
> order to reflect new growth and insights."
>
> *Sex Addicts Anonymous*, page 16

I've been coming to SAA for nearly four years, and as I write this meditation, I have four days of sexual sobriety. That doesn't seem like much, and yet, it's progress. My inner circles have changed over the years, getting tighter to better reflect my evolving sexual ideals. With each change of my circles, I reset my sobriety clock as I begin progress on another area of my life and sexuality.

When I first came to SAA, I engaged in many risky sexual behaviors. These were and still are the bull's-eye inner circle behaviors that I've managed to cut out of my life. Four years ago, porn was in my middle circle and I couldn't imagine giving it up. Now it's in my inner circle, and I'm slowly but surely making progress, with lots of starts and stops along the way. But that's progress. Recently, it's been three steps forward, one step back, which seems like even more progress.

I can't claim years of sobriety like others, and I don't have the chips to show for it, and yet, I've come a long way. It's not perfect, but it's progress. It's recovery, from shame to grace, and for that, I'm thankful.

~

I'm grateful for the progress and recovery I've made, and for the opportunity to grow and learn in the three circles.

> "Our experience has shown that we move
> forward in our recovery when we take action.
> Understanding our addiction benefits us
> in many ways, but ultimately, we can't
> think our way <u>out</u> of the problem."
>
> *Sex Addicts Anonymous*, page 63

With shame and embarrassment after each relapse, I promised myself that this time it would be different. As long as I think I can fix my problem by myself, I cannot stop the insanity of my addiction. If thinking about change were enough, I would have fixed myself a long time ago. I've proven, over and over, that just thinking about it gets me nowhere.

My recovery is based on a series of decisions to keep on track. These decisions about my newfound way of life must be followed by action. Taking action is what actually sends me along the path of change. Using my outer circle as a guide to healthy actions, I can keep myself on the recovery track. I cannot think my way into right action, but I can act my way into right thinking.

The book *Sex Addicts Anonymous* says that we can put the decision of Step Three into effect by taking small but significant actions. They include meetings, prayer, meditation, phone calls, literature, step work, sponsor work, service, etc. Making this small commitment and being accountable for my actions move me closer to turning my will and my life over to the care of a Higher Power. Each choice toward recovery that I act on creates space wherein my Higher Power can guide me.

~

Today I choose to recover. I pray for willingness to act on my choice.

ા

> "As we gain sobriety by having clear boundaries
> and working our program, it becomes much
> easier to stay sober and to truly
> enjoy recovery."
>
> "Three Circles"

SAA is about so much more than continuous sexual sobriety. The Twelve Steps are a way of living happily sober and giving life meaning. When I am fearful, I am suffering from the basic problem of all addicts: chronic self-centeredness and a lack of faith. Through the power of the Steps I have been given a life that is secure and deeply satisfying, and a relief from acting out that is not a struggle. This path enables me to enjoy what life has to offer.

This program reminds me I am but a small part of a greater whole, and as I stay sober I grow in two life-giving ingredients of enjoyable recovery: humility and responsibility. From my morning gratitude list and meditation to my evening review and prayers, with the opportunities to help other addicts in between—these are the things that enable me to truly enjoy recovery.

~

Today I will not sell myself short; I will take the actions I need to bring meaning to my sexually sober life. I will not be afraid to enjoy what is beautiful, and I will open myself up to this by practicing the spiritual principles of the Twelve Steps of SAA.

> "Developing our creativity helps us play and
> heal. We express ourselves in different ways."
>
> *Sex Addicts Anonymous*, page 65

How many artists, musicians, and writers have we
discovered sitting right next to us in SAA meetings?
For some of us, our sexual addiction whittled away
at our creative lives, leaving us with fantasy, obsession, and the compulsion to act out sexually. We told
ourselves we weren't good enough. We could not show
people our art, we could not let them hear our music, we hid our poetry. We found shame and isolation
everywhere.

In recovery from our sexual addiction, we try to live in
our outer circle. We learn that expressing our creativity connects us to other people, and we begin to feel the
presence of our Higher Power through our creativity.
We sing, we write, we read, we paint, we garden, we
hike, we sew, we bike, we surf, we dance, we build,
we garden, we listen, we cook, we relax, we laugh. We
laugh! We share these and a thousand other acts of
creation with the people we love. We take these actions, and we feel different.

In our creativity, we realize that playfulness is another tool of our recovery. We find wonder, awe, and
gratitude for our sober lives and the gifts we have been
given. We play imperfectly, but we play, and we begin
to heal.

Let me have a playful heart today.

රෑ

> "God willing, we may experience the
> forgiveness of those we have harmed. If we
> have been diligent in our amends, we will
> certainly grow in self-forgiveness too."
>
> *Sex Addicts Anonymous*, page 52

I could not do Step Nine until I was ready to let go of the pain and resentment that I had used for forty years to justify my actions. I needed to look at what I had done, not my rationale for doing it.

Looking at what I had done was humbling. I had treated everyone, including myself, with contempt. I had thought the world a lousy place and most people fools. I turned my back on the good and saw only the bad. From Steps One through Eight, I was able to see what I had done, and how I had harmed others and myself. I was now ready to start Step Nine.

This is what I found. There is a spiritual principle that applies whether I like it, believe it, or want it to be so: forgiveness = forgiveness. The chain of forgiveness started when I began making amends to people I had previously used as excuses for selfishness.

Until I was ready to forgive, I was not able to accept forgiveness.

œ

"The key to Step Two is not just believing
in a Higher Power, but believing that this
Power can and will restore us to sanity."

Sex Addicts Anonymous, page 27

I saw it at my first meeting—people who were sane, serene, and at peace. Such hope! I wanted it. Meanwhile here I was—tormented, possessed, and literally insane. How did they do it? I saw them being honest, and being willing to accept new ways of thinking and behaving. As I listened, it became apparent that these people did not escape the shackles of their addiction single-handedly. I continued to attend meetings, hoping some of this good fortune would rub off on me. Little by little I surrendered.

I experience the solution with each honest share, and I start to feel connected to something bigger than myself. I discover that I am not doing this on my own. There is a power moving through these meetings and through this program. I've seen this power reflected in others, and I've seen it move in my own recovery as unexplainable miracles. It was this power that led me to this program, and this power is leading me into a new life. I've seen the miracles. I believe. I am ready to be restored to sanity. I am taking action.

~

I pray for willingness to accept and embrace the grace that accompanies this program.

∽

"When life seems to be more than we can
handle or when we feel pulled toward our
addiction, reconnecting with our Higher
Power is a powerful course of action."

Tools of Recovery, page 18

After years in another program, my life was more un-manageable. I blamed everyone else, including God, and I was in denial about my sex addiction. When things didn't go my way, I became depressed, anxious, and oftentimes enraged.

One day, I was at a hospital for my father's chemo-therapy. I was worried about him and angry over an argument with my acting-out partner. I felt completely alone. I started texting a program friend, "This 'let go and let God' stuff stinks!" I wanted to call and pick a fight with my partner, but there was no cell reception. Fixated on my phone, I wandered the hospital until, finally, I had enough bars. I looked up and saw that I was at the hospital chapel. I lost my breath for a mo-ment. The irony of where I'd ended up jolted me out of myself just long enough. The pit of anger in my stom-ach began to dissipate.

I sat in the chapel and realized that, when I seek God, even in doubt or anger, I open up a space for God. God can handle my anger, fear, and confusion. Soon, God led me to SAA. I got a sponsor and began working the steps, and amazing changes started in my life. I have a long way to go, but I will keep coming back because the solution to my addiction is a spiritual one.

∼

When I seek God's help, I am led in the right direction.

૭

"By being willing to identify instead of compare, we not only break the bonds of our own isolation, but we help others."

Tools of Recovery, page 30

In the Twelfth Step we acknowledge a spiritual awakening as a result of the steps and try to carry this message to other recovering sex addicts. We also seek to apply these principles in all areas of our lives.

The mirror's reflection is a good analogy for the identification of one addict with another. In the face of every newcomer, I am given the chance to see myself as I have been. Because I have been down that treacherous road, I can readily identify with the struggles of my fellow travelers. I can relate to the pain, the fear, the shame, and the despair. I am humbled by the recognition of my own potential for relapse if I do not rigorously work the program. I need to stay in touch with my own powerlessness.

I can also share my experience, my strength, and my hope. I can model through my own stories and behavior a method for transformation. I can share gratitude for the opportunity to see progress through the pain.

~

I give thanks for the opportunity to see myself in the reflection of a twelfth-step call.

ଔ

"We learn to deal with conflict and to be honest."
Tools of Recovery, page 13

Sometimes I despair that my recovery will ever progress. It seems an enormous task, and I think of giving
up. But just a little honesty, a little courage, and a
little faith in my Higher Power can make an enormous
difference. Suddenly there is hope that things can
change. It doesn't take much light to guide me through
a dark passage in life.

This is one of the miracles of our program. Our disease is so overpowering, and we are so weak in the face
of it, yet just a little surrender to the program can give
us the momentum and hope to move forward, even
when that seems impossible. The rewards of this small
effort are a hundredfold, for they allow me to move on
to the next stage of recovery where new possibilities
and challenges exist.

Courageous honesty is like grease that unbinds me
when I get stuck. Perhaps there is a fact I don't want
to admit, or a feeling I'm trying to avoid, or I just want
to get my way. One little bit of honesty, acknowledging
how I am, might feel overwhelming and un-natural,
but it is a part of growing in recovery, and a perfect
antidote to sex addiction. With the help of my Higher
Power, my sponsor, and the fellowship, I can do it.

*Today I trust that a little bit of honesty will be enough
to help me move forward in my recovery.*

"Humbly asked God to remove our shortcomings."

Sex Addicts Anonymous, page 21

I am just beginning Step Seven and my first thought, after the previous steps, is how can I humbly ask when my character defects include pride, willfulness, grandiosity, and shame? Humility is not in my repertoire. I can talk the talk, but can I really walk it? No, I cannot humble myself by myself.

Intellectually, I grasp the helplessness, and even the irony of this predicament. Just as I had to pray in Step Six for willingness to be willing, I see that I must pray for the humility to even ask humbly. I have prayed to God for much of my life, and my Higher Power has been there for me despite my glaring moral flaws. Yet, through the Steps, I realize that my defects have not only led me into sex addiction, causing much suffering to myself and others, but have also kept God out of my life, at a "safe" distance. I have lived my life in my will, not God's will.

Seeing myself more honestly in the Steps has been difficult. I find I have to ask God for the humility to ask God for humility! My Higher Power has graciously led me to the fellowship and to this step. I am ready to have God remove these shortcomings and to be fundamentally changed.

~

I trust that God will give me the grace I need to grow steadily in humility, no better or worse than others. It's up to me to ask."

> "At meetings we emerge from our shame,
> secrecy, and fear, into a community
> of people who share the common goal
> of freedom from sex addiction."
>
> *Sex Addicts Anonymous*, page 10

I was a little apprehensive about going to my first meeting of Sex Addicts Anonymous. I was afraid I'd find a room full of unshaven, drooling perverts in trench coats. What I found instead were perfectly nice, ordinary people who happened to have the same addiction that I have. I met people who used to act out the way I did, but some of them had been sober for years. I heard members share honestly and openly about things that I never talked to anybody about. Their openness gave me permission to get honest, too.

As I shared about my secret life of acting out, the embarrassment and shame fell away. I was able to face my problem and to accept help from other members and from a Power greater than myself. It was in meetings that I heard about the solution in the Twelve Steps, reconnected with my spirituality, and began to rejoin the human race.

Today, I will stay connected to my SAA community and share the solution with others. I will make it to a meeting.

CR

"If we engage in middle-circle behavior, we have not lost our sobriety, but it's a signal that we need to reach out to others and use the tools we have learned in SAA to get us back on track."

Sex Addicts Anonymous, page 18

We often say of the program that, "It works if you work it." That idea might be extended to the thought that "it works as hard as you work it." The more honest and humble effort we expend on surrendering control and working the program, the more good results we are likely to see. We can gauge both our effort and the quality of our recovery by looking honestly at its results in our lives.

As part of our Tenth Step practice, we may reflect on today's behavior and honestly consider which of our actions were in our inner, middle, and outer circles. If we've been in our inner circle, we have slipped or relapsed, and we honestly admit it. For outer circle behaviors, let us be grateful to our Higher Power that we did the next right thing.

And we can be mindful of our middle circle most of all. For there we see the clear and helpful warning signs that something is amiss. We needn't feel shame or despair, or lose hope. Rather, let us recognize and accept our character defects as they are, and humbly ask God to remove them. Through the freedom of rigorous honesty, we can be grateful to our Higher Power for these middle circle signals that warn us of the path toward danger, and that have helped us to right our steps on the road to recovery.

May I consider my actions with rigorous honesty, acknowledge my middle circle behaviors, and take skillful action to keep my program of recovery on track.

ભ

> "This process of becoming willing to make
> amends involves a deeper surrender to our
> Higher Power's will than we have known before."

Sex Addicts Anonymous, page 48

Working Steps Four through Seven clarifies our responsibilities to those we have harmed. Nobody really
talks about Step Eight; usually we run right into Step
Nine. However, my sponsor of twelve years died recently, and this step brings back a flood of memories.

I had just finished my rather long Fifth Step and had
done the subsequent Sixth and Seventh Steps. When
I asked her how to do Step Eight, she said to go back
over my Fourth Step and make three lists. On the
first list were the amends I thought I could do—one
of which was repaying my mother $5,000 that I owed.
The second list included the amends I wasn't sure I
could do—those included an employee that I had fired.
That one was tougher. The final list was the "no way"
list. Here was my gentle, soft-spoken sponsor acknowledging that we all have our stubborn sides, too.

One of my amends was to do affirmations toward myself. I thought that was the most ridiculous amend to
do. That went in the "no way" list because of my utter
rejection of myself. Step Eight asks me to become willing. As the years go by, I become more willing to make
amends to all those on my list, including myself.

~

Willingness is the key to recovery. Help me become
willing to make amends to those I have harmed.

&

> "In Step Eight we claim both our integrity and
> our compassion, and become willing to free
> ourselves from the <u>guilt</u> we have carried."
> *Sex Addicts Anonymous*, page 46

My Eighth Step list of those I had harmed included people I knew I might never be able to find, and people that I knew how to find, but wasn't sure my amends wouldn't cause more harm. There was a couple in this latter group. It was clear to me that any attempt to contact them would surely bring harm to them and their relationship. With my sponsor's guidance, I prayed and prayed about it, even as I drove by their house almost daily.

After several years, my Higher Power caused a sudden shift and transformation in me. Now I could feel at a very deep level the harm my actions and my addiction had caused them. I became aware of the destructive force I had been in their lives. It was a profound moment for me. Though I still knew that initiating communication with these persons would cause them additional harm, I had become willing to make amends. I had found compassion and empathy I had not had before. I was also free of the guilt and shame I had carried for so long. I was now ready to make Ninth Step amends should my Higher Power bless me with that opportunity.

~

Infinite provider of all that I need, guide my steps each and every day.

ଉ

"As long as we seek to stop our addictive
sexual behavior, we belong in SAA."
Sex Addicts Anonymous, page 81

In my pursuit of religious learning and spiritual fellowship, I have often been frustrated by the admissions
requirements of the organized institutions. For several years of a prison sentence, I worked in the chap-
lain's office as a clerk. In this position I was exposed
to a wide variety of religious organizations. During this
time, a close friend of mine wanted to deepen his commitment to a specific practice. He was blocked by a
complex initiation ceremony and by the sewing of a
religious garment, which the prison authorities would
not approve. Neither the prison nor the religious authority would budge on this situation. As a result, he
was incapable of being recognized as a member of the
religion he loved.

Thankfully, I've never experienced any membership
requirements except the desire to stop addictive sexual
behavior, or any initiation ceremonies in Sex Addicts
Anonymous. I have been a member from the moment
I declared myself one. Nobody can declare me out. No
matter who I am, no matter how grave my emotion-
al complications—or even my crimes—Sex Addicts
Anonymous can't deny me membership. What's more,
Sex Addicts Anonymous doesn't want to keep me out.
I am welcome here, just as I am.

*Do I offer the same welcome to newcomers that I
received that desperate day at my first meeting?*

ରଏ

> "Most of us know that we are ready to sponsor
> when another member asks us, or when our own
> sponsor encourages us to take on a sponsee."
> *Sex Addicts Anonymous*, page 14

Was it something I said? I recall asking this silently
to myself just after my sponsor stopped me for a quick
chat as we left a retreat workshop. He simply smiled,
placed a hand on my shoulder and said, "I think you are
ready to sponsor someone else now." Despite a warm
wave of appreciation, I stood partially in disbelief. I recall asking if I should be completely through the Steps,
or be where I was at that time, which was working Step
Nine. My sponsor's answer almost shocked me until I
thought about what he had said.

At the workshop, I was one of three speakers sharing
their experience, strength, and hope. When it was my
turn, I spoke of working the Ninth Step and how it felt
to finally come face to face with those who suffered
from my addictive behaviors. I had tears in my eyes
and could barely finish without crying.

My sponsor later explained that what he heard in
my sharing and saw in my expressions told him I was
ready. I had simply shown what he called the three
H's: humility, honesty and healing. He then told me I
was ready to help others recover.

~

*Spending time with my sponsees and guiding them
through recovery is an opportunity my Higher Power
gives me to share respectful honesty and loving
humility.*

ea

> "There really is no point at which I stop and
> God starts. My ego-centered life is based
> on fear and scarcity, but a God-centered
> life is based on love and abundance."
>
> *Sex Addicts Anonymous*, page 323

During my formative years I experienced manipulating and shaming behavior from people who were presented to me as spiritual leaders. In many cases, I had been told these people were chosen or called by God. I came to blame God for this, and chose not to have that God in my life.

I also decided not to put people in a position of spiritual authority, and this helped quiet the loud voices of others. But refusing to accept their idea of God also kept me resentful and resistant to the process of discovering my own Higher Power.

In recovery I have found that my Higher Power does not try to control me with abuse or shame, but rather provides learning opportunities. By accepting a loving Power greater than myself, I can turn from resentment and resistance to acceptance of the learning opportunities life presents me. I can reach out to my sponsor and others in my group, and find the hope, understanding, and strength that are always available to me in recovery. I can nurture and benefit from a connection with my own Higher Power. Letting go of the resentment that lingers from spiritual abuse is the key to this spiritual life.

~

I am discovering a Higher Power that is free of shame and abuse, and instead loves me as I am, providing new paths to grow in love.

ଔ

> "We recognize that our shortcomings are
> not unique, and that we are not better
> or worse than anyone else. When we live
> with this knowledge, we do not expect
> perfection from ourselves or others."

Sex Addicts Anonymous, page 43

I marvel at the miracle evolving and unfolding in my life as I work the Steps. I was stuck in my resentments. The word forgiveness, in any form, was a triggering word that couldn't pass my heart, blocked by a strong, locked, metal wall. Part of me still told the lie that the only power I'll ever have is to resent deeply and remember, forever.

After Steps Four and Five, I was still stuck with my inability to forgive. I wanted someone to perform some magic that would make me willing to clear my heart of these toxic resentments. It didn't happen.

When I got to Steps Six and Seven, I had no choice but to climb down from my pedestal. Awareness of my character defects brought new and uncomfortable feelings. I understood this to be the beginnings of humility, and that helped. Every day waking up, absorbing the new, detailed awareness of my imperfection gave way to self-compassion, understanding, and acceptance of my imperfect, perfect humanity.

From there, somehow, the miracle happened. This compassion and humility cast light on the darkness of my resentments, granting permission for other people to also be human, make mistakes, and be spiritually ill. I now know what it is to view others with love and compassion.

~

Lord, help me stay humbly aware that, in your transforming miracles, the void left by surrendered defects can reveal a treasure of character assets.

ભ

> "We look honestly at the defects that drove
> our behavior, such as selfishness, desire
> for control, an attitude of entitlement, or
> feelings of inferiority of superiority."
>
> *Sex Addicts Anonymous*, page 33

When I got to the Fourth Step, I felt overwhelmed at the idea of examining in detail the sexual harms I had committed and the character defects that drove me to commit them.

My sponsor gave me a prayer and instructed me to say it every day during this process. I was to ask God to give me "the strength and the courage to see what I need to see about myself, remember what I need to remember, and do what I need to do to complete my Fourth Step inventory."

This prayer was the key to my being able to do this painstaking work. On my own, I would not have had the courage to look at all the harm I had done to others and myself in this addiction. I did not complete the Fourth Step inventory on my own. By the time I arrived at the Fourth Step, I had a Higher Power that works. All I needed to do was plug into that Higher Power with prayer.

～

For today, I know that my Higher Power will always assist me in working the steps, no matter how daunting the task appears to be. All I have to do is surrender my will and ask.

ભ

"Maintaining the freedom we have found
requires daily conscious contact with the God of
our understanding, expressed by practicing the
spiritual principles we have learned in recovery."
Sex Addicts Anonymous, page 62

My compulsive sexual behavior created a self-imposed prison where I languished for years. Even after
getting sober, I would beat myself up over my past and
be overly anxious about my future, thereby ruining my
day and staying behind bars.

The solution is in the Steps. Among other things,
working the Steps taught me to apply the principles of
this program to my daily life—principles like honesty,
willingness, love, and perseverance. At this point on
my path, I find special help in the Eleventh Step. I cannot be conscious of God's presence if I am living in the
past or overly anxious of the future. In other words,
conscious contact is right here, right now, this very
split second of living. When I get still and quiet, I can
become conscious of God's presence. Hence I become
free from all worry and concerns.

My Higher Power's creations, including me, are not
here for me to use or abuse. Having conscious contact
with God helps prevent me from acting out and helps
me see this moment as the miracle and the gift that it
truly is. Thanks to the Steps and the program of SAA,
I have learned to invite loving power into my life and I
experience freedom I never knew before.

~

I consciously invite God into this moment.

> "Our character defects...have caused us a
> great deal of suffering throughout our lives
> and prevented us from completely aligning
> ourselves with our Higher Power's will for us."
>
> *Sex Addicts Anonymous*, page 43

Today I am at a fellowship retreat where I hope to experience relaxation, rest, and renewal. Unfortunately, this morning, a number of tenacious character defects reared their ugly heads. Among them are self-pity, feeling like a victim, and taking things personally. I now know that it's my choice to either stay in this negative space or ask my Higher Power for help in getting out. Yet the negative space is so familiar, it can seem nearly impossible to break free.

At a workshop, I have a moment to pray and really reach out to my Higher Power for help. I can act as if, which for me is a way of surrendering to my Higher Power. It doesn't mean that I have the power to get rid of my own character defects; it just means that I have a way of surrendering, of doing my best not to be in them. My Higher Power always, always lifts me out of that negative space when I make that effort and surrender.

I believe God's will for me is to feel peace, joy, and bliss. Anything less is just my ego. By the grace of God and this program, I can let that go, one moment, one character defect at a time.

For today, I act as if I do not have to respond in my old ways. I surrender those old ways to God.

CR

> "As the reality of our shortcomings
> sinks in, we can bring them, in
> humility, to our Higher Power."

Sex Addicts Anonymous, page 38

Humility is one of the gifts I have received from the program, not to be confused with humiliation. The consequences of my acting out brought humiliation, especially when needing to admit my behaviors to my spouse and others. I felt ashamed of myself and of my actions. But to me, humility has meant surrendering my pride and ego and trusting that my needs will be met in spite of my shame.

In Step Seven, we humbly ask our Higher Power to remove our shortcomings. The inventory steps provide awareness and acknowledgement of our mistakes and weaknesses as well as characteristics of ourselves that we appreciate and like. In taking the Seventh Step, I asked my Higher Power to help me let go of the behaviors, beliefs, and resentments that had fueled my addiction. I did not insist that it was owed to me. I did not expect some particular response. I did not tell my Higher Power what I needed. I simply asked for help making changes. I knew I could not do it on my own and became willing to ask for help and surrender the outcome.

I remember that surrendering my shame is one of the changes I wish to make. In doing so, I make an effort to be of service to others because I am no better or worse than they are. If I could use some help, maybe they could also.

~

For me, being humble means letting go of my
expectations, judgments, and resentments.

◈

> "If we feel overwhelmed in this way, we
> turn to the God of our understanding
> and to our program friends for support in
> facing the pain of our actions and finding
> the willingness to make amends."
>
> *Sex Addicts Anonymous*, page 48

Looking over my Eighth Step, I felt overwhelmed. My Fourth Step revealed the defect of dishonesty in all but two of my resentments and harms. I knew I needed to be honest when I made my amends, but I just didn't want to. I had been honest with myself, God, and my sponsor. I wished that were good enough, but my heart said otherwise.

Turning back to my Eighth Step, I felt different, more willing. Yes, I had harmed these people, but today I had not harmed anyone. I rested in that fact. This is how I wanted to live—not harming others.

Any willingness I felt, I rested in, and prayed God would build on that willingness. I contemplated the good that can come from making my amends. I could right wrongs I had done, clear my conscience, and have a closer relationship with my Higher Power. I felt hopeful.

I was careful not to fantasize about outcomes from these amends; I can't control the response. I reminded myself that I'm making amends for me because it's the right thing to do and because God wants me to learn and experience love. I became willing by sitting in the serenity I felt that day, and I realized that this peace will continue to grow as I do the footwork.

～

Grant me willingness to be willing.

> "Meetings are places where we can
> drop our emotional defenses and get
> honest in a way we are rarely able to
> experience outside of the fellowship."
>
> *Sex Addicts Anonymous*, page 12

Before my recovery from sexual addiction, I had built a wall around myself. I rarely shared thoughts, feelings, or opinions with others, believing that if anyone really knew me, they could not possibly love me. Not surprisingly, all of my relationships were shallow, empty, and without emotional intimacy. My fear of being open and vulnerable did not allow for honest relationships.

When I began attending SAA meetings, I heard members being honest about their experiences, struggles, and emotions. I could connect with what they shared, and their honesty encouraged me. As I began to drop my emotional defenses, to risk sharing my feelings, experiences, and struggles, I found the honest, intimate relationships that I had previously longed for but had been too afraid to allow.

As I become more comfortable sharing who I am within the fellowship, I am removing barriers in relationships outside the fellowship. I am moving slowly, and I am careful to choose appropriate people, but I am starting to see the value of being myself in this world. The fellowship is helping me drop my emotional barriers.

I can risk being open and honest with others. My relationships will deepen, and life will be richer as a result.

ରେ

> "Admitting that our willpower is
> insufficient allows us to be open to
> new ways of thinking and living."
>
> *Sex Addicts Anonymous*, page 23

I came to SAA a devout atheist, but I was in despair and willing to try anything. When I read Step Two, I felt doomed. I was expected to believe in a Higher Power that was interested in me and my life.

I came to believe the program works because I heard it in the experience, strength, and hope shared in meetings. In good faith, I acquired a sponsor and worked Step One. Without understanding who had power over my addiction, I was willing to admit that I did not. Step One left me willing to change but with nothing to fill the void. Now Step Two loomed. How could I reconcile it with my upbringing and intellectual beliefs?

Flying home from Thanksgiving with my family, I was hungry, angry, lonely, and tired. I decided to act out. On the shuttle to the parking lot, I was on my phone seeking an acting-out venue when a voice behind me said hi. It was a man I had met in the program. Robert was returning from a different side of the country, yet here he was, right when and where I needed help to save me from myself. This could not be coincidence.

I did not need to seek my Higher Power. Admitting my powerlessness and surrendering my addiction opened room in my heart for my Higher Power to step in.

~

Help is here. May I be open to it.

ଔ

> "Now I'm hanging out with people who know my secrets, and it's the safest place I've ever been."
>
> *Sex Addicts Anonymous*, page 261

Isolation has always been part of my story. Even in recovery I can find myself isolated at work and at home. In the presence of the fellowship, however, I am immediately energized and connected.

It's not surprising then that I felt even more connected while attending the SAA convention. I felt tremendous strength and support looking around the room and seeing 200 sex addicts all with a familiar problem, history, and sense of belonging. At the convention I began to form friendships and bonds that will continue to grow and develop.

One of the speakers shared the breakdown of his life and eventual surrender. He said that he couldn't believe that people would still like him after hearing his story. I could connect with his pain and shame, and I was not embarrassed to cry. Neither were other addicts in the room. During the telling of that story, all my anxieties and worries faded, and I felt the power of the program and my Higher Power coming through that speaker.

I sometimes forget the joy and energy I get from connecting with my fellow addicts. I take back my will and end up alone, battling with addiction. My greatest moments have been with other addicts, sharing openly and being vulnerable. Staying connected with others and sharing intimately is the only way I can continue my spiritual journey of recovery. It is truly a gift from God.

I was alone in my addiction, but I am deeply connected in SAA.

> "In making this inventory, we take special
> care to identify those aspects of our character
> that have caused harm to ourselves and
> others, so as to bring them forward for
> healing and change in later steps."
>
> *Sex Addicts Anonymous*, page 32

A guy in my group likes to say, "Our greatest weaknesses are God's greatest doorways into our lives. Why? Because our greatest weaknesses are where we most need God and where we find God."

I tend to run from my weaknesses, to seek comfort and safety in my strengths. But if my addiction has taught me anything, it's that my strengths aren't enough to keep me from acting out. I desperately need a pPwer greater than myself to deal with my addiction. Somehow, deep inside, I knew this. I searched for that power and begged for help. Unfortunately, I wanted that power to do magic, to fix my addiction without me having to lift a finger.

When I was finally ready to give up on magic and do my part, the question remained: how do I open myself to this power? Step Four is my answer. Through my moral inventories, I delved into my character defects and found my Higher Power right there for me, and not just for my addiction. Through the doorways of my greatest shortcomings, the best of me has been brought out by my Higher Power. That's more than I ever dreamed possible. I had it all wrong; my comfort and safety became available when I searched my weaknesses.

Higher Power, help me to be open to you where you are, and let go of looking for you where you are not.

ଔ

> "We have seen it happen time and time
> again that people relapse when these simple
> needs of living are not considered."
>
> *Tools of Recovery*, page 24

I was convinced I had to be superhuman to feel adequate. I would work past the point of exhaustion, often triggering feelings of entitlement followed by acting out. I didn't exercise, my sleep suffered, I beat myself up for any mistake, and my anxiety was high.

I had heard for years that exercise would lift my spirits. How ridiculous, I thought; that would just make me tired. But on my doctor's advice, I started a regular exercise regimen. Guess what? I started feeling less depressed, even happy at times.

So it went with many things I now routinely do as self-care. I start my day praying, meditating, and reading spiritual literature. I stop work-like activities at a reasonable hour so I can unwind, meditate, pray, and read spiritual literature before going to bed, also at a reasonable hour. Aware of my disease's tendency to beat me up, I make a conscious effort to be gentle with myself. I call people on a daily basis to break the isolation and check in with my program friends. It adds up to more self-love. I feel better and I am a better person.

I've heard that I should love my neighbor as myself. Before I made self-care a priority, I would have felt sorry for my neighbor if I had!

Self-care is an act of love. I feel better and I am a better person for it.

ରେ

"Every aspect of outreach...is a potential
lifeline for a sex addict who may not
know that recovery is available."

Sex Addicts Anonymous, page 95

For me, sex addiction is a disease of relationships
and of perspective. The more I isolate, the more distorted my perspective becomes. The more distorted my
perspective becomes, the more I isolate.

I just heard of another brother who committed suicide. His home group meets on the day he killed himself. Why couldn't he have persevered just long enough
to make it to a meeting? When I hear about things like
this, it makes me more determined than ever to carry
the message to the addict who still suffers, as encouraged by the Twelfth Step. But for someone carrying
the message to me, I might have gone that same path.

Too many times I have allowed my fear or pride to
keep me from reaching out when I wasn't sure someone needed my hand. Or I don't reach out to the silent
one at a meeting because I might be rejected. However,
I believe that my Higher Power wants me to reach out
even if it risks embarrassment, even if the hand that
reaches out is rejected. I don't want my fear or pride
to keep me from this. The feelings that haunt me if I
don't are not worth the cold comfort of not risking just
so I won't get hurt. When I reach out, it strengthens
my recovery, and it may just save a life, maybe mine.

~

*God, grant me the courage to make the gesture that
may save a life.*

> "For some, negative consequences of
> addictive sexual behaviors can become
> the motivation for change."
>
> *Sex Addicts Anonymous and the Lesbian / Gay /
> Bisexual / Transgender Sex Addict,* page 6

When I approached SAA for the first time, I was full of fear. I, like many others, was afraid of being judged or condemned by those in the meeting. I was afraid of friends and family finding out I had a problem. I was especially afraid I'd see someone I knew at the meeting. Furthermore, many of my actions were illegal, and I feared someone breaking anonymity and reporting me to the police. On the other hand, the thought of continuing the status quo of my addiction had also become terrifying.

I felt like I was being pulled between two poles of fear. On the north pole is my addiction with its fears: arrest, disease, losing those I love, and the unending misery and shame. On the south pole are the fears of recovery: being judged, losing friends and family when they learn of my problem, being vulnerable, and facing myself.

The time came when I had to weigh the two poles and decide which I feared more: my addiction or my recovery. Recovery can be frightening, and the journey is often painful, but, unlike addiction, the path of recovery offers light, hope, and serenity—an actual life. There I can become a real transgender in the real world.

Since I must face fears, I will choose the path with hope.

"If we are fearful, we can gently and courageously allow ourselves to consider the possibility of surrendering our familiar defects, trusting that our Higher Power will not give us more <u>than</u> we can handle."

Sex Addicts Anonymous, page 40

In Step Six, I learned that I wore my defects like an old, worn out blanket. It may be smelly, torn, and discolored, but it was also familiar and deceptively comforting. I learned that my defects were born out of survival and that becoming ready meant I was ready to learn new behaviors. This terrified me.

Despite my fear, I had to learn to trust God even more than I already did. I had to trust that if I gave up the false protection of the blanket—the self-loathing and fear and shame—that God would not leave me shivering in the dark. This took a while for me to do, but when I was ready to surrender and throw away that old blanket, miraculous things started to happen. I had opened the door to change.

I trust that my Higher Power will protect me today.

ᘓ

> "One of the most direct and profound
> ways we can serve other members
> is by sponsoring them."
>
> *Sex Addicts Anonymous*, page 60

Sponsoring people is a great responsibility. For me or any other sex addict to return to our old life means more agony, misery, and insanity.

A sponsor's primary purpose is to help the sponsee work the Twelve Steps. After working the steps with my sponsor, I began to sponsor others, and I have found it to be spiritually challenging. I have learned what I am capable of doing and not doing for another recovering sex addict. I have become more compassionate, direct, and honest. In addition, I have learned that I cannot keep anyone sober, including myself.

When I first started to sponsor, I wanted to save every sponsee from the life I had lived. But now, more than ever, I realize that sponsorship is a two-way street. Recovery requires the willingness to do different things, such as working the steps. If the sponsee isn't willing to do whatever's necessary to stay sober, I have to be willing to let the person be. This runs counter to my character flaw of people-pleasing, but, from hard-won experience, I am more accepting of my limitations and thus able to let go. Like all sex addicts, I need spiritual help on a daily basis to stay sober. Today, I focus on sharing my experience working the steps, and I let God do the rest.

~

Am I doing what I can to help the newcomer find recovery?

"They can help us see shortcomings that we have been unable to recognize on our own."
Sex Addicts Anonymous, page 44

Other people are a great tool for my recovery, not just my program friends but also the folks who drive me crazy.

It's easy to maintain serenity when everything goes my way, but when someone does something that bothers me, that's another story. At an SAA convention, I woke up earlier than my roommates. I decided to leave our room to meditate so I wouldn't disturb them. Surprisingly, the only public hotel space without loud country music blaring at 5 a.m. was the pool area.

The first day went great. The next morning, I slept until six, and things were different. As I meditated by the pool, I realized someone nearby was smoking. The smell of cigarettes bothers me! Then a hotel employee began cleaning loudly. Then a father and son jumped in the pool, playing and yelling enthusiastically.

I became angry. Didn't they realize this was the one place I could meditate? But it was a hotel pool, not a meditation center. My lack of peace was due to my character defect of thinking I should be in charge of the universe. Other people weren't the problem; I was.

When I lose my serenity, it reveals a character defect. It is an opportunity to discover ways I keep myself in darkness and a chance to do something about it. I became grateful that these people reminded me of this shortcoming.

Today I am grateful for people who aggravate me. They offer a window into me that allows me to grow.

ଔ

> "For most of us, *coming to believe*
> is a gradual process."
>
> *Sex Addicts Anonymous*, page 26

Early in recovery, I had a Step Two crisis. I was struggling to leave a relationship. Leaving meant leaving the house, the car, and the place where I conducted my business. I could not see how I would be taken care of if I left. I was still in the process of coming to believe that a Power greater than myself could restore me to sanity. Even though I said that my Higher Power created the universe, I did not see how this Power could solve my housing, transportation, and work situations. Somehow, I thought that my little problems were too big for God.

In coming to believe that a Power greater than myself could restore me to sanity, I had to surrender and give up my ego. I had to come around to the fact that I am no less than, nor better than, anyone else in the fellowship or on the planet. Most importantly, I am not so powerful that I am beyond God's power. The God of my understanding created the universe; how arrogant of me to think that this awesome power could not solve my life's problems!

Today my belief that my Higher Power can restore me to sanity is more than a belief. It is a deep knowing, based on many experiences, over time, of being restored to sanity, one day, one situation at a time.

~

As I see the power of God working in others' lives, I gradually come to believe that God can restore me to sanity. My problems are not too big, or too little, for a loving and caring Higher Power.

ငာ

"We don't need to be experts about life, or even
about addiction, in order to sponsor someone.
We simply share the knowledge and experience
we have gained from working the Twelve Steps
and using the tools of the program, and we
pass on the wisdom we've learned from our
own sponsor and others in the fellowship."

Sex Addicts Anonymous, page 14

Our sponsors share their experience, strength and
hope with us, they show us by example how to live in
sobriety, and, most importantly, they guide us through
the Twelve Steps. Often, we first meet our sponsors
when they share at meetings. We identify with them.
In a moment of courage, we ask them to be our sponsor. This may be our first act of trust in another human being. Over time, maybe for the first time in our
lives, we create a relationship of trust with another
person. Our sponsors encourage us, and we begin to
learn our true worth.

Our sponsors encourage us to pass this gift on to other recovering sex addicts. When someone asks us to
be their sponsor, we say yes because that is what our
sponsors did for us. We share freely with our sponsees and guide them through the Twelve Steps. We give
away the program of recovery, and we maintain our
sexual abstinence. In all things, we remember that we
are in the care of the God of our understanding.

*Do I seek to learn from my sponsor's experience and
hope? Am I willing to be a sponsor? How have I shared
my knowledge and experience with other recovering
sex addicts?*

○ℛ

> "Anonymity is the spiritual foundation
> of all our traditions ever reminding us to
> place principles before personalities."

Sex Addicts Anonymous, page 95

When I am willing to break away from all the items I identify as a part of myself—my job or profession, my wardrobe, the car I drive, my status in the community, my need to be right—I can stand in solitude with my Higher Power in absolute surrender. In this state I experience an honesty that is pure.

To be a worker among workers or to have compassion for my fellow suffering addicts brings a feeling of connectedness and completeness. One anonymous being united with others. The fulfillment that I crave is satisfied with this surrender. I experience a new sense of what is important and find my heart filled with gratitude.

～

Today, I can let go of ego based validations and experience the unity of the fellowship if I am willing to let go.

"As long as we can be honest, even a little
bit, we can move forward in our recovery."
Sex Addicts Anonymous, page 23

Because of my addiction, I have spent most of my life
lying, denying, and living a secret life. Being honest
was a convenience to be used when it suited my pur-
poses. My primary motivation was to continue acting
out and to keep that part of my life a secret. When that
way of living came crashing down around me, I was
scared, alone, and had no idea of how to save my life.
SAA and the Twelve Steps were the lifeboat that res-
cued me. All that was required was a desire to stop my
addictive sexual behavior, and honesty.

My commitment to the Twelve Steps was sincere, but
my desire and honesty were not complete. After a lifetime of addictive behavior, I questioned, even feared,
what life would be like without it. I admitted and accepted responsibility for my actions, but found reasons to explain or rationalize them. The Twelve Steps
are ordered for a reason. Recovery is a process, and I
became better at as I progressed. So it is with honesty,
especially to myself. It takes time to give up old ratio-
nalizations and self-pity. Each day I was as honest as
I could be, even if it was just a little bit. Each day the
honesty grew, especially with myself.

*God help me to be gentle with myself as I grow in my
recovery.*

ℝ

> "The God of my understanding requires
> that I take action. Just showing up was no
> longer sufficient. It was time to grow, to put
> my feet on the ground and not be a victim
> any longer. Again, <u>easier</u> said than done."
>
> *Sex Addicts Anonymous*, page 243

When I was presented with Step Eight, I thought I would just begin. *Au contraire.* I had reasons to postpone, incidents and accidents. A year later, I had not sincerely even begun.

What was stopping me? In a word, resentment. I believed I had set my resentments aside, but that was not the case. I had to become sincerely ready let go of any excuses, looking only at what I had done, not why I had done it.

This was the spadework for Step Eight. Until I became willing to do it, I did not even begin Step Eight. Willingness was the key. Once I had become willing, everything flowed from there.

~

Willingness is the key.

ભ

> "By surrendering our addiction to a
> Higher Power, we receive the gift of
> recovery, one day at a time."
>
> *Sex Addicts Anonymous*, page 1

When I hit bottom, I felt gut-wrenching shame. It was a hopeless feeling that I was trapped, being destroyed, and that there was no way out. As I attended the meetings, learned from my fellow addicts, worked the Steps, and accepted the help and guidance of my sponsor, I learned to surrender my addiction to my Higher Power.

Day by day my life improved. I learned to be present, enjoy the moment, and I found the weight of unhappiness and doom lifted from my shoulders. I learned to have love for myself, and true intimacy with my wife. Day by day, I receive the gift of recovery, and I find peace.

I feel blessed that, one day at a time, my Higher Power gives me this gift of a better life.

"Recovery, in the full meaning of the word,
comes through practicing the principles
outlined in the Twelve Steps."

Tools of Recovery, page 2

I found that, for me, humility is feeling equal to the rest of the limited and human people who are trying to do and be the best they can. I'm not less than anyone else; I'm not more than anyone else. I accept my human limitations, striving for alignment with my Higher Power's will for me.

It also means accepting that I cannot do some things on my own, and this means accepting being loved and being worthy of asking this Power greater than myself for help. I ask my Higher Power for help, and I let go of the outcome, whatever it may be, without deceiving myself into thinking I can control it, and trusting that it's for sure going to be the best for me. This feels riskier than many of the destructive risks I took in my addiction because it involves deep trust.

This act of trust brings me to my "intimacy, deeper-heart section" where nobody was allowed for decades. I thought this room would be forever out of reach, but I realize that the Steps melt the locks, shake off the dust, and gently polish those rusty places in my heart—in healing, in hope, in grace.

Today I'm willing to try to stay open, honest, vulnerable, willing, teachable, patient, faith-filled, trusting, and be a positive-risk taker.

～

God, grant me courage to take the biggest risk—learning to trust again. If it's okay, I will start with you.

ભ

> "Gratitude is an attitude we
> choose for living well."
> *Tools of Recovery*, page 23

My overall wellness today includes the healing power of coming back to the present moment. Whether I am drawn to a place of fear about the future or shame about my past, being fully surrounded by the gifts of today helps me come back to the place where I truly live: right here, right now.

The tool I use to shift me back to here is the gratitude list. Whether writing down or meditating on all the gifts of my sobriety today, living in gratitude is one of the most spiritually fulfilling ways I live in the present. A connection with my Higher Power, my friends in recovery, my family, with myself, or with a total stranger can be gifts I can celebrate today.

~

Today I will remember to thank my Higher Power for all of the gifts of sobriety. I am grateful.

ca

> "We learn to accept that reality is not
> tailored to the limitations of self, and
> that hardship and loss are as valid a
> part of life as joy and pleasure."
> *Sex Addicts Anonymous*, page 58

In my addiction, I thought the universe had wronged me in some way, allowing me to suffer more hardship and loss than I believed was my share. This sense of entitlement kept me out of the solution for years. In recovery, I have found acceptance. Who am I to determine whether hardship and loss are fair?

In recovery, I see a blessing I could never have imagined. The hardships and losses are bridges that have brought me the tools and serenity to help others going through similar situations. Grief enables me to comfort others. Abandonment reminds me to be present for those I love. Being a sex addict gives me the ability to help those still suffering, and remind them that recovery is possible through working the Twelve Steps. Our hardship and loss, paradoxically, can ultimately bring joy to ourselves and to others.

Embracing my struggles and pain, and helping others has brought another, even greater gift. I found a connection with something that I had buried and forgotten many years ago—my heart.

~

Today I can embrace hardship and loss as schoolmasters, preparing me to benefit the people I will come in contact with in the future, including myself.

❦

> "Unacknowledged fear is often a pervasive
> aspect of our addictive thinking and behavior."
> *Tools of Recovery*, page 21

Whenever I find myself at a loss for how to do the next thing before me, I feel at once the lure of drowning the peril in addictive practice. I may fear the tedium of doing the dishes. Or, I may fear my own stupidity—not knowing how to solve a task, which I have, in fact, not even yet defined, for goodness sakes! Postponement is the garment I don to meet the emergency—and then another postponement and then another—until I am stifled under the weight of them all. Sleep, entertainment, and certain virtuous evasions also work. But, for this addict, the ideal way of eluding of fear was sex addiction. It was exciting, it was diverting, and it was time-consuming.

If I wake my day with a sober eye, sit and visit with God, pray for God's care, ask for blessings on others, and make a couple of program calls, then I find the energy to allow myself to breathe. I find the high and active energy of serenity. In short, I find I can postpone procrastination. I find I can walk towards my fears. And when I do, those fears are often not dragons at all, but worms, if that. I can read my day as it comes, as its pages turn, as it really is; and I am well.

~

The program helps me stop stalling and start striding forth, head held high.

ଙ୍କ

> "The stigma for female sex addicts can be even
> greater than it is for male addicts, just as it was
> for female alcoholics in the early years of AA."
>
> "A Special Welcome to the Woman Newcomer"

Is it odd or is it God? My acting out was predominantly with men, yet I found myself the only woman at an SAA retreat and conference. It was a joyful and deeply peaceful recovery space to focus and connect with my program and the fellowship. All the people (men) were easy-going and appropriately friendly, and I identified with every share, story, and workshop I experienced.

My recovery from sexual addiction is God-driven. Who but God would come up with such a powerful opportunity? Having so many men to share this path of recovery teaches a new, healing way to connect that surpasses anything I could have imagined for myself.

~

I am grateful for the opportunity to experience and form relationships that are based on our mutual desire to stay sexually sober and to grow spiritually.

ભ

> "Step Six builds on the recognition that
> our malady has roots that run deeper
> than just our acting-out behavior."
>
> *Sex Addicts Anonymous*, page 40

I knew for a long time that something was wrong with me, but I could not pinpoint what it was. I wanted my life to be different, but the deeper I got into my sex addiction, the less I was willing and able to look at my part. Naturally, my life continued to get worse. However, once I got into recovery, I instinctively knew there were underlying problems I had never dealt with. I also knew that, if I faced them now, I would find the help I needed and maybe some serenity.

I trust the program (that is, God) to help me deal with what I found out about myself from doing Steps Four and Five with my sponsor. As uncomfortable as it was, I saw the pain I had caused, and I knew I could not run away from my problems anymore. In trusting the process, I had to be willing to do different things to get different results.

Getting down to the causes and conditions helps me change my life for the better. Today, I am no longer under the delusion that my life will get better because I wish it, or if I just stop acting out. I know today that I need fundamental change in my life to find the happiness and serenity I so desperately sought when I first came into the program.

～

Help me to face myself, that I may come to face this life as the gift it is.

ଷ

> "We can live life on life's terms, without
> having to change or suppress our feelings."
> *Sex Addicts Anonymous*, page 61

Sometimes the present moment feels too annoying, too boring, too lonely, too blank. Sometimes a tension builds up without my even noticing it, and then all I know is that something has to change, and it has to change NOW! On cue, my addictive imagination rushes in, promising a numbing release from the tension, or a quick, exciting spectacle to pull me away from all this. If I choose to use the tools of the program—call a program friend, read literature, repeat a slogan, take the first three Steps— I am often relieved of the addictive impulse, at least for the moment. And that feels like a miracle.

But honestly, the present can still be filled with that same tension or sadness that had triggered the addictive impulse in the first place. A different sort of imagination can rush at that point —an imagination that takes the guise of self-care, but which is really just another desperate attempt to change how I feel. I may, with great sincerity, ask for new ways of thinking and acting, for the removal of my character defects, for a spiritual awakening. Anything! But what I really want is to change the way I presently feel. Which for some reason I can't abide.

I heard a wise old-timer say that when her feelings are too much, she throws up her hands and prays: "Higher Power, please just be with me, right here in these lousy feelings." Simply hearing her say this made me relax. I have practiced her suggestion, and little by little, the desperation has lessened. I have found a growing acceptance and peace around my present, whatever feelings it may contain.

My caring Higher Power will never turn away from me because of how I feel.

ça

"It is the feeling that we are never good enough,
that there is something wrong with us, that
we are bad people. Shame played a part in the
addictive cycle, undermining our resistance to
acting out."

Sex Addicts Anonymous, page 8

Sometimes, after a disappointing date or a party where I felt out of place, I would get a panicky empty feeling in my body, sometimes accompanied by thoughts like, "I'm alone," or "I don't belong anywhere." I used to call this feeling loneliness—not the sharp pang of missing someone or feeling homesick, but a kind of intolerable dread that I imagined would break me apart or dissolve me into nothingness.

As a sex addict, it seemed obvious that the solution to this "lonely" feeling was to seek company, either through a hookup or a pornography-aided fantasy. After all, I often thought, wasn't "seeking companionship" the answer to loneliness?

I now believe that the fearful sensation I get when I feel rejected or isolated is not so much loneliness as shame: a sense of being socially and personally defective. Acting out sexually could not relieve this feeling; it could only distract me for a short time before the shame came back as strong as ever.

Daily working the program of SAA in recovery with my fellows has allowed me to experience a new sense of value. I look at the trajectory of my daily interactions—more compassionate and increasingly accountable—and I can feel the iceberg of my unwarranted shame start to melt.

~

Higher Power, help me to see myself not as I fear, but as I am today—a work in progress, an accepter of grace, and a person willing to change.

> "Best of all, I now see my life and experience as a gift. My past, as awful as it was, is a tool that I can use to help others with similar problems."
>
> *Sex Addicts Anonymous*, page 212

That statement reminded me of prison and just how far the disease of sex addiction had taken me. Early in my recovery, I used that awareness to build resentment toward myself in a most destructive way. I wanted to know how and why I had gotten so sick and completely out of control. The fact is, it doesn't matter; all that matters is what am I willing to do about it today.

It has only been through working the Steps and practicing the principles of the program that I have finally forgiven myself for that horrible bottom of prison and insanity that had become so familiar to me even after getting into the program. That feeling of prison and the experience it gave me has a completely different power now. I use it for my recovery; I share it with newcomers in a way that alerts them and me of just how bad my disease will get without the program of Sex Addicts Anonymous in my life.

I can be grateful for those terrible reminders from my past—they help me remember why I'm here, and they help me help others.

ᏀᏒ

> "Our experience has shown, however, that the shame and compulsivity associated with sexual addiction can best be healed by sharing openly with others who understand and accept us as we are."
>
> "A Special Welcome to the Woman Newcomer"

Having made the decision to walk through the door, sit in the circle, and face fourteen men, I was not ready to share my story as a woman addicted to sex. Don't misunderstand—I knew I was in the right place, but I did not know how to share my own shame and guilt. So I listened. What I heard was that, regardless of gender or specific behaviors, these men had the same feelings of desperation, regret, and remorse that I had. But more importantly, they had hope that through the program, the Twelve Steps, and sharing, they could stay sober one day at a time. It started with a declaration, "I am a sex addict," and I was welcomed and accepted.

To me, recovery is an artistic gift to the world. It allows me to make beautiful life music. I make the world better by practicing my daily recovery plan.

I have since found my voice and openly share in meetings. By sharing thoughts and feelings that could lead to acting out, I bring them out of the shadows of secrecy and into the hope and strength of the group. Openly sharing helps me stay accountable to the group and my Higher Power. By sharing my own experience, strength, and hope, I offer the newcomer the same acceptance I was given.

～

Higher Power, help me remember that I am worthy of the acceptance given by my brothers and sisters in recovery, and that by sharing, I help myself and others.

September 30

"In recovery, we rediscover our creative side."
Sex Addicts Anonymous, page 65

My creativity is the best gift that God gave me. To use it makes me more authentically myself. To spend my time in this way is to allow God's investment in me to be made worthwhile. When I can creatively be of service to my fellows in this program, I am participating in the transformation, not only of my own life, but also of others' lives. What greater privilege could there be!

Let my creativity continue today to help me be of service. It is what I am meant to do.

"If you are uncomfortable speaking at meetings,
we strongly encourage you to talk with a
member one-to-one after the meeting, to get
a sponsor, and to use the phone list between
meetings. Remember: <u>you</u> have a right to speak."

"A Special Welcome to the Woman Newcomer"

I learned from a young age to be seen and not heard.
I began to silence my feelings by acting out sexually. In
my addiction, my shame kept me even more silenced
and isolated. Eventually, I forgot I had a voice and the
right to use it.

In recovery, I am finding the voice I lost so long ago.
When I share in a meeting, give encouragement to a
newcomer, or call my sponsor, I am using my voice
and I like how it sounds. In recovery, I can speak and
be heard.

Today, I will remember I have a right to speak.

℮

> "We feel victimized. And each time we play the
> event over in our minds, we feel victimized
> again. From this victim attitude, we often
> slip into an attitude of entitlement."
>
> *Sex Addicts Anonymous*, page 34

Resentments are contamination from the past that block healthy choices in the present. Memories of abuse linger and can be transferred to today's interactions with people who have not abused me in the past. Sometimes I hold these resentments like trophies from old battles. I wonder at times if these resentments aren't my most valuable possessions, because I can hold onto them even when I lose many other valuable relationships or possessions.

The phrase "just for today" can be a reminder that I only need to work my recovery for this day rather than for the entire rest of my life. It can also remind me not to shape and view today's choices and personal interactions by the worst experiences of my past. By letting go of resentments, I can free myself of contamination from the past so that I can be a loving person today in all of my interactions with others.

Rather than make my resentments my most valued possession, I can let my relationships and daily interactions provide me with valuable memories and relationships that are loving and kind.

~

Letting go of resentments is not a loss, but rather a freedom to be in the present.

ca

"Another gift of the program is the
emphasis on developing a new way of
life through a spiritual awakening."
Sex Addicts Anonymous, page 135

I recently read the Twelve Steps in a meeting. I've read them a hundred times, but Step Twelve spoke to me in a way I desperately needed that night.

After months of freedom, I was again struggling with obsession and cravings. Sure, I had just moved across the country, bought a new house, changed jobs (stay-at-home parent), and recently become pregnant with twins! The pregnancy was taxing and I had tapered off some medications for the health of the babies. But, I was working my daily practice, attending meetings, and using the tools. So, what was I doing wrong?

When I read Step Twelve that night, I realized that it promises a spiritual awakening as the result of working the steps. It doesn't say, "You will never again experience obsession or cravings, you will never face challenges to your sobriety, and your life will be easy and carefree." No, it doesn't say any of that.

So what does that mean for me? Right now, my spiritual awakening means that my Higher Power is with me every second, provides everything I need to live sober in reality, no matter what, and loves and accepts me exactly as I am. I am good enough, I have enough, and I do enough, always. Period. Those core truths allow me to walk through anything that life brings with strength, courage, and hope.

~

Today I can engage my life thanks to the spiritual awakening I found through the Twelve Steps.

October 4

> "We can't recover alone."
> *Sex Addicts Anonymous*, page 78

I spent a great deal of time and effort trying to quit compulsive behaviors and obsessive thoughts. I was convinced that if I tried hard enough, if I willed hard enough, I would be able to quit. I even thought that, if I got religion, I would be able to quit. So I dove in—I began a decade of religious learning.

I was still alone, though. I was alone in my thoughts, and isolated in my religiosity. On my own, I defined the religious path, and even God. Recognizing that I was still unable to quit, I added mysticism and meditation to my religiosity, convinced that I just needed an enlightenment experience.

What I needed was a spiritual awakening, all right. The problem was that I was trying to do it alone, and define the awakening myself. During my religious study, I once read that "a prisoner cannot free himself." I cannot free myself from the prison of my addiction. Hitting rock bottom and seeking the program of Sex Addicts Anonymous, I found recovery in the unity of a fellowship committed to the common welfare of each addict.

Helping others is the foundation of my recovery, not demanding that recovery, or others, conform to my desires, opinions and preferences. My personal recovery is tied to the recovery of others, and I realize this in a united fellowship.

~

Am I willing to vest my personal recovery with the recovery of others?

ଔ

"We need faith and strength to carry out
God's will, for we cannot always foresee the
results of the actions we are being led to
take, or take into account all possible effects.
Our belief that our Higher Power knows
what is best for us, and that more will be
revealed, grows as we work this step."

Sex Addicts Anonymous, page 58

The idea of powerlessness often escaped me until I
reached the Eleventh Step. Prior to this, I was terrified
of my lack of personal power and had little faith there
was any power greater than my compulsion to act out.
As I remained abstinent and worked through the pre-
ceding Steps of SAA, I slowly began to awaken to a
connection with a Power greater than myself. Along
with that came the power within me to choose more
and more aspects of sobriety. As that power grew within me, so did the layers and lengths of my sobriety.

As I continue my spiritual practice through prayer,
meditation, and service, I am filled with a sense of
purpose and clarity around the proper use of my will.
There are so many choices available to me that were
previously non-apparent. I am aware that all this
comes from my Higher Power and that my life is a work
in progress.

~

*Through practice, I open to the power to carry out
God's will.*

> "The real fears of life which we did not face—
> losing a job, financial insecurities, death of
> a loved one, rejection by someone significant
> in our life—seemed far, far away."
>
> "The Bubble"

The slogan "From Shame to Grace" is used many times in our literature and printed on our medallions. This process is one I will continue to practice everyday of my life. When I was young, medicating uncomfortable emotions was a survival skill I carried into adulthood in the form of avoidance, denial, and procrastination. I believe this skill was needed to move past deep emotions of fear, anger, and unworthiness from my youth. Each day with the support of the fellowship of this program, I gain more and more confidence that the God of my understanding will give me the guidance I need to move from shame to grace. My part is willingness.

God, grant me the power and strength to face my fears, both real and imagined, one day and one fear at a time.

> "In the long run, the most effective amends
> we can make to others and to ourselves
> is in our commitment to recovery."
>
> *Sex Addicts Anonymous*, page 51

The time span between hitting my bottom and the moment I spoke the last word of my amends to a close loved one was nine long years. I will always recall the evening I first spoke a confession of my actions through an insurmountable veil of pain and regret. I shared my worst addictive behaviors and I could barely stand to look at the tearful face across from me.

Backed by a loving God, years of recovery, and the help of my sponsor, I revealed to a loved one the regret I had felt over my actions and how much I wanted my life to reflect the changes I sought.

The program then gave me gifts I could not have foreseen. Following my explanation of feelings, hope, and a desire for continued spiritual growth, it was time for my loved one to share. What I received was, at first, hard honesty. Pain, disappointment, and betrayal were words used that cut through me with the hot blade of truth. But I also heard the words change, healing and even proud.

I now found myself able to accept positive words of affirmation and encouragement from another. Giving and receiving respect, love, and thankfulness had become natural as I began to walk a path of living amends.

A living amends continues to gently surround me with serenity—a gift from the program and my Higher Power.

"No one can judge whether a person is a sex addict, or make decisions about someone's fitness for membership in SAA. In order to belong, all we need is a desire to stop addictive sexual behavior. Since desire is subjective, it can't be determined <u>by anyone</u> but ourselves."

Sex Addicts Anonymous, page 81

I began my journey knowing what was wrong but not how to fix it. Something drew me to search online for "sex addiction." The first web site was SAA. Any other number of sites could have appeared, but something greater than me led me there.

I was skeptical at first, certain there was some requirement that would make the answer unobtainable. I thought, "Surely I had to believe in a specific religion. Or perhaps this was only for those worse or less afflicted than I was." But no, there it was, printed in black and white—all were accepted, and that included me. It mattered not what Higher Power I believed in, nor how I had acted out. All that mattered was that I knew I was a sex addict and had the desire to stop.

O Higher Power, show me the way to be accepting of your wisdom and of all those who come before and after me into the program.

> "Our closest relationships may offer
> the most challenges to our honesty,
> compassion, and integrity, but we are often
> rewarded beyond our expectations."
> *Sex Addicts Anonymous*, page 61

Today a fellow addict called and told me she is having contact with a man she used to live with. In the past she has asked the group and me for support in staying away from this man. I am afraid. I am afraid someone I care about is behaving in a way that has a history of hurting her.

She did not call for permission; she doesn't need it. She knows that the program we follow requires rigorous honesty. She knows that, if the group is to be an important tool in her recovery, she needs to be honest.

She also knew what my reaction would be. Honesty is a two-way street. If I am to be of any use in her and my recovery, I need to be honest with her. I respectfully told her I was scared that she was setting herself up to be hurt and to relapse. I also reminded her that, regardless of the outcome, I still care about her and she is always welcome at the meeting.

Perhaps her relationship will be different this time, perhaps not. But I know that, if her anguish returns, she has a safe place and caring people to turn to. I also know that, if this relationship turns out to be something delightful, she has people who will celebrate with her.

Today I will remember the importance of honesty tempered with humility.

October 10

> "And by sharing our recovery, we offer
> hope and show that there is a way
> out of our common addiction."
>
> *Sex Addicts Anonymous*, page 60

Before coming to SAA, I did not believe recovery was possible for me. I had the addict notion that I was terminally unique. In SAA, I came to understand that such thinking is egocentric and that a spiritual awakening is in store for me if I follow the Twelve Steps.

Someone had to be there to carry the message to me. The first meeting I went to was vacant—no one was there. Fortunately, I did not give up and found a wonderful network of people at other meetings. And, fortunately, the person I asked to sponsor me said yes! I am eternally grateful to her for sharing the message of recovery in word and example.

Now I have the opportunity to carry the message of recovery to other sex addicts. What a great joy! I talked to my first sponsee last night. I know it is imperative that I carry the message to her—not for her sake, but for mine. In working Step One with her, I remember what it was like, and in so doing, remember that, no matter how long I'm sober, I can act out again in a flash because I am a sex addict. Carrying the message keeps me sober and helps the still-suffering addict find a solution. What an ingenious program!

~

I am filled with the joy and awe of carrying the message to the sex addict who still suffers. Thank you, God, for this blessed opportunity!

"We allow ourselves to be known when we take this risk."
Sex Addicts Anonymous, page 25

I am a specialist at taking risks, something I share with others in SAA. We've boldly gone where no one in their right mind would want to go. I practiced these skills daily in the business of sexual addiction, putting myself and others in danger, enshrouded in a fabric of lies and secrets. At the same time, I hid the real me for fear of exposing myself and becoming vulnerable.

After years of successful recovery, I noticed that sobriety had become interlocked with risk avoidance. Recently I came across a spiritual principle: the universe wastes nothing. The God of my understanding wastes nothing. I welcomed this idea into my life, but it meant I must unite new conviction with action in order for it to be real for me.

Healthy risk-taking was born there. I risked falling back in love with my wife and even saying, "I love you." What a new kind of outing oneself! I left my lifelong profession only to have it given back to me at the insistence of others. I am sustained in the sometimes-frustrating work I do, seeing it all as part of taking healthy risks. I try new ideas and approaches and I no longer fear making mistakes. I have also learned to let go of losses and successes, and embrace being in the moment.

Taking healthy risks builds trust.

ॐ

> "For our group purpose there is but
> one ultimate authority—a loving God as
> expressed in our group conscience."
>
> *Sex Addicts Anonymous*, page 79

If, before I got into recovery, somebody had said I would encounter God in a room full of sex addicts, I would have thought they were crazy. But the language of the Second Tradition makes it plain that the conscience of our groups is one way our Higher Power expresses love to us.

What is our "group conscience?" On the surface, it means the decisions our groups reach together, after discussion and consideration. But group conscience has a larger meaning, too. It refers to the collective wisdom, strength and compassion that arise when we join together.

Certainly each of us has his or her own opinions, viewpoints and ideas. Just as every member has experienced sex addiction in a unique way, everybody's recovery program looks different. Yet when we meet together, I experience something far larger. That something is a shared willingness to become healthier, happier people—together. There is a shared commitment to support and accept each other, just as we ourselves need support and acceptance. We work together to make our meetings a safe, loving, healing place.

So when I look beyond the surface, I directly encounter a loving Higher Power in my group, always there to welcome, affirm and guide me.

May I see God more clearly in the love and support of my group.

ఐ

> "Effective amends are as selfless and sincere as
> we can make them, with no hidden agendas."
>
> *Sex Addicts Anonymous*, page 49

Service work and acts of love are living amends that are also incredible validations to my spirit. I can bring joy and love into the lives of others as an amends to my past where my fear-filled actions brought suffering and pain.

When I have done a thorough housecleaning and know in my heart that my actions are grounded in love, I can freely give my time as a means of assisting someone along the path of their life journey. The added benefit for me is a boost in my spirit, an increased degree of self esteem, a stronger connection to my fellow human beings, and ultimately a stronger connection to my God.

Today I will commit to at least one anonymous act of kindness for the sake of love.

Ê

> "To be intimate is to let go of control and begin
> to have trust—trust in another person, trust
> in ourselves, and faith in a Higher Power."
>
> *Sex Addicts Anonymous,* page 72

While co-workers, classmates, cousins, and neighbors were forming life-long friendships, I stood on the relational sidelines like a spectator and watched. My fear of rejection and deep distrust of others and myself paralyzed me, so I made excuses for remaining distant and disconnected. I beat myself up for wanting to connect with others and when I passed up opportunities to be intimate, I beat myself up for feeling lonely. I couldn't win. Eventually, I settled for something short of intimacy—dehumanizing and pain-numbing compulsive sex that left me more isolated, empty, and lonely than before.

I did not start attending SAA meetings to get close to a bunch of sex addicts. Life pushed me into these rooms, and though I started to see myself in other members, I resisted the idea of reaching out to others or accepting their offers to reach out to me.

But I kept coming back. Very slowly, I began looking forward to seeing my friends and hearing about their struggles, progress, and feelings. I learned to listen without judging and to share my heart without shaming others or myself. These skills have not just helped me connect in meetings, but they have allowed me to find the path leading to something that I spent my life simultaneously chasing and avoiding: intimacy.

~

When I reach out to others in the program and they accept me, they remind me that I am worthy of acceptance and intimacy.

ca

> "In particularly challenging moments,
> committing to our sobriety for just an hour
> at a time is what we may need to do in
> order not to give in to our impulses."
>
> *Tools of Recovery*, page 11

About six months into SAA recovery, I was riding my bicycle along a canal. Exercise had become an integral part of my recovery program, but after six months, I was no longer riding the so-called pink cloud of recovery. I was about to be tested.

My bike route took me close to an adult establishment that I had frequented in my addiction. Suddenly, I felt the "imperious urge" to stop and go in. I knew that going in would inevitably lead to my inner circle. The compulsion was visceral, powerful, and terrifying. I was powerless to resist, so I asked God to help me.

When I asked God for help, I sensed the suggestion to continue on my bicycle route for another fifteen minutes. Then, if I still felt the urge so powerfully, I could return to the current spot, which would take another fifteen minutes, and see how I felt.

By the time the first fifteen minutes had passed, so had the urge. God had relieved me of my craving. This was a turning point in my recovery. I learned that, with God's help, my cravings would pass, that I did not have to be a slave to them. That fifteen-minute God break between craving and action has become a fundamental tool of my recovery and has saved me from relapse on many occasions.

~

God, grant me the willingness to pause and ask for help before acting on my craving.

> "Emotions are an important part of my life today. They help me to understand myself and my relationship to the world."
>
> *Sex Addicts Anonymous*, page 212

One of the most toxic factors feeding my addiction was my avoidance of emotions, especially unpleasant emotions. I avoided painful emotions because I feared they would never go away, but I also shunned positive emotions because I was afraid they wouldn't last. I told myself that it is better to be cynical so I won't be disappointed, and I numbed everything by acting out. Now, noting what emotions I have felt throughout the day helps me understand my deeper emotional life.

In recovery I have learned to accept all my emotions, knowing they will all pass. I have also learned that feelings are not facts, but they can show me how I perceive the world. The critical tool for me is to acknowledge them to myself and to someone else—someone who might understand or at least accept me as I am.

I can share my feelings in meetings, finding others who understand and have also faced such feelings. I can call my sponsor and find support, encouragement, and insight by facing and sharing my emotions. I can call other program members who will also have hope and strength to share. When I do this, I practice emotional sobriety, and I become more connected to the person I lost in my addiction—me.

I accept all my feelings, trusting that I can face the painful ones and enjoy the pleasant ones.

ରେ

"Each group should be autonomous
except in matters affecting other
groups or SAA as a whole."
Sex Addicts Anonymous, page 77

Each meeting that I attend is self-governing, with different formats, different readings, and different methods of sharing. Each meeting, however, is distinctly identifiable as an SAA meeting, clearly following the SAA Steps and Traditions.

Since we have the autonomy to develop our meetings in different ways, each group can meet the individual and collective needs of its members. As I attend various groups, I marvel at how the variety of formats can still maximize the recovery goals of each member within the greater framework of SAA. My home group is my basic vehicle for recovery, along with working the Steps with my sponsor and sponsees. As long as we retain our adherence to the spiritual principles of the recovery program, each member will find an appropriate recovery path.

~

Within the spiritual principles of the SAA Steps and Traditions, I thank God for providing me a multitude of formats to achieve my own sexual sobriety and to carry the message to other suffering sex addicts.

ℭ

> "We address our sharing to the whole
> group, not to one or more individuals."
> *Sex Addicts Anonymous*, page 12

Crosstalk: somewhat vaguely defined, often disturbing, sometimes well-intentioned. At a meeting, I shared a struggle I was having, ending my share in a manner that put myself down. Immediately afterward, someone shared that he used to put himself down in conversations, but that a girlfriend who was breaking up with him had lambasted him with this knowledge, doubtless among other observations. The person took it to heart, and now he no longer did that, and boy, was he grateful! I felt ashamed.

Was this crosstalk? It sure felt like it to me. He never referenced me directly, but it seemed clear who he was talking about, and that everyone else knew. For months afterward, I felt uncomfortable any time he and I were in the same room. When I shared, I was careful not to give him any grounds to single me out again. The irony, though, is that I became more aware of my self-defeating behavior, and began addressing it.

So, was this crosstalk? Was it harmful? It was certainly painful and disturbing, but ultimately, some good came out of it. It also gave me a new appreciation of the potential effects—good and bad—of crosstalk.

Even with best intentions, if I engage in crosstalk, it can have a chilling affect on another's feeling of safety. I will make sure I share only my experience.

~

I am the subject of my shares. Help me temper what I say with respect and consideration.

> "For example, work may require that an employee use the Internet, or an SAA member might live with other people who subscribe to an online service. If we had legitimate need for Internet access, we found it helpful to be accountable to a sexually sober member of the fellowship."
>
> "Sexual Sobriety and the Internet"

Filtering software, passwords, using only public Internet access—these are some of the methods I used to try to control my compulsive sexual use of the Internet. I found that, until the compulsion to act out had been removed, there was always a way around these controls.

In the end, the answer to acting out with the Internet was, for me, the same as any other acting out—a spiritual experience that relieved me of the compulsion to act out. The spiritual experience started when I was able to admit complete powerlessness and surrender my addiction to a power greater than myself.

Victory comes from complete defeat.

ର

"The Ninth Step can be a project of some magnitude."

Sex Addicts Anonymous, page 49

In my Ninth Step to my wife, I took responsibility in detail for the damage and danger I had caused. To my son and daughter, then in their mid-twenties, I was less specific. My wife and I worried that full disclosure could harm them.

Last year, I learned that my daughter had discovered years ago that I had been seeing prostitutes. She kept this secret for years. Here was more damage I caused, damage I had never imagined—the shock she must have felt, the uncertainty and pain of holding such a dark secret for so long. I knew I owed her amends, again. I made amends and hoped she would see that she had no part in it, that it was all on me. I still don't know the full scope of her pain because she broke down, sobbing throughout my amends.

I then realized I owed more amends to my son. Either he knew, and I owed him amends, or he did not, and the rest of us now held a secret from him that could only erode our family's trust.

My son responded immediately to my amends. He was angry. I struggled. Why wasn't he glad to hear my honesty? Why didn't my wife tell him how wonderful our relationship was now?

It helps when I remember that successful amends are defined by honesty, thoroughness, and thoughtfulness, not by the reactions of others.

～

With my Higher Power and my sponsor's help, I accept responsibility in this project of some magnitude.

"When we were active in our addiction, it was difficult to stop our <u>sexual</u> preoccupations."

Sex Addicts Anonymous, page 5

My acting out degraded my life and wounded those I care about, but I think the greatest loss from this disease is years of precious time. My life is rich and there are never enough hours in the day to do everything I want to do. When I was in my addiction, those same opportunities were there, but only a fraction, if any, ever got attention. I was preoccupied with sex: planning, acting, regretting, dreading discovery, fabricating lies, avoiding people and places, wondering why I couldn't stop, blaming others, etc.

I calculated the time I spent just downloading porn (not planning or disposing or using or worrying), and it came to well over a year of my life, a year compulsively chasing something that harmed others and me in its creation, pursuit, and possession. If I add the time spent worrying and obsessing, it comes to years, many miserable years.

Thanks to my Higher Power and the program of SAA, I can now be present in this moment. This present, fleeting moment is all I truly have, a gift. If I look within and around, there are opportunities for gratitude, reflection, learning, love, creating, sharing, receiving... the list is endless. All I have to do is choose to be here, now, and ask my Higher Power for guidance.

～

This is a beautiful day when I ask for guidance and do what I can.

ଔ

> "These last two years, I have felt more hurt than at any previous time in my life. But I do not feel the guilt and shame and lack of control of actively <u>living</u> out my addiction."
>
> *Sex Addicts Anonymous*, page 305

I used my sex addiction to run from difficult feelings, situations, and life in general. In retrospect, I realize that I had been ducking emotions since elementary school. So in many ways, I spent years limping along, resembling a child emotionally.

It all started to change in recovery. After some time, I began to feel my Higher Power urging me to take some healthy but scary risks to further my recovery. As an exercise in willingness, I did these intimidating things.

One of them was service work. Although I am good at some things, human interaction has never topped the charts. Service work brought dealings and sometimes conflict with other addicts. I was, and often am, anxious. Things didn't always go well. I made mistakes and felt terribly uncomfortable at times. I have had to grow.

I soon realized that this growth stuff wouldn't be easy or painless, especially for this emotional adolescent. In fact, looking at the word "growth," I noticed that "ow" sits smack in the middle of it! It would seem that the workout slogan "no pain no gain" applies to recovery as well.

It is absolutely worthwhile. I now have good friends, a sense of community, and relative acceptance of and comfort with myself as I am today.

~

I will take the "ow" in growth over hiding from life any day.

"I am encouraged to focus, not so much
upon not acting out, or even avoiding
middle-circle behaviors, as on practicing
a new way of living that brings wholeness
and integrity to everything I do."

Sex Addicts Anonymous, page 135

The first task of my recovery was to eliminate sexual behaviors and thoughts that harmed me and those around me. I spent the first year of my recovery saying no to myself a lot. With the help of my sponsor and group I was able to stop acting out. After a while it was no longer a struggle to stay within my boundaries. Although I was in a relationship, I decided to be celibate. I learned to say no to sex altogether. It was an important lesson and I'm glad I learned it. Later, I realized that just saying no was not the answer to my problem.

Although I was celibate, I was still a sexual person. My next lesson was to learn to say yes to healthy sexual thoughts and behaviors. I found this more difficult than merely not having sex. I wasn't even sure what healthy sexuality was. I did a lot of talking, thinking, and meditating. I also had to be willing to take some risks and make some mistakes. After a while, I redefined my boundaries in terms of what is good for me as well as what is bad for me.

Today I will remember to say yes to healthy things.

"To be restored to sanity is to rediscover the
spiritual nature we have always had but which
was hidden by the insanity of our disease."

Sex Addicts Anonymous, page 26

I discovered that my powerlessness runs much deeper than my acting out, that the behaviors are but a symptom of a greater spiritual disease. I thought that I was self-reliant, but self-reliance is a myth, the biggest lie of all. For decades I unwittingly made sex my highest source of power, relying on it for comfort, satisfaction, worth, meaning, security, control, you name it. Replacing my creator with something created as my Higher Power is the spiritual sickness that fed the acting-out and -in and made chaos and misery of my life.

My life has shown that I am designed to depend upon a higher power. My only choice is over which power I will turn to. Sexuality is an important part of human experience and a gift from my Higher Power, but sex was never meant to solve my problems. Working the program of SAA, especially the Twelve Steps, gives me tools and freedom to choose dependence on the Higher Power of my understanding.

After so many years serving a compulsive obsession, I can easily fall back into that pattern if I fail to maintain my spiritual condition. The symptoms will surely resurface and will again run and ruin my life. I suffer from a spiritual disease. Fortunately, it has a spiritual solution.

~

Today I choose dependence, not on an obsession, but upon my creator.

⚮

"One way in which God's love has been
evident is the support I have received from
friends with whom I have been honest."
Sex Addicts Anonymous, page 269

I have long had difficulties with authority figures, and
in some part of my mind, God is the ultimate authority
figure. When I think of all the suffering in this world, I
may ask, "Where is God?" So I also bring trust issues
with God.

However, through recovery, I have developed a sense
of gratitude. I am especially grateful for the recovery
relationships I have come to cherish. These friends accept me, no matter how crazy I am at that moment.
They listen to me without judgment, and trust me to
do the same for them. We share experience, strength,
and hope; and we heal.

Program friends are gifts from God. All I have to do is
be open to the opportunities, accept them with gratitude, show up, and be honest. Here is tangible proof
that God wants to see me healed and is willing to use
me to help heal others. What more proof do I need that
God truly loves me? God wants healing, and the healing grows out of a beautiful dance among my friends
and me.

~

When I am open to the gifts God is presenting me,
I experience healing and discover gratitude. I am
grateful to be grateful.

> "Throughout this process, we carefully examine our motives, always balancing the willingness to take full responsibility for our wrongs with care and concern for the well-being of those we have harmed."
>
> *Sex Addicts Anonymous*, page 50

I entered recovery in another program. In my first Eighth Step, three former partners topped the list. The perceived wisdom at the time was that my amends would be to stay out of their lives. Twenty years later, in SAA, my current Eighth Step was fairly short. My new sponsor asked me if there were any from earlier Eighth Steps still un-amended. I immediately mentioned the three former partners. My sponsor suggested I start drafting letters to them. I consented adding, "But we're going to burn the letters and throw the ashes in the ocean, right?"

His response was, "Well, actually, I was thinking you might try to get their contact information while you're drafting the letters." I was dumbstruck and felt a strong resistance rising up in me. However, I'd been in recovery long enough to know that the resistance was the disease talking. I had also learned, the hard way, to follow my sponsor's lead on all amends.

I agreed and began, haltingly. I started with the letters—that was emotionally easier. I had no contact with these good people for almost twenty years. Over the next month, one of them pinged a website where I am a charter member, and the other two contacted me! I didn't have to search for contact information—it was handed to me. Needless to say, with my sponsor's guidance, I gratefully made the amends.

They're right—miracles do happen. All I have to bring is willingness and an open mind.

**"What lies have you told to conceal
your sexual activity?"**

"First Step to Recovery"

Maintaining my addiction usually led me to covering my tracks by lying to my family, coworkers, and friends. As the compulsive nature of my sexual addiction engulfed my life, I compounded the lies on top of previous lies. Ultimately, when I forgot the specific details in the chain of lies, I had difficulty separating fact from fiction, and I hit rock bottom. That is when I decided to come clean with my conduct and speech.

As I traveled through the Steps with my sponsor, I learned rigorous honesty as I strengthened my relationship with my Higher Power. With the guidance of my sponsor, I learned, one step at a time, to take responsibility for myself. I noticed that my conscience, that "still, small voice within," got stronger, too. I became accountable to myself, to my sponsor, to my group, and to my family and friends. Others, who heretofore suffered from my lies, slowly saw my growth in the truth and began trusting me. I will learn honesty through practice, and I will marvel at how much my memory improves!

Today I will practice honesty as an underpinning of my total recovery.

ଔ

"SAA is open to all people regardless of age,
race, religion, and gender or sexual preference."
Getting Started in Sex Addicts Anonymous, page 3

I was hoping I'd outgrow my sex addiction as I got older. I mean, lower hormone levels have got to help, right? And guys don't look at me as much as they used to, which is sometimes a relief—when I'm in avoidant mode, anyway.

But it only took one, and I was off and running. Anorexia? What's that? Lower hormone levels? Not so you'd notice. Even at my advanced age, I managed to get into one of the unhealthiest relationships of my life. There I met some of my worst character defects mirrored in my would-be partner. Right in my face.

So, okay, I get it. I'm not going to outgrow addiction any more than I can outrun it or push it away. And denying my sexuality just drives me deeper into the sexual, emotional, and social isolation of avoidance. And just to be clear, isolation is very different from my natural and healthy introverted self.

Sex addiction doesn't respect age any more than it respects any other human characteristic. I can't outgrow it, I can't outrun it, but I can be in recovery from it.

～

Since I am a sex addict, for today, I choose recovery.

> "As addicts, we are accustomed to seeking
> instant gratification. But in recovery, most
> of us experience gradual improvement
> rather than sudden transformations."
>
> *Sex Addicts Anonymous*, page 44

Part of the humility in asking my Higher Power to remove my defects is willingness to practice daily patience and complete trust. Hanging a sign that says, "Believe with all your heart," helped me remember and affirm this.

As an addict I am comfortable in my familiar ways of thinking: black and white, all or nothing, now or never. To be willing to experience little baby steps of growth requires willingness, trust, an open mind, and surrender. I need to practice these on a daily and hourly basis. I'm learning to adopt new ways of thinking—the ones that actually work.

In this process, I see the infinite mercy and love of my Higher Power. God's gentleness teaches me I'm respected, worthy, and trusted today. I'm enjoying and trusting my Higher Power's pace, timing, and rhythm.

God's gentleness teaches me I'm respected, worthy, and trusted today.

ભ

"We may, out of a genuine concern for the fellowship, want to take control of what happens in our groups and service committees."

Sex Addicts Anonymous, page 80

As I observe myself in action, I have been amazed to discover a complete lack of self-acceptance coexisting with incredible arrogance. How can this be? Because I feel intense inadequacy and insecurity, my addict overcompensates with self-defeating attitudes such as self-righteousness and a complete self-assurance about what others should do with their lives or their recovery. It never ceases to amaze me.

I have observed that, the more sure I am about being right, the more careful I need to be about saying anything. I try to keep in mind that everyone present has a Higher Power, and I am not it! The group as a whole has the guidance of a loving God, as expressed in our group conscience. If I can open myself to the guidance of a loving Higher Power and to the process of group conscience, my urge to control outcomes passes. After the urge subsides, I often see the wisdom of the group conscience. I see how things worked out just fine, usually for the best.

Maintaining connection to a loving Higher Power brings serenity and leads to emotional sobriety. Since acting out had been a way of coping with uncomfortable feelings, maintaining emotional sobriety now helps me maintain sexual sobriety.

~

How important is it? Good question!

"While the inner circle relates to behaviors
which keep us in permanent isolation and
fantasy, the outer circle refers to behaviors
which help us move out into the real world."

"Three Circles"

At first, I didn't think I belonged in SAA. I brought
many negative pre-judgments, and I was embarrassed
when we would go around the room to share. After
several months and with the help of my sponsor, it
started to sink in. I now look forward to meetings and
feel empty if I miss one.

Each time I admit my inner-circle behaviors and how
they have affected my family, I feel a deeper sense of
regret for the pain I have caused. Because I am no
longer hiding from this disease and its effects, I am
free to establish positive counterparts: my outer circle.
I wasted so much time and energy acting out. Now I
am concentrating on my outer circle with a renewed
awareness of its power.

For me, hobbies that I enjoy give me pleasure and
a sense of accomplishment. Putting my thoughts into
writing reveals abilities I had buried and neglected.
Meaningful, honest conversations with my partner
bring us closer. Prayer and meditation reveal that life
is good. Acknowledging both the inner and middle circles keeps me aware.

As I tend my outer circle, new rewards and possibilities appear.

Just for today, I will live in my outer circle.

⚪

"In taking the First Step, we admit that our
addiction is destroying us, and that we are
unable to stop it. We surrender, raise the
white flag, and accept that the battle is over."

Sex Addicts Anonymous, page 22

Many of us sought a remedy for our compulsive acting out behavior long before we finally surrendered.
We were convinced that if only we could figure it out,
we would do whatever was necessary to be rid of our
affliction. We only needed to dial it back some, so
that it didn't completely overrun our lives. Many of us
wasted precious years trying to control our addictive
behaviors. These attempts at control led us through a
maze of failed experiments and trapped us in the insanity of trying the same things over and over with the
same failing results.

The day I realized willpower and knowledge had little or nothing to do with sobriety was the day I understood powerlessness. Sobriety was not something I
could get for myself. I was forced to seek help outside
myself. Sobriety is a gift of mercy and grace we receive
from our Higher Power just because our Higher Power
loves us. I didn't do anything to deserve this mercy
and grace. In fact, I did everything not to deserve it;
and yet, I received it. And in the process of receiving
undeserved mercy and grace, I learned a little something about the Higher Power I would come to know
better.

~

*I don't have to know how or when or why or for how
long. My Higher Power's grace is sufficient.*

"I was opened up, and for me that
was the secret of spirituality."

Sex Addicts Anonymous, page 123

My Higher Power has never forsaken me. I walked
away because it was the best I could do. Little did I
know I was walking in a circle, right back to my Higher
Power.

People expressed bewilderment that parts of my life
were in such chaos while other aspects were ordered
and conventional. I doubt they knew that I couldn't
make sense of what seemed so natural to others, that
my life was in unfathomable turmoil, and that I was
paralyzed to change. I knew I was powerless before I
knew the power's name was sex addiction.

In SAA, I found courage and support to merge my
splintered lives into one, open, honest life. By allowing my Higher Power in, I affirm that I am not merely
molecules, I am a spiritual being, created to love and
be loved.

I've been heard to say, "I'm ready to dig in and fight
the addict!" My sponsor smiles and gently ushers me
toward letting go instead of fighting. Have I ever won
a fight with the addict? Instead, I use the love of my
group, my Higher Power, and my sponsor to gently
shine a light so bright that there are no shadows. This
is one way I become open and allow the scattered fragments of my being to unite.

For the first time in my life, people know me, and that
makes their love even more powerful.

~

*Being honest and vulnerable allows me to love and be
loved for who I am.*

ભ

> "With anonymity as our foundation,
> we dedicate our efforts to something
> much greater than any one of us."
>
> *Sex Addicts Anonymous*, page 96

One important reason for anonymity is to avoid cults of personality. I have found that certain people tend to exhibit leadership qualities, while others tend to be followers. This dynamic can lead to the dominance of some personalities with others providing a following.

Anonymity can help us avoid forming such cliques or groups. When nobody in the group is a leader, or when leading the meetings is rotated through the membership of the group, the hierarchy is flattened.

I have also seen attempts to achieve status by announcing in meetings who a sponsor is, as if we could achieve a higher level of recovery with a popular sponsor. Comparisons are sometimes made between the people with the longest continuous abstinence as a method of achieving rank.

While I may be interested in appearing to be more experienced, or to have all the answers, it is important for me to remember that I am a sex addict just like the others in the meeting. Like all of us, I need to surrender my ego and grandiosity, and ask for help. The spirit of anonymity and humility provide a framework for leaving the trappings of status and ego at the door of the meeting room.

~

Our primary purpose is to achieve abstinence from our compulsive sexual behavior. By keeping my ego out of the message, I provide a clearer message of recovery.

ભ

> "The First Step is a matter of honesty and
> openness—in the shadows of aloneness we
> can trip and bury ourselves in shame."
>
> "First Step To Recovery"

After acknowledging I was an addict and beginning recovery, I believed my years of dishonesty were over. Yet after a slip, my pride of reputation and fear of failure prevented me from telling the truth. Over the next year, I lied about my sobriety and acted out in secret. The more I acted out in secret, the harder I worked to save face. And I tried everything except honesty to make up for lying: working the steps, speaking at meetings, sponsoring, and attending retreats and conventions. I sought solace in others' approval, but the problem was (and always has been) that deep down I don't approve of myself.

As my shame from acting out and lying heightened, I ultimately feared failing at life more than losing my reputation. Thanks to my dishonesty in program, I discovered what rigorous honesty means: telling the truth to my sponsor no matter the consequences; honoring the trust and love of others; not twisting reality to gain affection and approval. And I learned that rigorous honesty is not an achievement but a daily practice.

When I came clean, I was not kicked out of the program or abandoned by my sponsor and friends in the fellowship. It was painful to share my dishonesty, but today I can hold my head up in meetings because my slate is clean.

~

I'd rather be courageous about my lies than cowardly about the truth.

> "Instead, we come to accept that making mistakes is a fact of life and an essential part of recovery. Step Ten says 'when we were wrong,' not 'if we were wrong.'"
>
> *Sex Addicts Anonymous*, page 55

There may not be a simpler step in all the Twelve Steps. We are asked to quickly admit we are wrong when we are wrong. We are all human. We are all going to make mistakes. We used to strive for perfection, but the myth of perfectionism is shattered by the time we reach this step. Making mistakes, acknowledging our errors, learning from them, and earnestly trying to avoid making the same mistakes in the future is what we strive for now. And what if we make the same mistake again? We celebrate the fact that we're still human, repeat the steps above, and keep moving forward.

The freedom to make mistakes and the ability to clean them up immediately are practices we learn in recovery. What a gift! What a gift it is to be healthier, more responsible, productive contributors to society. And we know that, when we make a mistake, we have this most wonderful tool with which to clean up our mess, however large or small. At this point, recovery just keeps getting better and better.

I cannot be perfect, but I can work the Tenth Step to the best of my ability.

> "It isn't always easy to know when we've
> been wrong. We may not discover the
> truth about our behavior until later."
>
> *Sex Addicts Anonymous*, page 54

Impulsiveness, a cunning component of my sex addiction, manifests itself in various ways. Therefore, it is vital that I review each of my days with either my sponsor or another member of the fellowship because I can only amend a potentially harmful behavior if I am aware of its presence.

Verbalizing the actions and decisions of my day with another person allows any middle-circle behaviors to be brought into the light. Some of the day's good ideas that I acted upon can swiftly reveal themselves to be foolish once they have been reflected on with a trusted friend in the program.

The actions I take each day propel me towards either shame or grace. I accept that I will make mistakes along the way, but through vigilant implementation of the Tenth Step inventory, I can promptly adjust and redirect the path I trek. With the help of my Higher Power and program accountability peers, I am learning to be honest, open minded, and willing to receive feedback. I am moving toward grace, serenity, and recovery.

SAA has given me an incredible tool kit. I will use these tools today.

"I cannot restore myself to sanity, so my
recovery and my life depend on a combination
of surrender, footwork, and grace. God gives
me guidance in my life if I look for it."

Sex Addicts Anonymous, page 178

I used to think that, if I could just get a few areas of
my life to go the way I wanted, I could control the whole
thing. Fortunately, that illusion got me to the rooms of
SAA and the door to a new way of life. Walking into my
first meeting was the beginning of a practice that has
never let me down.

I started in desperation. Now my experience and my
desire for a new way of life strengthens my relationship with a loving and much Higher Power. When I am
willing to relinquish the perception of control and the
insistence on knowing the answers or the outcomes, I
receive a gift of freedom.

Today, I trust that God has the answers.

> "There are some behaviors which, if not
> addressed, will eventually lead us back to our
> inner circle. We call these 'boundary behaviors.'"
>
> "Three Circles"

When I pray each morning to be shown God's will for today, I call upon my own higher self as well as consulting with a power greater than myself. Prayer and meditation are part of my routine upon awakening, and I can carry them with me throughout my day.

When a difficult person or situation crosses my path, I can make a choice to respond from my recovery or to react in my disease. Learning about my boundary behaviors is an ongoing process, and I am lovingly shown how to recognize these old habits that I no longer need in my life. If someone flirts with me or crosses my physical boundaries, I can pause and maintain my spiritual connection. When thoughts surface that, in the past, seemed like a good idea, I can check in with my Higher Power to determine what fits for me now.

Using prayer and meditation throughout my day to stay spiritually connected allows God a consistent opportunity to communicate with me. People are God's language, and my Higher Power talks to me through those who challenge me, as well as through sponsors and other program members. It's possible that someone on my path who seems like an obstacle may be a gift sent to help me learn more about my boundaries.

Higher Power, please show me what you want me to see, tell me what you want me to know, challenge me where you want me to grow, and carry me through all that I do as I go through this day.

ം

> "Through our experience of God's care
> and the love and care we find in the
> SAA fellowship, we learn the importance
> of being gentle with ourselves."
>
> *Sex Addicts Anonymous,* page 65

When I love my recovery friends and their imperfections, I am, sometimes uncomfortably, reminded that they may, in fact, love me and mine. Even after years with these people, I still cast my eyes away as I lay my failings and flaws bare before them. But always, when I return my gaze to their faces, I find in them what I still struggle to find in myself.

They are proud of me and of my honesty. They understand my pain. They do not forgive me for my weakness, my defects, or my deficiencies; they love me—unconditionally, and without reservation. And, purely because of who they are, I must accept this love as the truth. No longer can I insist that I am loved due to familial obligation or performance; no longer can I dismiss words of support and affection as being disingenuous. They are under no obligation to care for me, and have no reason to except that they do.

It is wonderful to be loved, but it is painful, too. Knowing that others love me more than I feel able to love myself is a bittersweet balm—another seeming defect that I cannot deny. But knowing I am loved, even as my weaknesses are exposed, gives me hope that I will one day love myself as much as I love my friends.

~

In loving others and letting myself be loved by them, I open the door to loving myself.

"With [Step One] we recognize that we have a
disease, not a mere weakness or character flaw,
and that we are powerless to change this fact."

Sex Addicts Anonymous, page 23

I entered recovery dazed and confused. I did not understand why I could not stop the compulsive acting
out behaviors which, at best, threatened to ruin my
life and, in the worst case scenario, kill me. My mind
seemed to be insane and my body appeared to be on
autopilot. My best thinking got me into more trouble.
My worst thinking used my shame and guilt to confirm
my beliefs about myself. Where was my will power?
Where was my inner strength? Why couldn't I stop?

As I began to understand the character of my disease, I thought to myself, "Cancer patients don't rely
on will power or inner strength to recover. They follow
a prescribed treatment program and make that program their number one priority in order to stay alive."
I would do the same thing, I thought. I had seen others
who did it—"Sex Addiction Survivors" I called them.

Like other people with life threatening diseases, it
was not my fault I had the disease. It was, however,
my responsibility to treat it. My road to recovery began with the realization that I am powerless over this
disease. But in that powerlessness, I found a Power
greater than anything I could have imagined.

*I treat this disease as I would any other life
threatening disease. I follow the treatment program
and I recover.*

"As we continued working the Twelve
Step program, we experienced the return
of personal integrity and found a new
sense of purpose in our lives."

"Sex Addicts Anonymous: A Pathway To Recovery"

Ever since I can remember, I felt something ominous looming in the future that I must prepare for, some sort of destiny that saw me playing the hero—a world to save, a war to fight, an enemy to overcome. Maybe I was watching too many action movies or reading too many comics. Maybe I was escaping the reality of watching my alcoholic father beat my mother on a regular basis. Whatever the case, I felt an urgent need to prepare for this future battle of epic proportions.

Now I am in the rooms as a fully surrendered sex addict, and one day it hit it me like a truck. This is the battle I was anticipating. This is what my subconscious foresaw. After thirty years, my eyes are open to my purpose on this earth. Generations of addicts and a family history of shame and repression have culminated in this moment of clarity.

Stopping this long line of self-hatred and shame is my great war. It's an inner struggle, much harder and more intimidating than I could have anticipated. The cycle stops with me, here, now. While I may not have planned for this moment, I am spiritually ready to see my destiny through to the end. All the essential resources I need are here in SAA. What could be more noble than stopping this cycle of shame?

~

I am open to whatever path my Higher Power intends for me.

"We also list people we harmed by our
neglect, by not 'showing up' for our lives."
Sex Addicts Anonymous, page 47

My character defects had led me to behaviors I never would have thought possible on a sane level. Many of those behaviors involved a victim, either directly or indirectly. The Eighth Step asked me to create a list of those I had harmed. In Step Nine, with the guidance of my sponsor, I would someday make amends from my heart, either face-to-face, in a letter, or indirectly without the injured party knowing.

My son was among those in my direct amends list. I recall my hand shaking with shame as I wrote his full name. While I had not missed his entire childhood, I clearly recall the many disappointments caused by my absences—absences when I was acting out. With encouragement from my sponsor and fellow recovering addicts, and the heart-felt presence of a loving God, I completed a list that was honest despite the pain of creating it.

Later, I stood across from a strapping young man who was two inches taller than me. I imagined that the shadow he cast was not of a man, but of the little boy whose father was absent too many days. I acknowledged my part, and expressed my regret and my sincere desire to make it right. I couldn't hold back the tears as we hugged and I told him how important our relationship was.

~

In showing others that I am not my old behaviors, I can heal old wounds and regain the greatest part of living—my relationships with others.

> "Admitting our wrongs to God opens the door
> to change within ourselves. We have found
> that God will help us find the courage and
> honesty we need in <u>order</u> to work this step."
>
> *Sex Addicts Anonymous*, page 37

Coming from active addiction into recovery, I was intimidated by the idea of being honest about the exact nature of most things about me, much less my wrongs. Experience has taught that being honest in the First Step brings gifts like trust, openness, surrender, and even some courage—courage to continue the exploration.

Working the Fifth Step with my sponsor helped me distinguish the things I had done from my true self. I did those things and I am responsible for them, but those actions are not my true self and do not spring from it. Rather, they reflect a diseased part of me. Seeing the things I had done as separate from the true me gave me hope that change was truly possible. Through this process I received the gift of more courage—courage to continue the journey into understanding and growth.

Working Step Ten on a daily basis helps me see more of the things that I do which are not in line with my values or my recovery. Seeing the nature of those wrongs helps me choose other actions, including Step Seven. As a result, upon reflection, I can see even more courage in my life—courage to live life on life's terms.

Higher Power, help me find the courage to be open to change.

ᏅᎥ

"When obsessive thoughts came into my mind,
I learned to say the Serenity Prayer or the first
three steps over and over, like a mantra."

Sex Addicts Anonymous, page 296

Recently, while driving through a small town, I received a speeding ticket. I had inattentively not seen the posted speed limit. Immediately, I felt embarrassment and shame, and began to emotionally kick myself for being so stupid. On the way to my destination, I repeatedly prayed the Serenity Prayer, trying to let go of the burden. It helped, but I knew I was still carrying some of the shame.

When I arrived, my hosts asked how the trip had been. I wanted to just say fine so they wouldn't know what had happened. However, I wound up saying, "Fine, except for one incident," and shared about the speeding ticket. They shared a similar experience they had been through. I no longer felt ashamed, carrying my own guilty secret. Instead, I felt connected and affirmed. Praying the Serenity Prayer and sharing what I was ashamed about with others helped me to let go of the toxic shame that could have sabotaged my recovery. I am grateful that in the SAA program, I have a safe environment to share my life and thereby break the cycle of shame that kept me bound all those years.

If I feel stuck, burdened, or trapped, the Serenity Prayer is a good place to start the path toward freedom.

ଓଃ

"The power of this step is in the asking, not in the result. Asking is a very powerful act—it expresses a deepening surrender on our part."

Sex Addicts Anonymous, page 44

I have helped many sponsees work Step Seven. I ask them to write their own Seventh Step prayer. Nearly every time, they write a beautiful prayer that leaves out one important part—the asking. They are always shocked when I point out that they forgot to ask God to remove their shortcomings. Sometimes they write it again, and again forget to ask.

In the past, I have asked God to help me get rid of my defects of character, or I have hinted around by describing the great pain and suffering my shortcomings are causing, but I would never simply ask my Higher Power to remove them.

Now, when I remember, I simply ask God to remove my character defects and trust that it will happen, perhaps while I am asleep. Picturing it this way allows me to leave myself and my power out of it. Remembering that the removal is God's action, not mine, also helps me be more willing for my Higher Power to do so.

Why is the asking so difficult and so powerful? Perhaps because it expresses a deepening surrender on my part. Because I tend to take things back, I usually have to ask more than once. So what is my part? What do I do after asking God to remove my shortcomings? I surrender the outcome by moving on to Step Eight.

Today I will simply ask. Nothing more, nothing less.

"Sex addicts like to rationalize a behavior by
saying I'm only hurting myself....First, you
have to ask yourself why is that okay?"

"Abstinence"

I have asked myself many times, "Do I really belong
in SAA?" The main excuse I use to prove I don't belong
is that I'm not hurting anyone but myself. I am single
and have no family. No one knows my secrets; therefore they don't exist. This is wrong.

I do belong. My secrets are hurting me. When I come
into the group and share my secrets, I realize the power they have had over my life. I see more clearly the
hurt that my addiction caused. When I go to meetings
and talk to other addicts, I get in touch with how much
my spiritual nature has been damaged by acting out.

I've heard it said that if a heart doesn't have a place
to break it gets harder. Sharing openly with other sex
addicts softens my heart and reminds me of where I
belong.

*Today I will reach out to someone in my program
because I belong.*

ℂℛ

> "Practicing the Tenth Step helps us
> continue to grow in self-acceptance, self-
> awareness, and rigorous honesty."
> *Sex Addicts Anonymous*, page 55

My wife and I are moving across town. We approach the process differently, and we butt heads on occasion. She thoughtfully plans and packs each box. I throw stuff in a box until it's full, fill the car, and go. I can organize it at the new house. To me, she makes this job even tougher. We clashed again Saturday morning, and then I headed to the old house for more stuff.

Alone in my car, I surrendered my internal harangue and simply acknowledged my disappointment in her, me, and the process. I started to ask my Higher Power for help and in a flash, the realization hit that she is not trying to undermine anything. She is bringing her most conscientious approach to this daunting slog. I then saw that my impatience and intolerance were making this challenging task truly unpleasant—for us, me, and especially her. I was the one making it stressful!

This program taught me that it doesn't matter who's right. If I have behaved poorly or thoughtlessly, I need to own it and make amends. When she got to the house, I stopped work. I acknowledged her thought-fulness and apologized for compounding her stress. I followed with tolerance and support for her efforts. It was probably the best thing I had done in weeks.

By the way, I moved three boxes for every one she moved, but now I can't find anything!

For today, help me be open, and help me think twice before I react.

"It is to be expected that from time
to time, you will feel irritated with
people both in <u>and</u> out of SAA."

Tools of Recovery, page 32

My two children many times will say, "He's irritating
me!" My canned answer has always been, "Only you
can allow yourself to be irritated." However, I often find
that I don't take that advice myself.

I've found it beneficial, if not essential, to remember
that I can't control the actions of others. I can only
control my reaction to the situation (God, grant me the
serenity...) The first SAA prayer I learned is often the
first one I forget in dealing with life on life's terms.

When I remember to use the Serenity Prayer, I sometimes get immediate clarity on what's mine to be concerned with. Even when I don't get that immediate
clarity, I often find that I've gotten through a difficult
situation with my serenity intact.

~

*God, help me listen to the wisdom behind the Serenity
Prayer, and let it not be only a chant after my
meetings.*

"Some suggest calling three people every day in order to build and maintain a support system."
Tools of Recovery, page 10

When I first came into the program, I didn't understand why there was such an emphasis on phone calls. Who has time for that, I thought. Isn't going to meetings enough? And who would want to hear from me anyway?

Fortunately, I was so broken that I was willing to try anything. So I started making three program calls a day: one to my sponsor and two more to friends in the program, folks who were struggling, or newcomers.

Amazingly, it worked! The very act of picking up the phone and calling someone breaks the bubble and establishes a connection with someone else. It takes me out of my head, which can be a dangerous neighborhood. And often, unexpectedly, it enables me to be of service.

Despite my early fears, no one has ever asked me why I'm calling. Every time, my calls are met with compassion and gratitude. I can't tell you how many times the other person has said, "I really needed a call. Thank you."

It's important for me to make program calls every day, even when things are going well. It's like I'm exercising a muscle, getting it ready for the day when acting out begins to look appealing again. Those are the days when the phone is at its heaviest.

Recovery is a team effort. By making program calls, I can lean on my brothers and sisters in the program, and let them lean on me.

ର

"It does mean that you are a female pioneer
in recovery from sexual addiction."

"Special Welcome to the Woman Newcomer"

Some years ago, we would have been hard pressed to find more than a few women here and there in our program. That is changing rapidly. However, it is still quite common for only one or two women to be in any meeting and yes, it can be scary, especially in the beginning.

I keep in mind that sex addiction is an equal opportunity disease, affecting all genders and every walk of life. Both men and women in the room are there for a common purpose—recovery. I also keep in mind that there is nothing between me and the door, and if I feel triggered, frightened, threatened, or uncomfortable in any way, I am free to walk out.

Normally, however, I find that at least one man in the group goes out of his way to make me feel welcome and safe. Pretty soon, another woman will come along and I can be the one with open arms.

~

God, keep me strong in unfamiliar situations and a
blessing to others when I can.

ଔ

"We need faith and strength to carry out God's
will, for we cannot always foresee the results
of the actions we are being led to take, or
take into account all possible side effects."

Sex Addicts Anonymous, page 58

Some talk of getting out of the driver's seat and letting God take the wheel. My experience indicates a different version of that analogy for my spiritual journey.

For me, God is in the passenger seat with the itinerary and maps. I am in the driver's seat waiting on the next opportunity and suggestion. I must watch the road, operate the vehicle, and check the rear-view mirror. However, God promises to direct and lead me, one turn at a time, to a place that is good for me, and promises to never abandon my vehicle. God also encourages me to enjoy the view whirring by. God gives me opportunities to pick up other travelers and give them rides until they find their own cars, and shows me when to slow down and let others pass or turn in front of me.

As an addict, I'd rather park the car, interpret the directions, and predict where I'm going and when I will get there. I may even get into others' cars and tell them how to drive. This effectively halts any forward progress and always irritates the other drivers! When I get back into my own seat, start the motor, and listen for God's directions, I am in the right place.

~

I have to drive my car, but for today, I will let my Higher Power be the navigator on this journey.

"As addicts, we were often all too ready
to shirk responsibility and allow others
to take care of us, clean up our messes,
and attend to the necessities of life. In the
program we learn instead to be accountable
for ourselves <u>and</u> our recovery."

Sex Addicts Anonymous, page 87

Early in recovery I considered the Seventh Tradition to be the money tradition. However, it is much more than money; in fact, it doesn't even mention money.

We all come to the fellowship with gifts and talents. Sharing these with SAA allows our groups and the organization as a whole to be fully self-supporting. Local groups need fellowship members to serve as officers, set up rooms, make coffee, and welcome newcomers. Intergroups may need a fellowship member to help design and manage their website. Conferences and retreats need workshop presenters and speakers, and service opportunities abound, including KP duty, registration, and on-site sponsorship.

Of course, our groups and the organization need money to operate. When the basket is going around, I sometimes find myself balking at how much to put in. Two questions I was taught help me with this process. (i) How much would it be costing me if I were still practicing my addiction? (ii) How much is this new life worth to me?

Any act of service allows a group or event to operate without outside contributions and this allows the message of SAA to be carried to the still-suffering addict.

I will honor the Seventh Tradition with my time, talents, and treasures.

ೞ

"We trusted that God would not give us more than <u>we</u> could handle."

"Recovery from Compulsive Sexual Avoidance"

When I came into recovery, I was overwhelmed. I had recently been separated from my husband, who had been unfaithful. I didn't think I could make it without his help, particularly as the parent of a young son with special needs. The first night our son went to spend the night at dad's new apartment, I picked up a man and brought him home. I was caught by my husband and six-year-old son because my son had had an asthma attack, and the medication was at my house.

I became increasingly depressed. I stopped my own self-care and that of my son. I almost lost custody. I believe God took care of me. A friend who was a sex educator listened to my panic over my acting out and responsibilities. She suggested recovery from sex addiction and introduced me to the woman who became my sponsor.

My sponsor suggested I write out the Serenity Prayer and call her daily. We worked together sixteen years before she died of cancer. My life has improved, as has my son's. My son says my sponsor saved his life because she saved mine.

～

I have faith that my Higher Power will never give me more than I can handle. Today I will trust in my Higher Power to take care of me.

&

> "Autonomy goes hand in hand with self-
> respect and a new sense of freedom, as
> we take responsibility for our groups
> and the carrying of our message."
>
> *Sex Addicts Anonymous*, page 83

As a practicing addict, I thought highly of myself, strutting around like I was king of the world. I was so convinced I was in control, that I thought I should control others. I spent countless hours daydreaming of my rise to political power. I wrote political platforms, manifestos, and even constitutions.

Two failed marriages and fifteen years later, through the program of Sex Addicts Anonymous, I am just coming to learn what control really is, and it is not control of others. When I turned my will and my life over to God, I was taking control of my life for the first time. I was told that I am not responsible for my addiction, but that I am responsible for my recovery. In Sex Addicts Anonymous, the Steps are not forced upon me; they are offered as suggestions that have worked for many others. As I've seen my recovery strengthen and grow through working the Steps, I've come to know freedom and gain genuine self-respect.

With Tradition Four as a guide, the same holds true for our SAA groups. The ISO of SAA does not compel groups to operate according to any specific protocol, though it may offer the experience of other groups. Our groups form and operate autonomously. As the group carries the message of recovery, it too experiences freedom and self-respect.

We are united in purpose, while free to serve in diverse ways.

> "We do not judge members who
> relapse, because we know that we are
> all powerless over this disease."
>
> *Sex Addicts Anonymous*, page 67

I recently discovered why I constantly judge others and compare myself to them. It stems from fear. Some part of me believes that if I can find out how I am different or better than someone else, I will be protected from whatever struggles they are currently facing. Of course, this is irrational. It is a habit that runs extremely deep, though, and I fall into it on many occasions.

Not too long ago, a fellow recovery partner relapsed. I felt like the two of us had been walking on water together, staying sober one day at a time by the grace of God. But the waves of addiction pulled my partner back under. I was paralyzed with fear for several days. The voices of my own disease chimed in, "You're next."

I started judging and comparing myself with my friend, trying to find the fatal flaw that led to relapse, a flaw that I didn't possess so I could be safe from that fate. I couldn't find anything different about me to explain why I was still sober and my friend was not. Just like everyone else, I am human, susceptible to all things human, and powerless over my disease. While it is not for me to judge others, perhaps my depending upon God a little bit more helps me stay sober.

For today, I accept my humanness and find guidance and courage in my Higher Power.

☙

> "The steps are the spiritual solution to
> our addiction—leading not only to a life of
> abstinence from our addictive sexual behaviors,
> but to a fulfilling life of service to our brothers
> and sisters in recovery and beyond."
>
> *Sex Addicts Anonymous,* page 99

When I first came through the doors of SAA, I was at my bottom, but I still hoped there was some way I could hang on to my behaviors without having to change completely. I hoped my new friends in SAA could show me how I could keep doing all my old tricks, but without unmanageability, pain, and consequences. I hoped I could learn how to have control over my addiction without actually giving anything up. Wasn't that what recovery was all about?

My new friends told me to keep coming back, to get a sponsor, to work the steps, and to do service. They handed me the format so I could lead the meeting, and suggested chores I could do, like keeping the key or updating the group listing in the directory. When I was ready, they invited me along to intergroup meetings and retreats.

I discovered that my Higher Power's plan for me is much bigger than my old deluded dream of managing my addiction. Through working the steps and doing service, I get a life full of love and purpose, friends, and true intimacy. As a newcomer, I thought this program would offer no more than a way to enjoy sexual thrills without consequences. I discovered that the greatest gift of the program is love.

~

*I thank God for my friends in recovery and the
opportunity to be of service to others.*

ca

"'Live and let live' reminds us that tolerance is an important quality to develop. It liberates us from being at the mercy of <u>other</u> people's behavior."

Tools of Recovery, page 33

I have always prided myself on my tolerance of others, but it bothers me when my spouse shows intolerance with me. Why can't she just get over it? It has been more than three years since I relapsed, and she has known about my addiction for twenty years. I am working my recovery through the program as I experience it, not as she envisions it. I wish she were accepting of the progress I've made rather than frustrated at my imperfection. I'm not the only one who's hurting here. My addiction caused her great pain and maybe even trauma. I can no more dictate how or when she will be healed than she can with me. I heard somewhere that the one with the greatest need comes first. If I am truly tolerant of others, I can start at home with compassion and patience for my spouse's pain and healing. If she's in pain, I can practice patience and acceptance and try to ease her suffering if she wants help. If she's abusive, I can gently set healthy boundaries. How would I like to be treated as I struggle? How might I react to others' struggles if I were well and not afraid?

I bring tolerance into my life by practicing it.

⚙

"Many of us experience a period of intense emotional upheaval and physical discomfort when we stop our addictive sexual behaviors. We call this withdrawal."

Sex Addicts Anonymous, page 66

A crisis led me to SAA, but the thought of living without my drug of choice was terrifying, and withdrawal was tough. Those with experience promised that the pain would pass, but that only I could travel this rough road. They added that they would be right beside me on the journey.

I agreed to a period of celibacy in our marriage. Initially, it felt forced and frightening, but again, the program offered hope. My sponsor gently guided me through tears and fears with the wisdom of one day or one hour at a time. He said the overpowering emotions were a great beginning to a life of emotional sobriety. When my addict chattered that I'd never stay abstinent, I comforted myself by developing my outer circle. As I began working the steps, I felt help from a Power greater than myself. Amazingly, I began to appreciate the gift of celibacy, and trust that I could be okay. The withdrawal symptoms subsided and my mind began to clear.

This principle applies to later experiences as well. If I stay sober and strive to learn from challenges, I will come out the other side healthier and happier. Thanks to this program, I can be gentle with myself as I journey through times of healing, learning, and growing.

I myself must walk this path, but I don't have to do it alone.

"My life is by no means perfect, but the tools
that I have received from our program have
given me the confidence and courage to
achieve goals I had <u>never</u> thought possible."
Sex Addicts Anonymous, page 214

Prayer and meditation can take many forms. In some situations, I can find great relief and strength in a short visualization I run on my mental screen. I'm sitting on the bench—dressed, practiced, and waiting. Our team is on the playing field. I so want to play. In the vision I say, "Coach, put me in. I want to play today."

That scene leaves me centered, peaceful, patient, and looking for an opportunity to be of service to my Higher Power and to the people I will encounter today. My will is switched from designing the world as it should serve me, to how "Coach" can put me in the game of life to get the most for our team today. Awe fills me every time I play this mental video.

I am grounded in my decision, today, to turn my will and my life over to the care of my Higher Power. The trust and confidence from being rightly aligned leave me wondering about my Higher Power's will for me in each situation. Outcomes include being joyful much of the time in the day, patient in traffic or with kooky drivers, able to listen attentively, and curiously drawn to investigate surprises, opportunities, and forks in the road.

Today, I'm patiently waiting for God's will for me to unfold. It's all opportunity.

ᔆ

> "The practice of making phone calls,
> even when you don't have any particular
> reason, will make it easier when you need
> support. If you are having a difficult day,
> consider using the _phone_ to do service."
>
> *Tools of Recovery*, page 10

Like many, I have struggled reaching out when I'm hurting—I didn't want to burden anybody. I had been sober in recovery for several years, active in step work and service; but there came an evening when I started to unravel. I was pacing the floor in my little two-room apartment, squirrel-caging, actually wearing a rut in the carpet. I was past being cognizant enough to call my sponsor or anyone else. I was, as they say, stark raving sober.

The phone rang. It was a guy from meetings. I barely knew him and there was no great rapport between us. He said his sponsor told him he had to call a different program person every day, and today he called me. I said something like, "Oh. So... how's it going?" He gave a brief check-in. I don't think I told him of my straits; I didn't have the courage. It was a brief and civil, if not pleasant, exchange.

After he hung up, I realized I was back on earth among the living. His call snapped me out of my spiral. I know my Higher Power had him call me that day because I was too far-gone to seek help. By taking care of himself, he saved me.

～

It's okay to call someone when I need help or just a friendly voice, and I never know whose life I might save.

> "We recover as individuals but we do not
> recover alone. We recover together. We
> recover helping others and being helped by
> others....And in this, the sponsor's recovery
> is helped just as <u>much</u> as the sponsee's."
>
> "Getting a Sponsor"

Sponsorship, for me, is an honor, a privilege, and an awesome responsibility—something not to be taken lightly. I currently sponsor a number of individuals in SAA, and have done so for years. I am always honored and humbled when someone asks me to be their sponsor. It may mean they see in me an integrity of commitment and a consistency in living the Steps, perhaps modeling the hope of recovery for them.

Sponsorship is also a privilege for me, as I get to foster an intimate partnership with another, and bear witness as we work together to peel off, layer-by-layer, the secrets, the deceptions, the hurts, the guilt, and the shame that keep this disease thriving in our lives. It's the most intensive accountability there is! I am forever moved to see and help someone blossom into who they really are.

Finally, sponsorship is indeed a welcomed responsibility. Besides being available for another addict, I am held to a higher standard when I sponsor someone, revitalizing my own recovery with renewed honesty, accountability, and congruency. I am helped by being of help to others. What a gift!

I receive the gift of recovery when I give it away.

> "Over time, we establish a relationship
> with a Power greater than ourselves, each
> of us coming to an understanding of a
> Higher Power that is personal for us."
> *Sex Addicts Anonymous,* page 21

I grew up with an all-knowing, all-powerful God; an ever-present judge, always ready to condemn me for my errant behavior. Even my thoughts condemned me. As I became older, I felt that God was there just to deny me any fun in life, especially after I was deemed unfit for leadership by the religious community in which I had been raised. I was determined to show everyone, including God, and proceeded to do so for the next twenty-five years. Ten years ago, God had had enough and knocked me off my prideful perch.

I then returned to God as a refuge from my persecutors and a comfort from the shame and degradation that had become my life. God led me to SAA and the Twelve Steps of recovery. By working these steps I have come to a personal relationship with a loving and merciful God who cares for me just as I am, and who keeps me on the right track in my recovery.

The over-seven-billion of us in this world can form a loving, working relationship with a Higher Power in over seven billion different ways. I know that my Higher Power will be with me as long as I remain humble and open to guidance.

Thank you, God, for taking me as I am.

"Our distorted view of ourselves led us to avoid responsibility for our actions."

Sex Addicts Anonymous, page 32

I clearly remember my sponsor telling me to get out my business card and write on the back, "If I'm not the problem, there is no solution." He then tasked me with holding this card in my hand until our next meeting. I reluctantly agreed, and was soon complaining about my sponsor's methods to anyone who would listen.

When I tell that story today, I smile and have a good laugh at myself. I recall how I even lamented that I couldn't hold my children with "that card" in my hand. I also recall how I came to accept it after a recovering friend told me he liked this idea—that it was like a prayer.

Of course, the prescribed inscription was not meant to inflict obsessive, debilitating guilt or morbid reflection. Instead, it gradually instilled the life-giving view that my own distorted perceptions were keeping me in perpetual martyrdom. Perhaps this addict had grown to love his own victimhood. I believe now that my sponsor was only trying to impress in me that nothing changes if nothing changes. I'm responsible for the actions necessary to change, and only I can make those choices. Carrying that card was an act of open-mindedness and willingness—a benign exercise in much needed humility in search of vital self-honesty. All great things have small beginnings, and my sponsor's spiritual plan for transforming my life began with a single sentence on a small card.

Great change is possible if I am open and willing.

"We find that we experience being sexual
as a way to satisfy appropriate sexual
needs and desires, rather than as a way to
manage anxiety, self medicate, or escape."
Sex Addicts Anonymous, page 72

Before getting sober in SAA, I would spend most of my day searching for opportunities to act out with sex. My life was a complete wreck, full of anger, fear, and chaos. I used sex as a means to avoid all of my feelings.

When I came into SAA, it was suggested that a period of celibacy, free of all sexual activity including with myself, would allow me to experience withdrawal. During withdrawal I worked the Twelve Steps of SAA and developed a relationship with my Higher Power. To my surprise the desire to act out with sex was completely lifted.

As a result of putting my trust in God, working the Twelve Steps of SAA, and carrying the SAA message to sex addicts who still suffer, I find that my anger, fear, and emotional disturbances get the treatment they need. And it allowed my brain to retool. Today I experience sex unlike any sex I had experienced in the past. When I choose to be physically intimate today, I know it is with a sober mind. I always ask myself, "Is what I am about to do selfish or not?" and I can trust my new-found sixth sense which I've been told is God-consciousness. Who knew that a person could grow from self-centered sex to God-centered sex?

I thank God for healing my life in ways I never thought possible.

ॐ

> "When we are quiet, we become receptive
> to wisdom that isn't available otherwise."
>
> *Sex Addicts Anonymous,* page 57

I was laid off from a job I dreaded going to but could never get myself to leave. The layoff was my worst fear, but I soon realized it was also a great gift. Nonetheless, every morning, my eyes opened to a wall of anxiety and the questions, "What am I supposed to be doing? Why am I here?"

Through recovery I've practiced prayer and meditation. During this time, though, my faith muscles strained under the weight of an unsure future. Prayer and meditation became vital just to face my day.

Through the Steps I've learned about my likes, dislikes, and desires. I've learned how I block myself and how I can be productive and useful. I am beginning to see the person my Higher Power created me to be. There is great dishonesty in denying that truth and living in fear. For many years my response to fear was paralysis or flight. Sobriety and recovery are about living in the world, part of a greater whole.

In the stillness, my fear and dread burn off. Clear thoughts surface bringing hope, cheer, and, most surprisingly, energy that propels me into action. I spontaneously took benign risks like telling someone what I think I do well, when asked. I sought help at appropriate times and felt healing with every action.

I cannot trade the glimpse of freedom I feel now for the security of a passionless existence. That would be a betrayal of my Higher Power.

Here I am, God. Where are we going today?

"We looked for ways to intensify the experience, forgetting that bigger highs will eventually lead to even greater suffering and unmanageability."

"Sexual Sobriety and the Internet"

My life as an addict is reflected in the quote above. Each time I acted out, I was trying to find a solution to a problem I didn't know I had. I applied one tool, sex, to solve all my problems.

If I was stressed at work, pornography was the answer. If I was abused at home, the bookstore was the answer. If I felt neglected or unwanted, prostitution was the answer. As the problems intensified, so did my acting out, and so, unknown to me, did the risks of being caught. I, of course, was finally caught, and my life in recovery began. At first, there was great suffering, divorce, loss of home, loss of children. But, my sponsor was there, telling me that I had to be willing to lose it all to gain it all. I gradually began to show up for my life.

Now I have many tools to solve my problems. The Twelve Steps frame the architecture of my new life. If I am stressed at work, meditation can be the answer. If I feel neglected or unwanted, a meeting is the answer. If my needs aren't being met, my sponsor is there. If I am lonely, I can call a friend in the fellowship.

I no longer seek ways to intensify the experience. I now seek ways to be present for the experience.

> "We gradually learn to be honest about
> our feelings with others, while being open
> to their feelings as well. In the process,
> we learn to express our affection rather
> than seek power and control."
>
> *Sex Addicts Anonymous*, page 72

Today, as I write this, I am quite depressed. The business I have worked for years to build is failing. If things continue the way they are going, in a short time, it will no longer exist.

The most painful part of this process is watching how it is hurting people I care about. I have worked, planned, laughed and grown old with these people. Now I am learning to cry with them. I am learning other lessons as well. I am reminded that my position, my title and my material possessions pale in importance to my relationships with my loved ones. When all else is gone, I will still have them. They do not love me for my title or for what I have accomplished. They love me for who I am.

The people in my group care about me because of who I am, not what I do. In fact, many do not know what I do for a living. We haven't gotten around to it. We are focused on other things like recovery, spirituality and emotions. These are the things that will remain, regardless of my business's fate. These are the things that matter to me.

~

Thanks to SAA I am able to have real connections with people. I think they call it love.

ભ

"When we admit our powerlessness, we start letting go of control and become more open to receiving the help we so desperately need."

Sex Addicts Anonymous, page 23

To me, our whole program is based on this first step. When I look back to the time I read my First Step in an SAA meeting, I realize that I was just beginning to understand what it means to be powerless. As I have continued in my recovery, powerlessness has become more clearly defined to me—both what it is and what it isn't.

Powerlessness is not the same as helplessness. Powerlessness is not an acceptance that I will always succumb to addiction, but rather it is a realization that I can't treat it on my own. I am powerless over my addiction; but my Higher Power, the Twelve Steps, and my fellow recovering addicts can give me tools to live life on life's terms.

As a recovering addict, I have had to embrace powerlessness, not as something that can be condensed into a simple, trite, slogan, but as a way of life. I live out powerlessness daily by praying, meditating, making calls to fellow recovering addicts, attending meetings, being honest in my sharing, and working the Twelve Steps with my sponsor. I do these things, not just as self-enrichment exercises, but because I am truly powerless. In return, I am given a freedom I had never known could be mine.

~

Powerlessness is the cornerstone of my recovery.

ॐ

"We strive to isolate and recognize each feeling, to the best of our ability, and we practice acceptance of all our emotions, rather than denying or fearing them."

Sex Addicts Anonymous, page 35

Through a Fifth Step I discovered I had no self-acceptance. But awareness of a defect doesn't create a light switch I can turn off at will. In addition, I beat myself up over this defect and my inability to turn it off. So what do I do? I had learned of three "a's" that can help. In order, they are: awareness, acceptance, and only then, action. I may have awareness, but without acceptance, I am unlikely to take appropriate or effective action.

I prayed, not for self-acceptance, but to accept that I don't accept myself. Once I could accept the situation as it is, I could start the footwork. It meant sharing openly in meetings, reaching out to others, and forming honest, open relationships. The way I figure it, if sex is on the table, what isn't? If what I felt most ashamed of is open for discussion, what is there to hide?

Whenever I put myself out there and make a genuine connection, I plug a hole in the sieve that holds my self-image. Gradually, conversation by conversation, relationship by relationship, I am healing.

I can't force myself to accept myself. I believe that happens through working this program, and in relationships with others and my Higher Power. But I can pray for acceptance of the situation as it is. Then, appropriate actions can become clearer.

~

Who I am and where I am are good places to start today's journey.

∞

> "History does not have to repeat
> itself in my life. I have choices!"
> *Sex Addicts Anonymous*, page 128

When acting out, I sometimes used the excuse that I had a high sex drive. I would also justify my socially unacceptable behaviours by telling myself I was extremely sexually open-minded. In reality, I was preventing myself from having a true sexual relationship with another human being and ensuring my loneliness and isolation. The phrases "high sex drive" and "open minded" made it sound like I had the power. But the drug of my sex addiction had the power, forcing me to repeat destructive behaviours and pulling me deeper into my own painful world. The only thing that seemed to bring light to that painful world was more acting out.

Finally, I hit rock bottom, came to SAA, and got the principles of the Twelve Steps into my life. I was rocketed out of the hell I was living in. I found more than sufficient substitutes for my acting out: the Twelve Steps, my home group, and service. I discovered true sexual freedom: to go on a date and enjoy being with another human being, to be free to experience the joy of intimacy, to experience true friendship with another. Such things were not truly possible for me before SAA—I had been trapped by my so-called uninhibited nature. Then, in the discipline of sobriety, I found true freedom.

~

By accepting the boundaries of my abstinence and the selflessness of the Steps, I am free to enjoy the beauty of other people.

&

"We are grateful for this opportunity to share the precious gift of recovery with our brothers and sisters in prison."

"Writing to Prisoners"

Prisoners convicted of criminal sexual conduct who have a desire to stop addictive sexual behavior through the SAA program are often the forgotten members of our fellowship. I know this from firsthand experience. I was a "consumer of correctional services" many years ago as a result of my victimizing and harming others through my insanity. I know the pervasive feelings of shame, guilt, loneliness, ostracism, fear, self-loathing, and hopelessness that engulf sex offenders who are incarcerated. Back on the outside, we are often stigmatized by our culture for our past, fueling those same emotions. Prison can take many forms.

I visit and sponsor a number of prisoners by letter. I offer them encouragement through my experience, strength, and hope; and I guide their work in the Twelve Steps. There are many challenges facing correspondence with prisoners, but they are manageable. I engage in this joyful task because it benefits my own recovery, and it affords me the opportunity to share the gift of recovery with those who are eager to receive it.

Despite my past, and because of it, I have much to give. Grant me compassion and courage to reach out to others.

ଔ

"The program tools being offered to you are
the same that kept your sponsor sober,
and they can keep you sober too."

"Getting a Sponsor"

I am grateful for the people who walked this path before me and paved the way for my recovery. A sponsor is able to introduce me to these precious gifts and walk with me on my journey of recovery. The tools that worked for my sponsor can work for me too. At first I needed to take this statement on faith. Later I came to know the truth of it through my own experience of being restored to sanity and finding joy through these tools. On days that I don't experience this joy, I remember the acronym Y.E.T. ("you're eligible, too").

The program tools are all available to me today because my sponsor chose to use them and to pass the benefits and wisdom on to me. Thank God that someone has gone before and blazed this trail for me and countless others! And thank God that it's now my turn to pass on my experience, strength, and hope with others coming to the fellowship today.

I once heard the phrase, "Have a sponsor, use a sponsor, be a sponsor." That slogan puts my program today in a nutshell. I can't keep the gift of recovery all to myself. I need to give it away in order to keep it.

~

God, thank you for my sponsor and others who have walked this path before me. Help me give as I have been given.

> "Throughout all of these ups and downs,
> I have had one huge blessing...I have had
> the loving support of the SAA fellowship."
>
> *Sex Addicts Anonymous,* page 157

After joining SAA and stopping my acting out, I discovered a deep hunger for connection. I'm sure it had always been there. Despite my insecurity and awkward emotions, I gradually reached out to others within the fellowship. Sometimes a great friendship would blossom. Sometimes a friendship didn't work out and I felt deeply discouraged, fearing that I had done something wrong. Regardless, my hunger for connection did not go away, so I resolved to keep reaching out.

I have made great friends this way. If I had not been willing to risk rejection and feel some very uncomfortable feelings along the way, I would still be isolated, lonely, and stunted in my ability to have meaningful relationships. I would not be living but merely surviving, just like before entering this program.

I am grateful for the friends I have made. And I am filled with wonder at the many good people in this program whose paths only briefly crossed mine. I believe all these friendships are gifts from God—gifts I had to be present to receive. I am reminded of the saying, "Thank you God, now I know that thorns have roses." The roses of my friendships are worth the thorns of the difficulties and painful moments I have had along the way.

Grant me the courage to reach out today. The thorns of my insecurities may lead to the blossoming of a friendship.

> "Through applying the Twelve Steps of Sex
> Addicts Anonymous with guidance from
> a sponsor, our groups and our Higher
> Power, sex and relation,ships slowly
> take their rightful place in our lives."

"Recovery from Compulsive Sexual Avoidance"

I coped with the addictions in my family by becoming withdrawn, quiet, and polite. Adults regarded me as well behaved. Even then, however, I sometimes engaged in impulsive mischief. Beneath my placid exterior a storm was brewing.

When I discovered sexual acting out behaviors, I thought I had finally found a way to meet my needs. I became something of a split personality. But my need for intimacy was not really being met. Hence, my behaviors became more severe until I eventually got into real trouble.

I was encouraged to try a Twelve Step program. With that and therapy I became successful in all areas except forming an intimate relationship. My current therapist suggested SAA. Sure, I had sexual issues, but that program seemed to be for other people. Nevertheless, I starting going to meetings, got a sponsor, and worked the Steps.

I took a good look at my fantasy behavior. Fantasy came between me and any meaningful relationships. A romantic connection was out of the question as long as I lived in a kind of bubble where I could dream of sex whenever I felt the need to be comforted. Today I have many good friends and get along with other people in my life. Although I still feel shy in various social situations, my strength in reaching out to people is growing daily.

I am open to a life based in the real world.

"Shame is a common experience for sex addicts. It is the feeling that we are never good enough, that there is something wrong with us, that <u>we are bad people</u>."

Sex Addicts Anonymous, page 8

Before coming into the fellowship and working this solution, I had no other choice but to continue acting out in order to mask the pain. This perpetuated even more feelings of shame, guilt, and remorse.

I remind myself that when I follow the Steps, I enter into a relationship which is unconditional, all-loving, and caring. My creator has done the impossible. It was only when I had no other way out that grace held me and whispered, "I've got this. I love you. I forgive you."

The path is indeed wide enough. It's up to me to walk it.

ℂℕ

> "This impulse springs from
> selfless love and gratitude."
>
> *Sex Addicts Anonymous*, page 59

I came to SAA a long-time member of another fellowship. I thought I knew something about recovery. Thanks to my Higher Power, I learned otherwise.

I got a sponsor, worked the steps, and sponsored others. Sobriety was a to-do list: check, check, and move on. At over a year sober, I relapsed. I barely made it back into the fellowship, but when I did, the gift began.

I stopped knowing things. I gave myself the gift of being a newcomer. I listened. I asked questions. I received. From that gift of nothingness, I was granted a new beginning, a new recovery, a new life, a new me—a me I could know, a me I could love, a me I could share.

When sobriety was a task-list with pre-defined objectives, I remained confined by my own thinking—barriers of addiction, limitation, and have-tos. When I became empty and simply surrendered to the process, I was filled to overflowing.

As I worked each step with the heart and mind of a beginner, I experienced gifts—gifts I could not have imagined.

I now work the steps, sponsor others, and do service, but my heart is different. I am acting, not because I have to or I'll act out, but in love and gratitude. I want others to receive and discover their unimagined gifts. It matters to me that others get the same opportunity for a new beginning and a life worth living.

From thinking I was something, I became nothing.
From becoming nothing, I was offered everything.

ॐ

> "Our best thinking got us into
> trouble in <u>the</u> first place."
>
> *Sex Addicts Anonymous*, page 63

"Dude, it's not about sex!" I heard this early in my recovery. Of course sex was about sex, wasn't it? Or was it? I couldn't believe it. So what was it about? It was mostly about self-medicating insecurity, beliefs of inadequacy, and uncomfortable feelings such as fear and anxiety. It was about coping with uncomfortable situations like arguments with my partner or bad days at work.

This was mind-blowing! If sex isn't about sex, then is anything about what I think it's about? Could anything going on between my ears be trusted? This attitude has changed my life. If I felt triggered to act out, I could ask myself what was really going on. I began praying for my Higher Power to show me the truth. That simple prayer helps calm me, putting space between my swirling thoughts and emotions on the one hand, and my actions on the other.

I began rebuilding my life by praying, talking to program friends, reading the literature, and trying new behaviors. Slowly I began to feel the feelings I had run away from for so long. Sometimes it feels like a punch in the stomach, but each time I face an uncomfortable emotion, ask for guidance, and practice patience, I emerge from the experience a little stronger and a little lighter. Now, there is an adult to protect and nurture that frightened child inside—me.

～

Feelings are not facts; they will not kill me. I can learn about myself from them, knowing that for this moment, I am safe.

☙

"For most of us, those moments of acceptance,
however or whenever they occurred, were
followed by periods of doubt and denial."

"First Step to Recovery"

I have been addicted to pornography since I was five.
My father was addicted. At first it was file folders stuck
in bookshelves or closets. By the time I entered puberty, he had evolved to file cabinets with fictitious labels
on the drawers.

Twenty five years later, I was recovering in other programs but had successfully compartmentalized this
part of my life so it never entered any step work. I
eventually got home Internet, and the first question
to the friend installing my computer was how to find
pornography. This was the same computer I used for
my research and education.

Many of us know what ensued—attempts to stop, de-
leting the images, promises to spend only thirty minutes, etc. Then came a day when the computer bogged
down because the drive was full of porn. Without
thinking, I bought storage disks and started migrating
and filing my images. During this, I had the sicken-
ing and demoralizing realization that I had become my
father. I had to develop disciplined filing practices to
manage my porn. It was still some years before I found
SAA, but this was one of the thousand blows that prepared me to be teachable when the time came. I now
realize that these blows were my loving creator trying
to show me the truth so I could find my true self.

～

*It takes what it takes, and I thank God for all the
lessons that got me here.*

ca

"We would use sexual fantasy to
deal with emotions and situations
that we didn't want to face."

Sex Addicts Anonymous, page 5

I had a serious problem with sexual fantasy, but never saw the connection between fantasy and acting out. In time, I saw that fantasy was acting like a gateway drug. When I "took" fantasy, I was highly likely to go to the harder drug of acting out sexually. For me, fantasy is a circling-the-drain behavior with one logical outcome.

I put fantasy in my middle circle. I then applied principles from the Steps whenever I would start to fantasize. I begin by admitting to God that I am heading into fantasy, and ask God to free me from it and show me the truth about the situation. Then I check in with my program friends.

I found that fantasy often masks feelings of insecurity, inadequacy, fear, etc. In this way, my sexually oriented thoughts and activities were acting like a drug to dull uncomfortable feelings. In recovery, I've learned to embrace those uncomfortable feelings as messengers and to learn from them, all the while weaving a closer relationship with my Higher Power.

I found the Steps to be a powerful weapon against this problem. Now I rarely spend time in fantasy, and acting out is not the powerful temptation it used to be.

～

*If I treat my middle circle activities as danger signals,
I can stay away from my inner circle, and I can open
the door to even greater freedom.*

> "Step Two offers hope that sanity is
> possible, and at the same time it implies
> that, in our <u>addiction</u>, we were insane."
> *Sex Addicts Anonymous,* page 25

When I first read this sentence, I had to pause and ask myself if I were truly insane. Step One required me to admit that I am a sex addict and a sexual anorexic, that I am powerless over these illnesses, and that my life is unmanageable by me. Since I believe that I am a sex addict and a sexual anorexic, that means I have a disease of the mind, body, and spirit that reacts very negatively to all sexual stimuli. For me, unhealthy sexual stimuli can lead to addictive sexual behaviors, and healthy sexual stimuli, such as sexual intimacy with my husband, can lead to sexual avoidance or addictive sexual behaviors.

But, being a sex addict also means I have a mental obsession with sexual stimuli of all kinds. To me, that's like someone with a peanut allergy having a mental obsession with finding and eating peanuts. Wouldn't I call that person insane? Yes, I would. So it clearly means that I am, in fact, insane.

Without God and the SAA program, my default desires are to harm myself with addictive sexual behavior and starve myself of healthy sexuality. Believing God can restore me to sanity means believing that God will change my whole being so that I no longer desire harmful sexual stimuli and I no longer avoid nurturing sexual stimuli, one day and one step at a time.

May I be willing to go to any lengths today to be restored to sanity.

"We can also work the Tenth Step by checking
in regularly with our sponsor or other
members, or by giving a thorough and rigorous
accounting of ourselves at meetings."

Sex Addicts Anonymous, page 53

I have struggled for years to do a daily Tenth Step,
thinking it needed to be done daily, perfectly, and in
a certain format. I now know that there are many different ways others in the fellowship work their Tenth
Step. I learned that from talking to others in recovery.

What I did not realize (until reading Step Ten in a
recent meeting, seemingly for the first time) was that
every time I reached out to a program friend, checked
in with my sponsor, or spoke honestly about my
strengths and weaknesses at a meeting, I was, in fact,
working that step to the best of my ability. I continue
to pray for willingness to be a little more on-task about
it, but I am happy with my progress and awareness.

*God, please help me review my day in whatever form
you see fit for me.*

ભ

"Belief in a Higher Power can be difficult
for many of us in SAA who come to
the program with a faith that was
damaged in one way or another."
Sex Addicts Anonymous, page 26

My son was sick with a cough that made sleeping very difficult. When I tried to give him cough medicine, however, he spit it right back out. The taste was just too unpalatable for him to handle. It didn't matter that the medicine was exactly what he needed to feel better, because he was too young to understand. After many failed attempts to get him to swallow the medicine, I finally mixed it with milk and he drank most of it without a fight.

I realized that, for me, coming to believe in a Higher Power who could relieve me of my sexual addiction and anorexia was kind of like that. Even though I knew from SAA meetings and literature that my only hope of recovery was finding and believing in a power greater than myself, I did not know how. My old religious beliefs and past experiences with God were just as unpalatable as my son's medicine. I spit them right back out. But through attending SAA meetings, working the Twelve Steps of SAA with a sponsor, and being patient with myself, I have slowly developed a relationship with a personal God of my own understanding. Finding God through SAA was like giving my son his medicine through his milk, gentle and kind, and for that I am so very grateful.

~

For today, I allow myself to experience God as I can understand and tolerate God.

ର

"In order to stay sober, I needed to
make sure that, one day at a time,
acting out was not an option."

Sex Addicts Anonymous, page 288

I was in sexual recovery for eight years before I realized I actually had to stop acting out. I thought being in the rooms was enough. Despite meetings, my life had grown ever more empty and painful, and I was desperate. I wanted something more or I wanted to die.

Then I heard someone speak who had thirteen months sobriety. We all listened quietly to her moving story. After eight years of meetings, I could finally hear people announcing their sobriety, and I wanted what they had. I finally realized that I had to stop my behaviors. Acting out was no longer an option. I was finally willing to go to any lengths to stay sober.

I went to nine meetings a week for two and a half years. I got a sponsor and worked the steps. In the morning I would check in with myself, and if I felt that acting out was an option, I went to a meeting, made a program call, and sometimes prayed in a house of worship until the feeling passed. This is the biggest gift I ever gave myself because, one day at a time, I have not acted out since. I came to realize that I couldn't have gotten the clarity one moment before I was ready. With clarity I gave myself the gift of sobriety.

Clarity comes when it does, not a minute before. Then it's up to me to act.

> "We can start to open ourselves to this idea by
> considering the forces that are clearly more
> powerful than we are, such as nature, society,
> or even our addiction. When we recognize that
> our own power is limited, we can more readily
> acknowledge the possibility of a Higher Power."
>
> *Sex Addicts Anonymous*, page 26

When I read this passage, Steps One and Two became perfectly clear. Is there a power greater than me? Of course! My addiction is proof. If I were more powerful than my addiction, then my marriage, career, and self-esteem would not have been falling apart. I no longer need to waste time wondering if a power higher than me exists.

This also relates to Step One because my addiction is proof that my life is unmanageable by me. If I were actually able to manage my own life, I would not have had to lean on sex in the first place for control, love, or meaning. I would have had, on my own power, everything I could possibly need. Obviously, that is not the case.

The evidence clearly indicates that I am powerless over my sex addiction and unable to manage my own life, and that there are powers much greater than I. I'm grateful to this passage for opening my mind to a new way of understanding Steps One and Two and my own recovery.

~

If I need proof today of my powerlessness, unmanageability, and need for God, I need only look at my life before recovery.

December 25

"Our specific words are less important than our willingness to make contact with a Power greater than ourselves and to let God's care into our lives."

Sex Addicts Anonymous, page 30

In asking for help from my Higher Power, I visualize myself in a small sailboat, using an oar instead of the sail. I can make some progress with a lot of effort, and even feel a sense of control, but I am constantly struggling to stay on course, and I am missing out on a limitless resource available to me. All I have to do is put up a sail and the wind is there.

When I ask for help from my Higher Power, I demonstrate willingness and an open mind. I am tapping into a force vastly more powerful than anything I have. That resource is always there, but I have to take the action of asking for help, or the wind just blows by. I am also still responsible for my thoughts, words, and actions, but any sail I raise opens directions and possibilities beyond my limited vision and my little oar's influence.

I pray for the willingness to ask for help, and to accept and use that help with grace.

✂

> "Most have found that during challenging
> times, if we look at what is going on and
> how we are conducting ourselves, we can
> usually identify <u>some</u> positive growth."
>
> *Tools of Recovery*, page 31

I was at a meeting once where the topic was "Progress, Not Perfection." It was a large meeting with a round-robin format. When my turn came, I talked about the positive changes the program had worked in my life and some of the struggles I was having with the Steps and life. I closed with, "Most nights now, when I go to bed, the dishes are washed."

The sharing worked its way around the large table until it got to a woman I did not know. She shared about her progress and struggles, and ended with, "And some nights, when I go to bed, the dishes are not washed."

I don't think I laughed out loud, but I know I sat there quietly chuckling for the rest of the meeting. This beautiful program does not define our recovery by specific external circumstances. There is no one-size-fits-all picture of progress. The progress is in how I treat myself and those around me. As the old-timers say, it's an inside job.

〜

Washing the dishes, not washing the dishes—the progress is in my heart.

᱐

> "We had become so used to defeat and
> despair that we lost touch with hope."
>
> *Sex Addicts Anonymous*, page 28

Coming to SAA, I knew I was insane and had papers to prove it. I had long-term sobriety in another fellowship, working the steps several times but never finding the hoped-for transformation. On Step Two, I said, "Well, God can do anything, so I guess God can do this," while thinking, "Nope. Sanity is not an option; misery and despair are my lot."

In SAA, this approach to Step Two ended in relapse. Next time around, my sponsor had me dig deep. I realized in Step One that I was also powerless over God. I had been trying to manipulate God to restore me to my definition of sanity, on my terms.

Simultaneously, I was writing letters to God and writing responses from God. A sober sister observed that I seemed angry at God. She suggested an angry letter, so I let 'er rip. I railed at God about all I had done to get sane, ending with, "What's up God?!" My Higher Power's simple reply struck me silent and changed my life: "Who are you to define happiness?"

At that moment, I got it. Recognizing and accepting that I don't know what sane or happy looks like, I no longer had to force some artificial construct. I surrendered my sanity and my definitions of sanity. When I let God set the terms, my sanity was quickly restored to so much more than I had ever hoped for or imagined.

~

Letting go of my old unworkable ideas opens the path to a new life.

ભ

"We then go back over the list of resentments,
looking at each incident, and ask ourselves
what role we played in the situation. We
must take responsibility for our part,
however small. Sometimes, especially for
resentments from childhood, we determine
we had no role in the problem at all."

Sex Addicts Anonymous, page 34

In my Fourth Step, I listed resentments against my
father. They were for the verbal, physical, and sexual
abuse I suffered from him during my childhood. I left
my part in it blank—how could I have a part in it if I
was a child?

At a meeting, I shared about my childhood trauma
and my feelings as a victim. I didn't realize the power this still had over me. Then someone else shared
her experience with childhood trauma from her parent
and the resentment it created. She shared how she felt
her role in it was not surrendering the trauma sooner
as an adult.

The abuse happened, it wounded me deeply, and it
negatively affected the rest of my life. But today I have
choices. I went back to my Fourth Step and put lack
of acceptance as my part in the resentment. I began
to feel empowered by taking ownership of my role. By
surrendering the trauma and not playing the victim as
an adult, I am reclaiming my childhood and my life.

Today, I'm open to seeing how holding on to past
traumas keeps me a prisoner of the past. With surrender, I'm learning to let go and move on.

~

Today, my life is mine. I have choices.

ᐃᐧ

> "In essence, our shared experience of this
> Power is one of <u>loving and caring</u>."
>
> *Sex Addicts Anonymous*, page 27

After several years of sobriety and recovery, I can still think "control of God" when I hear "care of God." When I cause hurt by resentment, self-pity, or other character defect, I often balk at admitting my wrongs because I feel I must do so to please God. This stems from shame, the belief that I have to earn God's love and that I am not intrinsically worthy as I am. It's the old idea that God is a controlling parent that I must appease in order to keep peace in my home.

One day, my sponsor told me that she thinks of it as turning her will and life over to love. Suddenly, everything changed for me. While the word God can trigger old feelings like shame and fear, love is something I can trust. Love is safe and caring, gentle and strong.

I'm beginning to understand and accept that turning my life over to a higher power, taking inventory, and making amends are not things I must do to earn love, but loving actions I do for myself because they will bring me the most joy and peace in this life. God loves and accepts me as I am, whether I do the actions prescribed in the Twelve Steps or not, but God gently encourages me to follow this path of recovery because it is the most loving thing I can do.

For today, I can turn my will and life over to love.

ભ

"We see that we are becoming better people,
and we begin to experience a new sense of
self-worth. We feel free to live in the present
and enjoy our lives, no longer having to carry
a load of despair, resentment, and fear."

Sex Addicts Anonymous, page 51

I love watching a TV show where people bring in their possessions to be appraised by experts. Someone brings an item in, not knowing its value and sometimes believing it worth little or nothing. It might have been passed down for generations, or purchased at a flea market. The appraisers research the item and tell the owner what they learned. Usually the owner is surprised by the informatio, and is often astounded by the value placed on their treasure. Their joy and tears move me.

Through the Twelve Steps of SAA, I brought my dusty, scraped, and scratched item—my life—to the ultimate appraiser: God. I felt my life was worthless and wanted to discard it. God took it and told me of its origins and true purpose. These revelations astounded me. I was further shocked by the value placed on my life: God found me to be priceless!

I also see my value in the eyes of my SAA brothers and sisters. Their joy at seeing me again astounds me. When they listen intently to what I share, I am humbled by the wonder of it all. Their friendship is priceless. I have value. This is serendipity at its best.

When they say, "Keep coming back; it works if you work it, and you're worth it!"—it's the truth.

ℭℛ

"You have taken a brave step walking in the door today, and we support your search for recovery."

"A Special Welcome to the Woman Newcomer"

When I was fearful, my sponsor would say, "Courage is fear that has said its prayers." I would get angry. If I prayed, it didn't seem to help, and I wanted relief! To me, courage meant the absence of fear, and I didn't see how I could proceed when I felt so scared.

I heard a talk recently that put things into perspective. The speaker's experience is that Step Six is an action step. He prays for release and for courage (what my sponsor was trying to tell me!), and then does the opposite of what he formerly did when his character defects were active. This way he demonstrates readiness to have them removed.

I have significant social anxiety, a manifestation of my self-centered fear. I fear how I will come across in conversations, meetings, or other social situations. My shame tells me I am a fraud, and I'm afraid others will find this out and believe it too.

My solution is to pray for release from my self-centered fear, then put myself in situations that my fear would make me avoid. This means praying a lot and living outside of my comfort zone a significant amount of the time. It's slowly getting easier, and I have grown tremendously. And apparently this is courage even though it doesn't often feel like it.

I pray for relief from my character defects, and for courage to put feet to my prayers.

We invite your feedback and your responses to this book. Although we are no longer accepting meditations for this project, we encourage your contributions to our newsletter, The Outer Circle. If this book has inspired you to write a meditation of your own, a story of service, sobriety, or recovery; or even a poem, you may submit it to The Outer Circle by emailing info@saa-recovery.org or writing to P.O. Box 70949, Houston, TX, 77270.

In Deep Gratitude,

The ISO Literature Committee

October 2018

1. We admitted we were powerless over addictive sexual behavior — that our lives had become unmanageable.

2. Came to believe that a Power greater than ourselves could restore us to sanity.

3. Made a decision to turn our will and our lives over to the care of God as we understood God.

4. Made a searching and fearless moral inventory of ourselves.

5. Admitted to God, to ourselves, and to another human being the exact nature of our wrongs.

6. Were entirely ready to have God remove all these defects of character.

7. Humbly asked God to remove our shortcomings.

8. Made a list of all persons we had harmed and became willing to make amends to them all.

9. Made direct amends to such people wherever possible, except when to do so would injure them or others.

10. Continued to take personal inventory and when we were wrong promptly admitted it.

11. Sought through prayer and meditation to improve our conscious contact with God as we understood God, praying only for knowledge of God's will for us and the power to carry that out.

12. Having had a spiritual awakening as the result of these Steps, we tried to carry this message to other sex addicts and to practice thse principles in our lives.

1. Our common welfare should come first; personal recovery depends upon SAA unity.

2. For our group purpose there is but one ultimate authority — a loving God as expressed in our group conscience. Our leaders are but trusted servants; they do not govern.

3. The only requirement for SAA membership is a desire to stop addictive sexual behavior.

4. Each group should be autonomous except in matters affecting other groups or SAA as a whole.

5. Each group has but one primary purpose — to carry its message to the sex addict who still suffers.

6. An SAA group ought never endorse, finance, or lend the SAA name to any related facility or outsidide enterprise, lest problems of money, property, and prestige divert us from our primary purpose.

7. Every SAA group ought to be fully self-supporting, declining outside contributions.

8. Sex Addicts Anonymous should remain forever nonprofessional, but our service centers may employ special workers.

9. SAA, as such, ought never be organized, but we may create service boards or committees directly responsible to those they serve.

10. Sex Addicts Anonymous has no opinion on outside issues; hence the SAA name ought never be drawn into public controversy.

11. Our public relations policy is based on attraction rather than promotion; we need always maintain personal anonymity at the level of press, radio, TV, and films.

12. Anonymity is the spiritual foundation of all our traditions, ever reminding us to place principles before personalities.